CHILKOOT TRAIL

Heritage route to the Klondike

This book is dedicated to the residents of Skagway, Carcross and vicinity, and all those who know the trail, have shared in its stories, are proud of its history, and care about its future.

CHILKOOT TRAIL

Heritage route to the Klondike

David Neufeld • **Frank Norris**

Yukon and western Arctic Historian
Parks Canada

Historian
U.S. National Park Service

LOST MOOSE

THE YUKON PUBLISHERS

1996

Published by Lost Moose, the Yukon Publishers
58 Kluane Crescent, Whitehorse, Yukon, Canada Y1A 3G7
phone (403) 668-5076, 668-3441, fax (403) 668-6223, e-mail: Lmoose@yknet.yk.ca
(Please note that our area code changes to 867 after October 21,1997.)
web site: http://www.yukonweb.com/business/lost_moose

Canadian Cataloguing in Publication Data
Neufeld, D.H. (David H.)
  Chilkoot Trail

Includes bibliographical references and index
ISBN 0-9694612-9-1

1. Chilkoot Trail--History. 2. Tlingit Indians--History.
3. Klondike River Valley (Yukon)--Gold discoveries.
I. Norris, Frank, 1950- II. Title.
FC3845.C49N48 1996   971.9′1   C96-910251-8
F1089.C44N48 1996

Design by Mike Rice
Production by K-L Services, Whitehorse
Printed and bound in Canada

Front cover photograph: Waiting their turn to climb the Golden Stairs, stampeders pose for the camera at the Scales.

Dedication page photograph: Today, as in the past, the Carcross-Tagish First Nation people remain closely affiliated with the Chilkoot Trail.

Photograph this page: Packing up the Chilkoot Pass.

Original spellings and phrasings have been maintained in all quoted excerpts.

The international character of the trail is reflected in the use of metric and imperial measurements and the terms First Nations (Canada) and Native American (U.S.).

Lost Moose gratefully acknowledges the receipt of a Canada Council project grant.

97 98 99 00 01 10 9 8 7 6 5 4 3 2

Forewords

The Chilkoot—a mystical, magical, marvellous piece of real estate. For the back-packing jock, not a great challenge. For the never-before-hiker, not recommended as a first. But for anyone who enjoys putting on a pack and spending time in the great outdoors, a must. The Chilkoot Trail is more than just a physical experience. The visual pleasure is only equalled by the weight of history extending back for centuries. There is a presence as you hike. Long dead travellers of the trail seem very near. You may commune with more than nature as you toil up the Golden Stairs.

My great-grandfather and his four sons were part of the teeming river of gold seekers in 1898. My family has lived in the Yukon since that time and I have hiked the trail over 18 times. Each trip is different. I always find or see something new and it is the unpredictable weather which offers the greatest challenge, demanding care when packing clothing.

This book brings new insights about the trail and those who have used it. The photographs bring an appreciation of the hardships experienced by those pioneers. The research highlights the skills and entrepreneurship of the First Nations clans who opened and owned the trail long before 1898.

Ione J. Christensen, CM

Together, David Neufeld of Parks Canada and Frank Norris of the U.S. National Park Service bring a quarter century of Klondike studies to fruition in this book. As research historians, they dredged up textual and graphic riches from gold rush archives. Then, as field historians, they used the old maps to follow stampede trails to overgrown sites. And there, with old photos and accounts in hand, they reconstructed the scenes and events depicted and described by those who, a century ago, joined "The Last Great Adventure," as it came to be known even then.

That is how this book was made. First, immersion in the documentation; then, immersion in the glorious and still-challenging landscapes whose names will always make the pulse race: Chilkoot, Klondike, Yukon, Tagish.

Neufeld and Norris have bitten off a bigger chunk than just conventional academic history. Their all-season explorations infuse their text with the feel of cold and barren days as well as those of riotous, life-packed summers. And their work with Tlingit and Athapaskan Indians, whose trade relations pioneered the coast-to-interior trails, adds cultural dimension to both the land and gold rush history. For, as usual on the frontier, the newcomers relied on Indian knowledge and muscle to help them across the mountains until trail improvements and, later, trams and trains, made the way easier. Nor did the story of the First Nations end way back when. It goes on to this day, enriching both the U.S.-Canadian borderlands and this book.

A good, solid narrative takes us across the trail and through the era. But that is only the framework. The authors have packed this volume with a simply outstanding collection of historical photographs, numbering in the hundreds. Throughout, the faces of that marvellous band of seekers and dreamers gaze at us from settings in camp or on the trail. Each face projects a story, many of them given substance by journal and letter quotations or sidebar essays relating to people and places pictured. So the general history constantly comes to point with individuals or groups who look back at us from each turning page. We wish we could talk with them, join their adventure.

This is a very personal book. It enfolds us in the high-voltage energy of people just like us, who came this way a century earlier and left a legacy along a trail we eagerly follow.

William E. Brown, former Alaska Historian, U.S. National Park Service

Preface

A century ago, the Klondike gold rush fired the imagination of a restless western world. Wearied by economic depression, unsettled by industrialization and urbanization, and struggling with the social unrest caused by massive immigration to the new world, the Klondike offered an escape to a dream—a place where individuals could regain an identity lost in the anonymous hordes in factories and cities. Thousands heeded the call and headed north.

Almost all who started on the journey underwent a transformation. Whether their dream ended in a pile of sodden supplies sold at a loss in a rainy forest on the Alaskan coast, or whether they struggled all the way to the goldfields, they were changed—changed by the hard, physical work of hauling gear through a rugged mountain pass in the depths of a northern winter, changed by the overwhelming sense of awe from such a great and rugged land, changed by their exposure to the self-confident and powerful Tlingit and changed by their meetings with the friendly and helpful First Nations of the Yukon River. For here, in the Chilkoot, was one of the last places on earth where Europeans and aboriginal peoples met on roughly equal terms and began the last negotiations for a set of relationships that affect all of North America today.

The inspiration for this work was the trail itself. The experience of the trail—hiking in summer, skiing and with dog team in winter—shaped every facet of our work on the written and spoken record.

And the record of human experience here is remarkable. The people of the Carcross-Tagish First Nation, the heirs to the trail on the Canadian side, carry a rich oral tradition

Camp life on the trail wasn't always a rugged struggle. Fine weather, clean clothes and a camera call for some light-hearted fun.

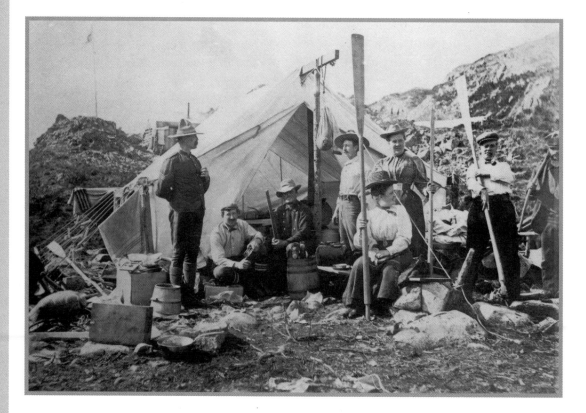

describing the land and their lives on it. Winnie and William Atlin, Edna Helm and Jean Desmarais, among many others in the community, all generously shared this tradition. Si Dennis, Sr., Andrew Mahle, and other Native Americans were likewise helpful regarding matters on the United States side. Their memories, stories and invitations to join them out on the land were critical elements in the attempt to gain an understanding of the human relationship to this special place. Judy Gingell kindly provided permission to share family stories with the readers of this book. The support and interest of the Chief and Council of the Carcross-Tagish First Nation in the research for this book always reminded us of the importance of taking a broad view of history.

We are also in debt to the Klondike stampeders, who left us such a rich legacy of hopes, dreams, pains and, sometimes, just plain exhaustion expressed in their letters, diaries and photos. Individuals, archives, museums and libraries preserving these records all deserve our thanks.

The people of Parks Canada-Chilkoot Trail National Historic Site and the United States National Park Service-Klondike Gold Rush National Historical Park always welcomed us to their offices and out at their camps. Whether undertaking field research on the trail, making ice cream at Lindeman in spring or baking a berry pie at Sheep Camp in late summer, their consideration in allowing us to accompany them and learn from them continues to be appreciated. Similarly, professional staff in archaeology, curation, interpretation and management all cooperated to make our work easier and more accurate. Our park service predecessors in northern research, Rick Stuart of Parks Canada and Bob Spude of the U.S. National Park Service, cleared a great deal of ground and contributed to the valuable research collections maintained by both parks services. A deep gratitude goes to Sande Faulkner of the National Park Service and the management team of the Parks Canada-Yukon District Office for supporting this initiative.

Advice and information from colleagues, especially Julie Cruikshank of the University of British Columbia, Frank James of the Carcross-Tagish First Nation, Sheila Greer of Edmonton, Karl Gurcke of the U.S. National Park Service, Patricia Halladay of Whitehorse, and Alice Cyr of Bellingham, Washington were important in the research, synthesis and presentation of findings. Longtime Skagway residents George Rapuzzi, Barbara Kalen, Ed Hosford, Edith Lee and Glenda Choate also deserve heartfelt thanks. Thanks, too, to the many friends and colleagues who took time to review the manuscript and offer corrections and clarifications. The people of Lost Moose, especially Wynne Krangle and Peter Long, who shared their electronic hearth with us for many hours, deserve applause for their contribution. We take full responsibility for any errors, misinterpretations or omissions that remain in the book.

Finally, we would like to thank our wives, Joy and Candy, and children, Erin, Andrew and Alice Mae. Their loving acceptance of long absences, irritable fathers and husbands who stare far too long at computer screens, and of our continued insistence on taking the whole family traipsing off into the bush are debts that can never be repaid. Thank you.

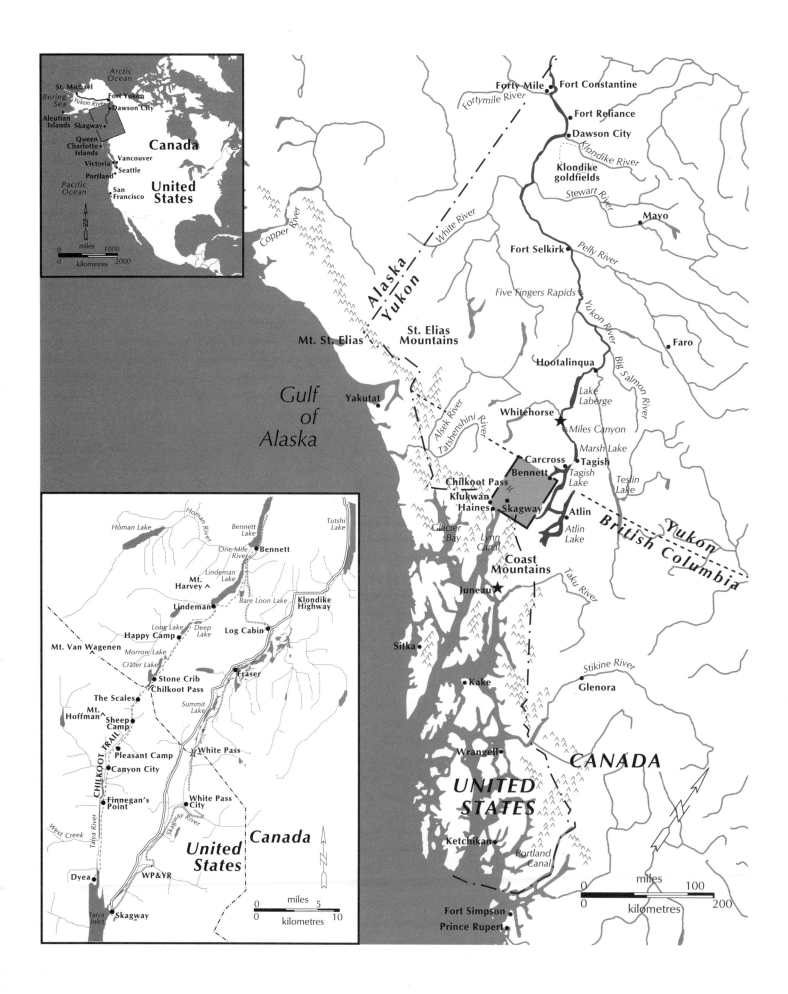

Contents

Native woman packing through gorge south of Long Lake, 1897. The Chilkoot Trail heads for a long distance over this kind of rock.

Native women and their young daughters and sons from ten years of age and up were also packing from fifty to seventy-five and one hundred pounds on their backs for miners, earning from ten to twenty dollars per day.

• J. Bernard Moore, reminiscing about the 1890s

Chilkoot:
The Mountain Trail

After climbing through misty fog, the view north from the Chilkoot summit is breathtaking. Blue sky and glistening white snow divided by the jagged crest of the coastal mountains, repeat and emphasize the contrast. While often thought of as a dividing point between coast and interior, between society and freedom, and between civilization and wilderness, the Chilkoot Trail is actually more important as a place of contact.

The Chilkoot Trail has a colourful history. Stretching 53 km (33 mi.) from Pacific tidewater in Alaska through British Columbia to the headwaters of the Yukon River, the trail is best

(preceding page) **In mid-June, the trail leaves winter at Morrow Lake and the warm spring of the interior invites the traveller farther north.**

(right) **Panorama of the Chilkoot Pass from the summit, looking north over Crater Lake. In the foreground are the ruins of a gold rush aerial tramway terminal.**

known today for its place in the Klondike gold rush. More than 30,000 men, women and children toiled up the Golden Stairs, the last daunting climb to the summit of the pass. Even before the stampede of miners, the trail was an important First Nations trade and travel route joining the Tlingit of the coast with the First Nations of the interior. Today, the region remains their homeland.

Each of these groups developed a distinct connection with the Chilkoot Trail. These relationships reflect their political, economic and social interests. Not surprisingly, there are

Tired, bone tired, and wet, I gladly dumped my 40 pound pack at Stone Crib. I had struggled against the wind-driven rain every step toward the pass. Finally, I could look forward to a warm cup of tea. The wind continued to howl and moan outside. Rain pelted the tarp-swathed patrol hut, but I felt completely at home. Solitude...Rare and precious, I savoured every moment of it in that desolate little haven. Finally, I was lulled to sleep by the wind's siren song.

Several hours later I was jolted awake—it was completely silent outside— the ever-present wind had stopped. The rain had cleared up, and I couldn't resist the urge to step outside. The northern lights cascaded across the sky, twisting and rolling their arms of brilliant green and pink. Below me, Crater Lake lay completely calm and clear, reflecting the dance above. A trillion stars glittered and shone in the sky, as the crescent moon's silvery light bathed the snowy peaks. Finally the chill air forced a retreat to the warmth of my sleeping bag. By next morning, a thick cloud of mist erased all but the memory of the night before.

• Candy Norris, ex-warden,
Parks Canada

Heading up the Golden Stairs at the Chilkoot Pass in the spring of 1898.

differences. This book explores these different perspectives on the Chilkoot Trail by reviewing the activities of the 19th century coastal Tlingit, the stampede newcomers in the late 1890s and both the First Nations and non-natives use of the trail through the 20th century.

Through the 19th century, the Tlingit were a powerful group in the Pacific northwest. They established major communities such as Klukwan on the Chilkat River, and seasonal camps at favourable fishing spots such as Dyea. In addition to harvesting of marine resources, the Tlingit were well-known travellers. On trading trips and military raids, they swept the northwestern Pacific coast. Especially important, however, were the highly profitable overland trading trips into the Yukon interior for prime furs and skins.

The Chilkat and Chilkoot mountain passes were two of the most important routes. The Tlingit warily protected these passes from both their trading partners in the interior and 19th century newcomers—Europeans anxious for furs. The Tlingit accommodated these desires, ensuring the maximum benefit for themselves.

In the summer of 1897, the explosion of interest in Klondike gold brought a stampede to the north. Most funnelled through either the old trading and fishing village of Dyea and the Chilkoot Pass or the neighbouring boom town of Skagway and the White Pass. Carrying enough supplies to sustain them for a year, they struggled up the rough trail and over the summit through the sharp, northern winter, suffering agonies of cold and exhaustion.

Along the way they created colourful trail towns like Sheep Camp, Lindeman and Bennett, where the comforts of home awaited them—for a price. After journeys as long as eight weeks, they reached the headwater lakes of the Yukon River. Here they decimated the forests for firewood, shelter and lumber. By spring, thousands of boats were ready, the travellers waiting for the ice to break up and the start of the frantic race to Dawson City and the Klondike goldfields.

Along with dreams of wealth, the stampeders also brought their civilization. The North-West Mounted Police struggled to maintain Canadian law amidst the swirling tide of humanity struggling north.

Investors saw possibilities here as well. Alaska's first railway, the White Pass and Yukon Railway, reached over the White Pass to Bennett by July, 1899. The railway effectively ended the Chilkoot's role as a transportation corridor.

Through the last century, the wounds of the gold rush have gradually healed, leaving only romantic scars of this fantastic adventure. For the stampeders, success was built upon their victory in the Chilkoot. Whether they found gold in the Klondike or not—and most did not—the Chilkoot passage was the climax of their stampede.

After the gold rush, the Yukon First Nations reclaimed their homeland. Interrupted by the stampede, they adapted their trading and harvesting patterns and social ways of life to the railway and sternwheelers, the continuing annual parade of tourists and other outside influences. It was the Chilkoot environment and landscape, the seasonal availability of natural resources and the extended family network that gave, and continues to give, meaning to their life, ensuring the evolving continuity of the annual round. Picking berries in the fall, hunting the family's moose, trapping through the winter and coming together for fishing and celebration in summer give both meaning and pleasure to First Nations.

All three perspectives—coastal Tlingit, stampeders and interior First Nations—divided by history and by purpose, have meaning today.

The real teacher is the trail. The long days of a northern summer obscure the passage of time, while the thick rainforest, sinuous windings and steep descents and climbs of the trail make a mockery of any measured distance. A day's travel ends at suppertime and suppertime comes just after the travelling is finished. Even more disorienting are the many and varied ecozones of the trail. Hikers can begin on a warm summer day in the Alaska rainforest and end up on the summit ploughing through thigh-deep snow with icy sleet blowing in their faces. From there they can walk through spring near Deep Lake and back to summer at Bennett.

Time becomes distance. Distance becomes seasons and in June and July there is no night at all. This delightful absence of regular order encourages the exploration of new ways of experiencing the world around us.

The Chilkoot is a meeting place. For thousands of years, the trail joined coastal and interior people in trade, marriage and travel. The Klondike gold rush merely added another ingredient to the mix. Alaska Natives, Yukon First Nations and newcomers continue to work on a social contract for the future.

The Carcross-Tagish First Nation hosted "Indian Days" near Tagish in 1989.

The Land

To most people, the area of Alaska and British Columbia surrounding Skagway, Dyea, Bennett, and the Chilkoot and White Pass trails is known because of its association with the Yukon's great Klondike gold rush. However, this formidable landscape has been here for millions of years.

The towering Coast Mountains, formed by the colliding plates of the Pacific Coast fault zone, began to emerge in the Jurassic period, 150 million years ago. About 10 million years ago, the great glaciers of the Ice Age began the first of their four descents from the north. By the time the last ice sheet retreated, some 11,000 years ago, thousands of peaks dominated the skyline, most of them 1,500 to 2,000 m (5,000 to 7,000 ft.) high.[1]

When the last ice sheets receded, the Coast Mountains formed a rampart separating the coast from the interior. They appear as a massive, impenetrable barrier with few breaks: the Tatshenshini and Chilkat rivers, the White Pass and Chilkoot Pass, and the Taku River.

The two passes at the upper end of the Lynn Canal, the White Pass and the Chilkoot Pass, gain their importance from their proximity to Bennett Lake, just a few kilometres to the north. With only a short overland journey, the trails through these passes make it possible to travel from the Pacific coast to the Yukon River watershed, and then, almost 3,200 km (2,000 mi.) north and west to the Bering Sea. The other routes, via the Taku, Chilkat and Tatshenshini rivers, each require more than 160 km (100 mi.) of foot travel to reach interior waterways.

The White Pass, 870 m (2,865 ft.) high, is 24 km (15 mi.) inland from the mouth of the Skagway River. Just a few kilometres to the west, the Chilkoot Pass, 1,080 m (3,550 ft.) high, is 27 km (17 mi.) from the mouth of the Taiya River.

The White Pass route is longer than the Chilkoot but lower. The trail along the Skagway River valley makes its way along tortuous valley slopes until it reaches the summit of the White Pass. Then it snakes between alpine lakes before reaching the north end of Lindeman Lake, where it joins the Chilkoot Trail.

On the Chilkoot Trail, the first 12.5 km (8 mi.) ascends the wide, flat Taiya River valley. The terminus of the valley is a logical place to rest; during the gold rush this was the site of

(preceding page) **The Taiya tidal estuary attracts many birds with its runs of fish. Pictured here are glaucous-winged gulls and a bald eagle.**

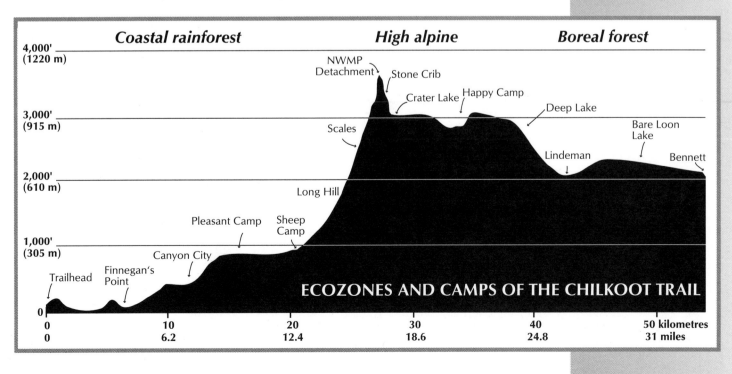

ECOZONES AND CAMPS OF THE CHILKOOT TRAIL

Canyon City. A narrow, precipitous canyon continues for the next 3 km (2 mi.). To this point the elevation gain is slight; the foot of Long Hill, 22 km (13 mi.) from tidewater, is still less than 300 m (1,000 ft.) above sea level. Here was another large gold rush campsite, Sheep Camp.

Long Hill forced stampeders to climb more than 500 m (1,650 ft.) in just 3 km (2 mi.). The ascent to the summit of Chilkoot Pass is steeper yet; the trail rises from 800 to 1,100 m (2,600 to 3,600 ft.) in less than 2 km (1 mi.). Beyond the pass, the trail drops to the shores of Crater Lake. From there it meanders around a series of lakes until descending to the shores of Lindeman Lake. The trail then continues to the far end of the lake. One mile beyond, 53 km (33 mi.) from salt water, lies Bennett Lake. From here, stampeders could float through the southern lakes down to the north-flowing Yukon River and on to the goldfields of the Klondike, 880 km (550 mi.) downriver.

The Chilkoot Trail is travelled most comfortably during the summer. Winter brings short days, dangerously cold weather, avalanches and huge snowdrifts. These factors make the hike difficult, tedious and risky between late September and early May.

This 1898 map, printed in Victoria, British Columbia, assumes that Skagway, Dyea and the Chilkoot Trail were all part of British Columbia, Canada.

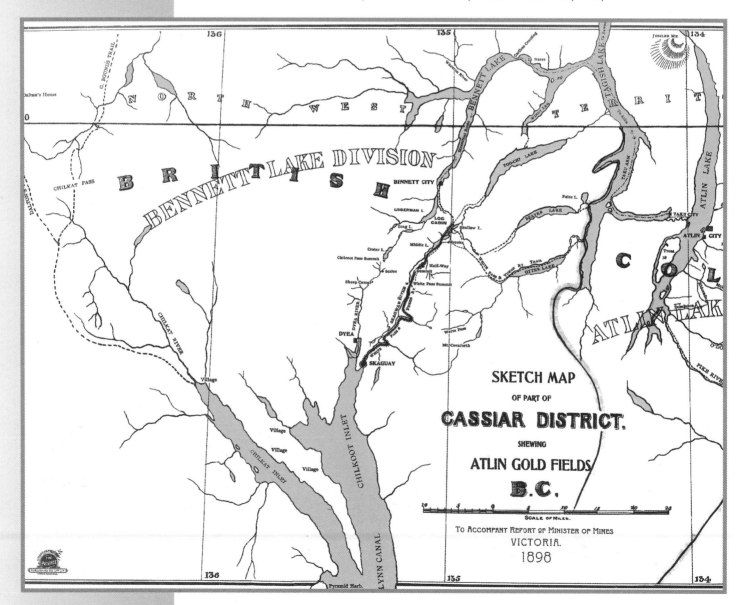

SKETCH MAP
OF PART OF
CASSIAR DISTRICT.
SHEWING
ATLIN GOLD FIELDS
B.C.

SCALE OF MILES.

TO ACCOMPANY REPORT OF MINISTER OF MINES
VICTORIA.
1898

COMING INTO SKAGWAY

THE DECK THROBS beneath my feet. The sound of the engine drowns out the calls of the seagulls sweeping ahead of the ship. Both sides of the Lynn Canal are dark green forest with autumn showing as irregular slashes of rust and yellow. Clouds reach halfway down the slopes, a filmy skirt of snow just visible below the mist, hinting at the winter to come. Occasionally a break opens and we see the rugged heights of these new mountains. Fresh snow dusting the tops highlights the creases and folds of continental plates—crushed and folded upwards.

The Dyea flats are out front, to the right the narrow cleft that is the White Pass. The sea is dark, a black green, choppy with small whitecaps and long, thin stringers of golden leaves luring us into the harbour. The docks and town of Skagway—a scattering of wooden buildings dropped amongst the trees—are almost lost in the steep rocky faces of the mountains and the low black clouds veiling the pass into the Yukon.[2]

(right) The 1900 Baedeker tourist guide to the Dominion of Canada described the Klondike routes.[3]

Skagway is a popular tourist destination, with over 400,000 visitors arriving each summer, mostly on cruise ships.

50. Route. 247

KLONDIKE REGION.

to Sitka

Lynn Canal ends in two prongs, named the **Chilkoot** and **Chilkat Inlets**, recently come into prominence in connection with the rush to the gold district of the Klondike. In these inlets the tourist reaches the highest latitude of the trip (59°10′36″N., about that of the Orkney Islands, Christiania, and St. Petersburg). At midsummer there are not more than 3-4 hours of partial darkness here. On Chilkoot Inlet (the E. arm) lie the new little towns of **Skagway** (E. bank) and **Dyea** (W. bank), the chief points of departure for the Upper Yukon and the Klondike. Each is furnished with rough hotels, outfitting establishments, and other accommodations for the miner. Owing to the opening of the railway (see below), Skagway, now contains about 4000 inhab., has completely outdistanced its rival, which seems likely to collapse altogether.—On Chilkat Inlet lie *Pyramid Harbour* and *Chilkat*, with prosperous salmon-canneries. There are also other settlements on the inlet. This is the district in which the fine Chilkat blankets are made. Good echoes may be wakened off the glaciers.

At Pyramid Harbour begins the *Dalton Trail* to the Klondike (to Fort Selkirk 350 M., to Dawson 530 M.), which is (or was) used solely after the close of the season of navigation.—The *Chilkat* or *Bound Trail* follows the *Chilkat River*, crosses the *Chilkat Pass* (3000 ft.), and unites with the Dalton Trail at *Fort Selkirk*.—The *Dyea* or *Chilkoot Route* is the shortest route to *Lake Bennett* (see below), where it joins the Skagway route, and in spite of the difficulties of the *Chilkoot Pass* (3500 ft.) was popular among travellers with little baggage. Latterly the pass has been facilitated by an aerial tramway. The distance from Dyea to Dawson by this route is about 585 M.

All of the above routes have, however, been thrown into the shade by the *Skagway* or *White Pass Route*, owing to the fact that the easy gradient of the pass allowed the construction of a narrow-gauge railway (*Pacific & Arctic Railway*; through fare to Dawson about $110), which was opened in 1899 as far as Lake Bennett. This line begins at *Skagway* (see above), the top of which (2600 ft.), it gains in about 15 M. more. It then descends to (21 M.; 40 M. from Skagway) *Bennett City*, at the head of *Lake Bennett*. Here we leave the railway and traverse Lake Bennett (26 M.), *Lake Tagish**(17 M.), *Marsh Lake* (20 M.), and a stretch of the *Lewes River* (25 M.) by small steamer. This brings us to the *Miles Cañon* and the dangerous *White Horse Rapids* (ca. 3 M.), which are avoided by portage (tramway). Below the rapids we board another small steamer, which carries us all the rest of the way.

——— *In 1899, the Canadian custom-house was stationed on Lake Tagish, but the whole question of the boundary between Alaska and Canada is still unsettled.

Since the Chilkoot opened as a recreational trail in the early 1960s, almost all who have hiked it have done so in the summertime. The coastal Tlingit, who used the pass for hundreds of years, usually travelled after the snow hardened in the spring and in early summer. However, many Klondike gold rush stampeders, hell-bent on reaching Dawson City, forced their way through during the depths of winter.

Although the trail through the Chilkoot Pass is relatively short, it traverses a remarkable variety of scenery and climate. The coastal end of the trail, in Alaska, has a temperate, maritime climate. Near the summit an alpine climate predominates, while the interior portion of the trail, entirely within British Columbia, has a dry, sub-arctic climate.

The coastal rainforest

The coastal region includes most of the lower stretches of the Skagway and Taiya river valleys. This area is undergoing a process of rapid rebirth known as glacial rebound. During the Ice Age, the weight of the vast glaciers compressed the land underneath. Today, thousands of years after most of the glaciers have retreated, the coastal areas of southeastern Alaska are rising again. The land in the Glacier Bay region, 100 km (60 mi.) west of Skagway, still partially glaciated, is rising more than 25 mm (1 in.) per year. The re-emergence is more gradual in the Skagway and Dyea areas, averaging just over 13 mm (one-half inch) per year.[4]

Summers at the foot of the two trails are mild while winters are cool but not extreme. Cloudy skies are the norm and both rainfall and snowfall are frequent. Summer days in Skagway have been recorded as hot as 33°C (92°F); the town's lowest recorded winter temperature was a frigid -31°C (-24°F).

Skagway receives 710 mm (28 in.) of precipitation yearly, one of the lowest levels in southeastern Alaska. While no historical precipitation records exist for Dyea, at the foot of the Chilkoot, the site probably receives between 1,270 and 1,520 mm (50 and 60 in.) of precipitation annually. Rainfall along the coast, even in January, is by no means rare, but

Many Tlingit families brought their canoes to Dyea for freighting in 1897. On the coast, the mountains drop straight down to the wide flat streams draining the narrow strip of the Pacific rainforest.

most of the precipitation between November and March falls as snow, which can build up to heights of 60 cm (2 ft.) or more. Occasional warm spells, however, can bare the ground of snow even in midwinter.

Wind is a major element of coastal weather. During the summer, high-pressure storm systems in the Gulf of Alaska contrast sharply with low-pressure areas in the Canadian interior. As a result, winds rush from the coast into the interior, and the mountain passes bear the brunt of them. Come winter, the process reverses itself, and strong, often gale-force winds,

Probably a Carcross-Tagish family camped near Sheep Camp during the spring packing season in 1897.

The stampeders usually established their first camp in the rainforest while they transferred their hundreds of pounds of goods up the trail in short stages.

streak south through the coastal valleys. The near-constant winds have left a permanent imprint on the region; the name Skagway comes from a Tlingit word meaning "home of the north wind."

The climate along the coast is ideal for both trees and smaller vegetation, and a temperate rainforest predominates. Brooding forests of Sitka spruce and western hemlock carpet the landscape, particularly on the mountain slopes. Black cottonwoods are often seen in the river valleys, and alpine fir, lodgepole pine, trembling aspen, and balsam poplar are also seen here and there. A variety of second-storey plants, such as alder, willow, devil's club, salmonberry and ferns thrive here as well.

This botanical diversity encourages abundant wildlife. Large mammals include black bears and an occasional mountain goat, coyote or lynx. A few moose live in the upper Skagway River drainage. Smaller mammals include porcupines, snowshoe hares, river otters, mink, marten, red squirrels, deer mice, voles, weasels, bats and shrews. The valleys are home to an extraordinary assemblage of bird life, both seasonal and year-round dwellers. The most common birds are bald eagles, goldeneyes, arctic terns, great blue herons, ruby-throated hummingbirds and both blue and ruffed grouse. Several species of fish inhabit the Taiya River and its tributaries, including pink salmon, chum salmon, Dolly Varden trout and eulachon. Mammals in the coastal waters include northern sea lions and, occasionally, humpback whales.

Frederick Schwatka, a U.S. Cavalry Lieutenant, extolled the Taiya River valley as he crossed the pass in June of 1883:

> ...high hills covered with spruce and pine nearly to the top, the latter predominating in the lower levels, the former in the higher, and capped with barren granite mountains, covered on the top and in the gulches with snow and glaciers.... The Oregon blue grouse could be heard hooting in the woods, and in the quiet evenings a perfect chorus of them filled the air. Trout had been caught in the fish-weirs of the "Stick" [Yukon] Indians, and offered us for sale.... The tracks of black bear, fresh and old, were very numerous, and one was seen but not secured. The valley....would make a favorite summer camp for those officers and men who wished to break away for a while from the routine monotony of garrison life. Mountain goats and deer can also be added to the game list. The river bed and the valley is filled with great bars of bowlders, sand, and coarse gravel, with here and there groves of poplars, willows of several varieties, and birch.[5]

Loaded freight wagon making its way through the rainforest.

Tappan Adney, a correspondent for *Harper's Weekly*, was one of the few gold rush observers to describe the valley's natural beauty. In August, 1897, he noted the "Dyea River" (Taiya River) ran:

> ...through a level valley of sand, gravel, and bowlders, with groves and patches of cottonwoods and spruce and birch, while along its banks are thickets of alders and a

species of willow resembling the red willow of the East. Its swift, milky, ice-cold waters [are] filled at this season with salmon, spawning, and with large, fine trout. The woods, to the unobservant, seem devoid of life; but though there is no song of bird, still if one listens he will hear the low chirp of sparrows, while the hoarse croak of the raven is borne to the ear as it flaps lazily overhead. There are also red squirrels, and if those who have hunted in this region can be relied upon, the country abounds in large game as well as small — grizzly bears on the mountain-sides, mountain-goats...on the summits that overlook the valley, and numerous small fur-bearing animals. There could be no finer place to fish for trout than along this Dyea River.[6]

Others wrote less, but were nonetheless impressed with the scenery. Julius Price, a correspondent for a London newspaper, walking up the Chilkoot in May, 1898, was positively exuberant. He noted that he "passed through a broad, smiling valley, that looked very beautiful in the glory of its spring verdure in the bright morning sunlight." Martha Louise Purdy (Black), later a noted Yukoner, was similarly impressed two months later. "For the first time in my life," she wrote, "I saw hillsides of wild blue iris and lupine."[7]

Although the trail through the lower Taiya River valley was muddy and rocky in spots, it was easily managed, and by the spring of 1898, a wagon road traversed its length. Beyond that, however, lay the real difficulties. The river, frozen in midwinter, "narrowed down to a gulch of only sufficient width to pass one man or wagon at a time," according to U.S. Army Sergeant William Yunera. Stampeders found the canyon ascent tortuous and slow.[8]

Those who climbed the Chilkoot in the summertime followed a trail perched on the canyon wall. Most fared little better than those who had braved the winter route. Robert Oglesby remarked that the summer route in 1896 led "through thick timber, over fallen trees, up and down hills, through snow-drifts and across numerous small streams." A reporter for the *Seattle Post-Intelligencer* stated: "Many people consider [this] mile and one-half the worst part of the Chilkoot Trail.... The surface is rough and [is] covered with decayed vegetable matter from the surrounding woods."[10]

The Yukon in winter is a death trap for the imprudent and inexperienced man, whether he be city-bred or mountain born. The story of the Klondike will be written in blood.

• E. Hazard Wells, 1898[9]

The rainforest is multilayered. Small shoots and flowers cover the floor, while devil's club and ferns reach up to the shoulder. The trees top out a hundred feet above.

On August 4, 1898, William Zimmer, a U.S. customs agent stationed at the Chilkoot summit, wrote to his superior, W.P. McBride:[11]

The weather here has been so [foul] that a person could not be seen twenty feet away on account of the rain and the fog which has prevailed for nineteen days without any exception, until yesterday afternoon when the fog lifted for a couple of hours when it again began to storm and up to this evening it has been almost impossible to be out as the fog is so thick and the wind has been blowing at a sixty mile an hour gait.

View looking south from the summit.

At the upper end of the canyon was "a romantic spot covered with spruce and cottonwood trees," known to the stampeders as Pleasant Camp. Beyond that, a narrow and level valley brought the traveller to Sheep Camp. Despite the difficulties, stampeder Georgia White found the scenery beautiful. She saw "numerous waterfalls, the most beautiful ferns and flowers," and marvelled at the glacier hanging from Mount Hoffman.[12]

The high alpine

At approximately 900 m (3,000 ft.), the rainforest gives way to a transition zone of stunted tree growth, shrubs and more tenacious forms of plant life. The alpine region above this zone surrounds the summits of the two passes and continues into the interior until tree growth resumes at lower elevations.

Harsh weather in the alpine region is common. Snow can fall in any month of the year, even in midsummer, and remains on the ground from mid-September through early July. Snow on the passes can reach incredible depths. Railroad maintenance crews, stampeders and winter hikers all attest to snow depths of 5 to 10 m (16 to 33 ft.) or more. In spring, the huge snow loads on the mountain slopes cause frequent avalanches, many of which cross trails, roads, and the railway. Winds are often fierce, and there is little cover to break their fury.

The weather is highly unpredictable at all times. Temperatures range widely; summer days can be quite warm. More commonly, however, they remain cool, even on midsummer afternoons. Winter temperatures can be bitterly cold, reaching -40°C (-40°F) with winds of up to 100 km/h (60 mph). Few Chilkoot trail hikers are lucky enough to reach the summit in sunny weather; most cross in high clouds or fog. Stone Crib, the abandoned gold-rush-era aerial tramway station just north of the Chilkoot summit, is one of the least sunny places in Canada.

Much of the area above treeline is covered by remnant glaciers or rocks which, at first, appear to be largely bereft of life. But mosses and lichens survive among the rocks, and algae grows even on the snowfields. Though vegetation is sparse, protected niches support a surprising wealth of specialized plant life. Dwarf shrubs and stunted trees manage to grow in some places. Various willow and heath species are more common. Sheltered areas contain a wide variety of herbaceous plants, grasses and sedges. And there are more than 100 species of alpine flowers, ranging from mountain avens to dwarf azaleas.

The severe weather of the alpine prevents all but the hardiest of animals from living here. Mountain goats are the most common, primarily in the winter; caribou, moose, and coyote are occasionally spotted. Dall sheep have also been observed, although not in recent years. Smaller mammals include pikas and marmots. The only known year-round bird in this area is the white-tailed ptarmigan, often seen along the trail in early summer near Long Lake. Seasonal birds include rock ptarmigan, water pipits, Wilson's warblers, gyrfalcons, snow buntings and golden-crowned sparrows.

Travellers crossing the pass before and during the gold rush period saw little of the area's biological diversity. They travelled during the relatively barren winter months. Most, intent on getting their goods over the pass, paid little attention to their surroundings. The sheer volume of human activity drove much of the animal life away from the trail corridor.

The weather in the pass certainly bothered us. All very wet despite rain gear; boots sloshing water....

• Lindeman Lake log book,
Dan Morrisey,
August 14, 1972

The Scales in late June. A good place to stop for soup and a snack before scaling the summit in the background.

Most travellers overnighted in the trees at Sheep Camp, the last place to camp before ascending the pass. Just beyond lay the infamous Long Hill, to many the worst part of the climb. Tappan Adney described the transition to alpine in September, 1897:

> From Sheep Camp the valley is a huge gorge, the mountainsides rising steep, hard, and bold to a prodigious height. The valley begins to rise rapidly, and the trail is very bad. A mile above Sheep Camp, on the left hand, a huge glacier lies on the side of the mountain, jutting so far over and downward that every moment one expects a great chunk to drop off and tumble into the river. But it does not, and only a small stream of water from its melting forces its way to the bottom. A mile farther on is "Stone House"—a large square rock, crudely resembling a house; it stands on the river's brink. At the base of the mountain is a great mass of slide rock, some of the bowlders being nearly as large as the one by the river.... The valley here makes a sudden turn to the right, and the trail begins to grow steep. The valley is filled with great water-and-ice-worn bowlders. There is no vegetation, save a few alders here and there, and these cease just above "Stone House."[13]

In 1898, a reporter for the *Dyea Trail* newspaper made a similar comment, noting the trail passed "over a rough surface covered with immense rocks which by some convulsion of nature have been detached from the mountain side and rolled down to the bank of the creek."[14]

The trail crossing the summit of the pass into Canada, winter, 1898.

After climbing Long Hill, stampeders entered an open bowl at the base of the pass—the Scales. Adney continued:

> The trail enters a cul-de-sac, climbing higher and higher. The valley seems to end; a precipitous wall of gray rock, reaching into the sky, seems to head off farther progress, seaming its jagged contour against the sky—a great barrier, uncompromising, forbidding—the Chilkoot Pass. We start with our packs up the side of the mountain. Chilkoot deceives one in this: it seems to tower directly over one's head, whereas the actual average slope is about forty-five degrees, consisting of a series of benches alternating with slide rock.[15]

In winter, the frequent storms dump prodigious amounts of snow on the summit. For stampeders with their piles of gear, making 10, 20 or more trips to the summit over the course of the winter, the snow was an enemy. J.W. (Will) Patterson summed his experiences in the spring of 1898:

> At the top [of Chilkoot Pass] the snow is very deep and many caches are covered and lost. Saw some holes in the snow where they had dug 30 feet and still not found the goods. Am acquainted with one man who got his goods on the top early in the 3rd month [March] and then came a snow storm and covered everything up smooth. He dug it from under 15 feet of snow and piled it on top. In a few days another storm buried it and he took it out of 8 feet of snow, piled it up and now it is buried with another buried still above it and one piled on the snow on top of that yet. The [Canadian] customs house is on top of snow 40 feet above the spot in which it first stood.[16]

Julius Price was the rare traveller who saw beauty in the pass environment. Price was fortunate to ascend the Chilkoot on a clear day, and he pronounced the view "simply magnificent" and the mountains "glorious." When the sun set, he noted the sky turned:

These tough stunted balsams are the first trees beyond the Pass. This group is near Deep Lake.

> ...a blazing glory of red, which gradually merged into tender opalescent tints till on the opposite horizon it finally merged into the most delicate grey-blue, against which the distant snow-clad peaks stood out in faint relief.... The bracing air of the mountains acted like a strong tonic, and one felt curiously less fatigued than one would have...after such an arduous walk.[17]

Just beyond the pass the trail, "plainly marked by scars left on the rocks by thousands of cleated shoes," descended to Crater Lake. After the backbreaking climb to the pass, most people were glad to descend. Martha Louise Purdy, however, remembered that portion of her July trip painfully: "Then the descent! Down, ever downward. Sharp rocks to scratch our clutching hands. Snake-like roots to trip our stumbling feet."[18]

Once beyond Crater Lake, the trail descended slowly to "a small, desolate valley" just south of Long Lake. The site was called Happy Camp, "a misnomer, if ever there was one." Here the alpine, treeless climate began to give way to the more diverse vegetation of the dry, boreal interior.[19]

The boreal forest

North of the alpine zone, the harsh alpine climate gives way to a warmer, dry subalpine climate in the boreal forest. Trees and different forms of wildlife start to appear. The boreal forest region begins to assert itself in the Happy Camp-Deep Lake area.

Stampeder Ed Lung said:

...for the last thousand feet...it was almost perpendicular. It was like climbing an icy stairway to hell![20]

During the summer, this section of the trail enjoys a favourable climate. Average temperatures are often warmer than those near the coast and consistently warmer than in the alpine region. It can, at times, be quite hot here. In winter it is often far colder than on the coast. Temperatures commonly drop to -30°C (-22°F). Because the interior lies in the rain shadow of the Coast Mountains, the area is relatively dry. Annual precipitation averages only about 380 to 760 mm (15 to 30 in.). Even so, enough snow falls over winter to reach levels of 2.5 m (8 ft.) or more. Winds are not as strong as in coastal and alpine regions.

Vegetation in the interior is quite different from the coastal rainforest. The predominant species in the boreal forest are lodgepole pine, alpine fir and white and black spruce. Black cottonwood, trembling aspen and balsam poplar are found in the wetter bottom lands. Trees are more widely spaced than in the closed canopy of the coastal rainforest. Understory plants include a variety of berry bushes, and reindeer lichen is a common ground cover. Vegetation is most sparse in localized sand dunes, located at the windward end of the major lakes.

Stampeders' camps on the shore of Lindeman Lake, spring, 1898.

WINTER IN THE BOREAL FOREST

WE'RE FINALLY ON our way—10 dogs, bounding in their harnesses and straining against the weight of the sled. Brusquely, John keeps the team going the right way. We follow on skis, carrying packs heavy with food and watching that the children don't fall off the sled.

After two hours of trail through the warm green of spruce and pine we turn downhill onto the ice of Lindeman Lake. Before us stretches a magnificent vista of brilliant blue sky and glistening snow, the contrast so sharp it hurts the eyes. Sometimes on this trip we see snow rollers. At the bend of the lake the mountain wind is so strong it lifts a lick of wet snow and rolls it into a hollow tube. Hundreds of them litter the surface of the lake in the morning. By afternoon the warm sun leaves only the caved reminders of this extraordinary phenomena.

The dogs can pull us across the hard, smooth snow of the lake. Grasping a line from the sled we crouch comfortably and watch the landscape drift lazily by. The children are fast asleep on the gear. We hear only the panting of the dogs, the creak of the leather harness and wooden sled as it bounces over the ice ridges and the crunch of our skis cutting through the windblown skiffs of snow. A sense of balance and serenity infuses the moment.

At the south end of the lake we can see the site of the ephemeral stampede city of Lindeman. A point of land reaching out into the lake, Lindeman is our camp for tonight. The dogs are tied down and after preparing their water and food we can relax. A simple hot supper is enlivened when our son, Andrew, leans forward over the candle. His hair smoulders briefly until a gloved hand gently sits him back down.

The sky is black now; a million stars spill from the Milky Way. A small patch of the northern sky brightens momentarily and then—sudden explosions of orange and unrolling sheets of purple and red aurora borealis. In awe we lean back against the runners of the upturned sled and watch the dance of the universe.[21]

March 17, 1988

Got to Lindeman today. Tomorrow will ski up the lindeman river valley and make camp. Will hopefully then climb Mount Vanwaganen on the border. Adios.

March 19, 1988

Back with our tails between our legs. Tent got flattened in 50 knot + gusts, and had over a foot of snow. Didn't sleep all night, we were holding up the sides. We got trashed.

- Lindeman Lake log book, Paul Christensen and Peter Hayes

Racing across Lindeman Lake.

Sept. 17/72 - 1st snowfall was the 16th but none of it has stayed low. Have had strong northern winds since then. Fall colors have really been standing out with a little snow. Large flocks of geese have been coming through.

• Lindeman Lake log book,
Mike Peterson,
Santa Barbara, California

Lindeman Lake with Bennett Lake reaching to the north. As journalist Tappan Adney noted during his September, 1897 passage, Bennett Lake "lies like a trench between towering, rugged mountains of great grandeur."[22]

Both grizzly and black bears inhabit the boreal forest, along with caribou, moose and wolves. Smaller mammals include beavers, snowshoe hares, porcupines, wolverines and weasels. Among the most commonly seen birds are golden eagles, hawks, ruffed grouse, juncos, redpolls, cross-bills and chickadees.

Travellers crossing the pass were usually glad to notice the first signs of timberline, just north of Happy Camp campground. Tappan Adney recalled the site had "wood and a little grazing for a few wretched horses. The wood is spruce, scrubby and sprawling, some of the trunks being a foot thick, but the trees themselves not over ten or twelve feet in height."[23]

Between Long Lake and Lindeman Lake, the natural landscape changes dramatically:

> *The drop of eight hundred feet in elevation from Long Lake to Lindeman puts one into a new and smiling country.... The river [north of Deep Lake] drops into a narrow canyon at tremendous speed, falling eight hundred feet in two or three miles. The trail strikes across a spur of the hill, striking the lake near its head. Lindeman is a beautiful lake, four and a half miles long, and narrow with a towering mountain on the opposite side. At its head, on the left hand, a river enters, and there is timber for boats up this river. Vegetation is now plentiful, but it consists mainly of willows and a dwarf cornus, or bunchberry, which at this season, with its purple-red leaves covering the whole ground, gives a rich look to the landscape.[24]*

Lieutenant Schwatka named Lindeman Lake after a German botanist and described it as "a beautiful Alpine lake, over 10 miles long, and picturesque beyond description."[25] Ed Lung, who camped there in June, 1897, described it as "a beautiful lake surrounded by snow-peaked mountains and dark green forests. What a haven it appeared to be!"[26]

One detractor was the exhausted Martha Purdy, who decried the trail between Deep and Lindeman lakes. The trail "led through a scrub pine forest where we tripped over bare roots of trees that curled over and around rocks and boulders like great devilfishes. Rocks! Rocks! Rocks!" Her excursion proved so debilitating she had to be assisted over the last mile.[27]

Lindeman Lake was also the point of introduction of the most common, and most feared, denizen of the northern woods. Schwatka noted:

> Mosquitoes now commenced getting very numerous, and from here to the mouth of the river they may be said to have been the worst discomfort the party was called on to endure. [The mosquitoes] often made many investigations, usually carried on in explorations, impossible of execution, and will be the great bane to this country should the mineral discoveries or fisheries ever attempt to colonize it. I have never seen their equal for steady and constant irritation in any part of the United States, the swamps of New Jersey and the sand hills of Nebraska not excepted. It was only when the wind was blowing and well out on a lake or wide portion of the river that their abominable torment ceased.[28]

The trail, in short, exposed those who crossed it to some of the best—and the worst—that the north country had to offer. During the short journey between Dyea and Bennett, travellers crossed through flat valleys, rolling hills, steep canyons, and rugged mountain slopes, and through portions of three dramatically different climatic zones. It took an enormous amount of effort to cross the Chilkoot Pass—the feat is not easy, as today's backpackers will quickly attest to—but the scenic beauty and the trail experience have remained a lifetime memory for all those who have participated.

Moose are often seen in the early evening browsing in the marsh at Lindeman.

Fireweed and yarrow in early summer.

The Coastal Tlingit
Trading Trails to the Interior

The coastal Tlingit trace their heritage back thousands of years. At the beginning of the 19th century, they were a wealthy and powerful group taking advantage of their rich environment to foster strong communities and a sense of cultural identity. The Tlingit flourished by working an extensive coastal trading network. They also made effective use of the resources available on the forested flats of land between the deep waters of the ocean and the rocky slopes of the high coastal mountains.

Each community had its own strengths. For the Tlingit of the Lynn Canal, one of the most important was their control over the trade and travel routes reaching through the Coast Mountains to the continental interior.

The Tlingit of the Lynn Canal

Plentiful marine resources provided for the basic needs of the Tlingit. Clear streams flowing out of the mountains and the quiet bays were the spawning grounds for many kinds of fish. The Chilkat River, for example, has major runs of five different species of salmon every year, providing fish from late May through the middle of November. Most of the Tlingit in the upper Lynn Canal lived along the Chilkat River to take advantage of this resource.[1] Through the winter and spring, people fished for flounder and halibut, netted or trapped large numbers of the oily eulachon fish, and harvested herring roe.[2]

They hunted and trapped animals in the thick forests and mountains behind their villages. Goats, useful for their wool as well as meat, were hunted in the fall as were deer. Birds and berries were important supplements to the summer diet.

The massive trees of the coastal rainforest were another feature of the Tlingit homeland. Villages had well-constructed buildings of considerable architectural sophistication:

> *One of the larger Tlingit villages is an impressive sight if one sees it from across the water and at a fair distance. The regular row of solid wooden structures on the shore, which is*

Potlatch dancers at Chilkat, 1895.

A traditional Tlingit house at Klukwan.

The eulachon harvest kept everyone busy during the spring run. This group is on the Chilkat River near Klukwan around 1895.

covered with canoes and fishing gear, presents in this wilderness, a friendly picture of a civilization that would bring thoughts of home, if the sight of an occasional totem pole or grave post and Indian figures wrapped in woollen blankets did not again transpose one into a strange world.[3]

The cold winters and heavy rainfall of this region demanded expert joinery and tightly constructed dwellings. Tlingit plank houses were among the most impressive aboriginal buildings in North America.[4]

The regular availability of food and shelter provided the Tlingit with a solid foundation

for their culture and an ability to both express and protect their vital interests. The basic unit of social organization within communities was the clan—extended family units following the maternal line.[5] Within clans, individuals had well-recognized status, generally based on their wealth and prestige. The clan provided for the protection and care of all family members and represented their interests. Important assets, such as canoes, fishing places, houses and control of the valuable mountain trails, were owned by the clan. Legal issues of liability or crime were the responsibility of the clan, not the individual. [6]

Routes to the Yukon

Trade and military excursions along the coast were regular features of Tlingit life. From other aboriginal groups to the south they obtained, both by war and by purchase, dentalia shells (used as currency in the trade to the interior), shark's teeth, mother-of-pearl and slaves. They also traded for canoes, especially the cedar vessels made by the Haida of the Queen Charlotte Islands. Status was measured in real wealth—the number of caribou skins, later, woollen trade blankets—an individual could distribute at a potlatch, a celebration involving one-sided gift presentation. Gaining this status was made possible by trade with the people of the Yukon interior.[7]

The Tlingit used five routes through the mountains. Each route was owned by a specific clan and the trade through it managed by the clan leader.[8] Farthest north was the Tatshenshini, reaching from Dry Bay to the village of Neskatahin. Another route, through the narrow valley of the Taku River and along mountain streams, led to Atlin and Teslin lakes.[9] It was controlled by the Taku River Tlingit living near present-day Juneau. Yet another route led up the Chilkat River valley to Neskatahin or via Kusawa Lake and the Takhini River to the Yukon River valley at Lake Laberge. It was owned by the Wolf clan of the Tlingit at Klukwan.[10]

At the head of the Lynn Canal were the last two routes. The White Pass route was not used often. The other route, owned by the Tlingit Raven clan of the village of Chilkoot, led up the rugged Taiya River valley to the headwaters of the Yukon River. This was the Chilkoot Trail.

These trade links to the interior are very old. The Tlingit took dried fish and eulachon grease, Chilkat blankets, cedar boxes, spruce root baskets and, in later years, European trade goods, to the interior.[11] They returned with copper, tanned moose and caribou hides plus beaver, lynx and fox pelts, prepared skin clothing and the goat skins and lichen needed for making and dyeing Chilkat blankets.

Klukwan graveyard. Grave markers indicated the clan identity.

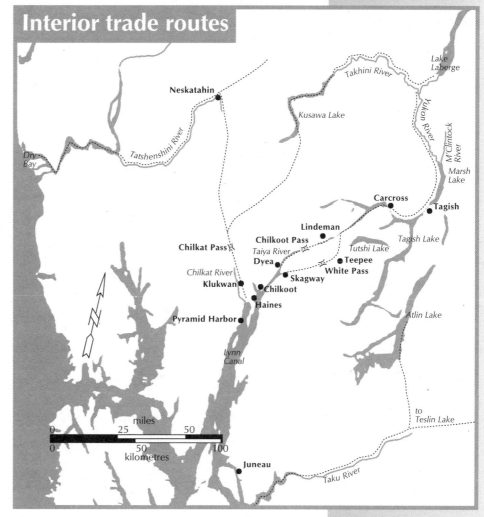

Interior trade routes

Trading into the Yukon

The Tlingit traded with several Yukon First Nations. These people of the interior, known variously as Sticks by 19th century European explorers, or Athapaskans by 20th century anthropologists, lived quite different lives than their coastal trading partners. In contrast to the rich array of concentrated marine and land resources of the coast, the Yukon interior provided more thinly distributed resources. The Athapaskans moved frequently to harvest the more dispersed sources of food and shelter of the interior.

A Tlingit family at Dyea.

Tlingit children near Klukwan.

In late summer, people began preparing for the coming winter. Berry picking and the annual fall hunt for moose or caribou took place. Food preparation and storage became increasingly intense as fall progressed. The first part of winter was a communal time; families settled together to relax and celebrate after the busy summer of activity. As winter progressed and food supplies diminished, families spread out to trap. Spring was eagerly anticipated. It meant a chance to get out of brush and skin shelters and hunt for fresh meat. It was a time to add to the diminishing—or empty—caches of preserved fish, dried meat and berries. In summer, families gathered in larger groups at river sites to catch and dry fish.

These camps were also often the meeting sites for the annual Tlingit trading trips. The Athapaskans prepared their prime furs and well-made skin clothing, often artfully decorated with porcupine quills, and later, beads, and waited for the traders to arrive.

The Tlingit usually made two trading trips per year into the interior. A small group might brave the fierce winter winds and

storms of the mountain passes in January or February to meet the Athapaskans at their winter camps. The longest trips, with more traders, came in the early summer between the eulachon fishing of April and the start of the salmon runs in late June.[12]

These arduous trips through the mountains were well-planned. Aurel Krause, a German ethnographer visiting the Tlingit in spring, 1882, described his participation in a Chilkat trip:

> *Before going, dances were performed, thorough bodily cleansing was undertaken, and the face was freshly painted; during the journey no one washed.... For weeks ahead preparations went on, ...trade goods desired by the Athapaskan were acquired...and, together with their own dried salmon, fish oil, and flour as travelling rations, were packed in large bundles which were carried on the back by means of pack straps across forehead and chest. The Tlingit manage perfectly astonishing loads of one hundred pounds and more on steep mountain trails and across broad snow fields on trips of several days into the interior.... In winter almost the whole trip is done on snowshoes, which are especially large to prevent the packer, who carries, in addition to his load, a gun and an axe, from sinking into the snow under his weight. Sleds were seldom used.... Each carrier was provided with a staff which he used in winter to knock the snow off his snowshoes and in summer to bend back the thick underbrush.*[13]

Once in the interior, the traders had to travel, sometimes quite extensively, to find their Athapaskan partners. The Tagish Narrows and the M'Clintock River fish camp on Marsh Lake were usual places for trade. During their trip, the Tlingit would leave a variety of bush signals to indicate their direction of travel and the

The interior of a traditional Tlingit house. Chinese tea boxes were prized possessions.

A new style clan house under construction at Klukwan, 1898.

number in their party. Once they reached the trading place they would build a smoky fire or torch a lone tree to signal their arrival.[14]

While the economics of the trade favoured the Tlingit, the period of trading was a time of great excitement and fun for all. The host chief would make a speech and a ceremonial exchange of gifts would be followed by a feast and an invitation to join in dancing, singing and games.

Trade was not simply an economic exchange. The Tlingit demanded, and received, the loyalty of individuals as trading partners. These relationships became bonds of trust, usually

Winnie Atlin of Carcross preparing a moosehide jacket for a Tlingit relative in Juneau, 1993.

Two youth from Tagish at the turn of the century.

First Nation houses at Tagish in 1897.

solidified with marriages between interior and coastal trading families.[15] Over time, the resulting blended families and increased trade blurred distinctions between cultural groups in the region.

Fur traders from Europe

During the 18th century, the Tlingit began to meet with European fur traders more often. Russian traders first entered the waters of southern Alaska in the 1700s. They pursued lucrative commercial ventures in the Pacific northwest by trading for sea otter skins. Initially reaching the Aleutian Islands in the 1740s, at first they traded with the Aleuts there and later forced the Aleuts to hunt for them. Their aggressive exploitation of both people and wildlife led to dramatic declines in the aboriginal population and in their own profits.[16]

At about the same time, Spanish, British and American explorers and traders were moving north up the Pacific coast of North America. Captain James Cook of the Royal Navy reached the area in 1778, reinforcing British claims to the region. As many as 15 independent American fur traders also cruised the coastal waters at this time. All of these newcomers reached into the Tlingit homeland.

The Russian American Company expanded into Tlingit lands at the end of the 18th century. It established settlements at Yakutat and Sitka. Although these outposts were attacked by the Tlingit, and Yakutat was permanently abandoned in 1805, the Russians persevered and gradually solidified their presence. They eventually began to trade with the Tlingit.

By the 1820s, the continuing exploitation of the sea otter had led to its near extinction. The Russians' main fur market had been the Chinese Empire. However, this market collapsed as a series of devastating internal wars and European invasions punctured the old Chinese state. The western European appetite for furs, however, continued strong to the end of the century.[17]

Sitka Tlingit were related to the Chilkat. Here they arrive at Klukwan for a potlatch in October, 1900.

The beneficiary of these changes was the British Hudson's Bay Company (HBC), which developed an active presence along the north Pacific coast. By underselling the American free traders, the HBC was able to clear the market of competitors. In 1839, the company signed an agreement with the Russian American Company to lease its lands along the Alaska Panhandle. A network of HBC posts was soon opened on the coast. The company's steamer, the *Beaver*, and subsequent vessels, then carried on the northwest fur trade until 1867, when the United States bought Alaska from Russia, ending the HBC lease.[18]

The purchase of Alaska brought no significant changes to the Tlingit fur trade. Independent traders from the United States began returning to coastal Tlingit villages as early as 1869, purchasing furs from the Tlingit. In 1880, the American North West Company established six trading posts in the region.[19] This continuing demand for furs from the Yukon increased the value of the Tlingit mountain routes. The fur trade remained an important part of the Tlingit economy until the late 1880s.

A Tlingit from Klukwan ready for an early spring trip to the interior.

The Hudson's Bay Company sidewheeler, the *Beaver*, steamed up and down the coast picking up furs from 1836 to 1858.

Maintaining the interior trade

Although Tlingit trade with coastal neighbours was generally carried on by individuals, the more lucrative interior trade was managed by the heads of certain clans. By tightly controlling the use of their trails and by defeating challengers to their monopoly, these clan heads maintained a strong negotiating position with the European traders on the coast. And with their ready access to attractive European trade goods, they could also demand high trading prices from their Yukon trading partners. The Tlingit retained this position as intermediaries from the 1830s to the late 1880s. The cohesive character of their communities, their knowledge of the country, and their ability to play competing traders against one another, made them potent and effective negotiators. In their relations with the HBC, individual miners and traders, they rarely had to use force; the strength of their position was well recognized.[20]

The Tlingit, wary of competitors' attempts to enter their territory, not only traded but also monitored their partners' trade. In the late 1820s, the HBC attempted to expand its interior trade network westward into the Yukon River basin. In the summer of 1848, Tlingit traders were displeased to find Robert Campbell, an HBC trader, with a post on their trading site at the junction of the Pelly and Yukon rivers. Determined to rout this competition, they undersold Campbell. For four years he carried on a limited trade at Fort Selkirk, but was hampered by the high costs of operating a post so far beyond the company's network. In the fall of 1851, he acknowledged his difficulties:

> I am sorry to report that a large party (31) of trading Indians from the coast who visited the Pelly and remained here 'til they got their loads traded made a clean sweep of all the furs and leather of the surrounding vicinity. Some of the same Indians even went down the river near a hundred miles. This long established trade, the very low price at which they dispose their goods, and their acquaintance with the language and the habits of these tribes afford them facilities for trade we are all deprived of.

The Tlingit, already annoyed by Campbell's trading, became alarmed in 1851 when he built a new, more substantial trading post across the river from the original site. The following year, a Klukwan war party went to Fort Selkirk, where they ransacked the post and chased Campbell from the country. Campbell was incensed by the loss of Fort Selkirk and made his way south to argue for re-opening the post. However, in 1851, the HBC had spent

By 1850 sea otter skins made up less than one tenth of the value of the fur packet dispatched from the main HBC post in the region, Fort Simpson. In the same year the HBC trading vessel, *Beaver*, traded no sea otter at all. Six years later less than 100 sea otter pelts were traded at Fort Simpson, out of a total packet of over 14,000 furs. The major species traded were beaver, mink and marten, all mainland species.

• *Historical Atlas of Canada*, v.2

Àndàx'w, also known as Mrs. Dyea John or Mary Hammond, a Carcross-Tagish First Nation woman, with two children at Carcross about 1905.

over £650 operating Fort Selkirk while the return in furs was only £240. Company managers saw little point in trading at a loss for furs in the Yukon interior when they could trade with the Tlingit for the same furs on the coast at a profit. Therefore, they chose not to rebuild the post.[21]

As well as keeping the European traders out, the Tlingit made sure their trading partners stayed in. The Tlingit exercised their control of the mountain passes and refused to allow Yukon First Nations down to the coast to trade. Even when some of the Athapaskans did pack their goods out, only those who were relatives of Tlingit families were allowed to trade directly with the white traders. Others traded their wares with their Tlingit partners at deeply discounted prices.[22] In addition to travel and trade prohibitions, Tlingit traders consistently warned people in the interior of the dangers of dealing with white men.[23]

As Tlingit access to European trade improved, more European goods were carried in to their trading partners. By the 1820s, there was a fairly regular supply of European goods into the Yukon basin. Metal kettles and pots, mirrors, flour, baking powder and coffee, knives and axes, guns and ammunition, calico and woollen blankets became common after the short-lived popularity of beads and other cheap jewellery. Robert Campbell noted the high quality of the trading goods the Tlingit used for their trade near Fort Selkirk.[24]

For six decades, this careful balancing of threats and service allowed the Tlingit to effectively compete with, and block, the trading efforts of aggressive European traders. Consequently, they were able to maintain their profitable and powerful position in the Yukon fur trade.

Only in the 1880s did the Tlingit economic position start to erode. Independent traders began travelling up the lower Yukon River from its mouth, eventually reaching into the Tlingit market. Fort Reliance, established on the Yukon River in 1874, was the first of an increasing number of new trading posts competing with the Tlingit trade monopoly. By the mid-1880s,

A winter camp along the Yukon River. In the 1890s, life for the Athapaskans of the Yukon River was radically different from that of the Tlingit on the coast.

much of the interior fur trade was drained away to the west and north. Mike Hess, a prospector living near the mouth of the White River, described the changing trade routes of the Athapaskans in a letter published by *The Alaskan* on November 28, 1885:

> The Tanana Indians come to this place to trade; they come across the headwaters of the White, then come down on rafts. They take that route because the portage is shorter, and it is easier to bring their furs 200 miles down the river than pack them on their backs [presumably down to the coast].

Although the Tlingit trading area was significantly reduced to those areas immediately inside their passes, they retained considerable power. In September, 1887, George Dawson spent several days in Dyea waiting for a steamer while on his way out from the Yukon. He noted local storekeeper John Healy's observations on the fur trade:

> Healey says $2000 to $3000 of furs come out now yearly by Chilkoot Pass. Prob. $10,000 or 12,000 by Chilkat. More would come by former, but Coast Indians are diverting the trade, as the Tagish formerly in a state of servitude almost to the Chilkoots have now managed to obtain direct trade with Healey. A rather large quantity of furs from interior comes out by Yukon R. Healey wishes to establish post E. of Mts, but does not think it safe to do so unless police protection, as Coast Indians would probably destroy as interfering with their purogative of trade.[25]

Even in this smaller area, the prohibition against direct trade between whites and the interior people was gradually overcome. By the late 1880s, small groups of Tagish regularly carried furs through the Chilkoot Pass to Dyea, to trade. The collapse in European demand for furs in the late 1870s and the ongoing depression in prices until the mid-1890s also reduced the importance of the fur trade, forcing the Tlingit to change the focus of their local economy.[26]

An imaginative sketch of Frederick Schwatka's 1883 trip through the Chilkoot Pass.

More newcomers

In the last quarter of the 19th century, many new people arrived in the Chilkoot region. The abundance of salmon attracted commercial canneries to the inlets and harbours of the southeast while the rugged, exposed geology of the coast and the mysterious promise of the Yukon interior drew miners and prospectors from the south. Travellers and tourists came to see the natural wonders and American Presbyterian missionaries arrived to convert the "heathen" Indians.

The Tlingit preserved their trade network by playing to their strengths. In July, 1869, the editors of the Sitka *Alaska Times* complained about the power of the Tlingit in the Lynn Canal:

There is a very large trading business carried on there, chiefly in furs and skins, the market, however, is not accessible to every one. The Indians rule and their fashions are law in that land.... At present the Indians govern to suit their own interests.

Healy and Wilson's trading post at Dyea opened in 1886. (inset) The expanded store on Decoration Day in 1899.

The newcomers had a highly-developed view of their own superiority as well as fairly detailed preconceptions of where they were going. The "wilderness" beyond the islands of settlement they established were seen as God's original handiwork. To some, it offered opportunity and freedom. One commentator at the time wrote about the Yukon:

> Upon this azoic land lay the laws of the universe in its uncontaminated state before the hand of civilization had spread its warping veneer or written its crooked code.... In the strong, pure, free life, no want of woman, no curse of caste, no rust of rivalry, no gall of glory, no edict of earth prevailed. There man, and woman, too, was ruled according to stark merit.[27]

For many newcomers, however, the natural environment of the Chilkoot was something to be feared, not celebrated. Charles M. Taylor, a Chicago newspaper editor, described his trip up the Lynn Canal in 1900:

> How repelling are those distant peaks, in their unchanging draperies of ice and snow! Their children, the glaciers, cling to their slopes, and though mist and fog oft times surround them, they are ever the same—bleak, barren, inaccessible.[28]

Newcomers felt that this unregulated corner of the world had to be brought under their control. Without "order," Alaska was a drain on national resources and a corrupter of national life as they knew it.[29]

"Order" arrived with the newcomers. Using dynamite, steel and money, they introduced the social and technological infrastructure to transform the wilderness. Bishop William Bompas, the Anglican missionary in the Yukon interior during the 1880s, was pleased with the growing number of doctors, more regular steamship service, the extension of roads and the introduction of government. He noted the transition of the Yukon "from a savage wilderness to a civilized white man's home."[30]

There were two schools of thought about northern Indians, both based on the then-prevalent notion of natural selection. At best, the northern aboriginal people were seen as frozen in time and stalled in the evolutionary process. This view, shared by most missionaries, inspired them to "civilize" the Indians by means of western law, education, temperance and Christianity. The self-sufficient Tlingit of the coast were often seen as intractable and arrogant. However, the Athapaskans of the interior were referred to as "ideal children of the forest, innocent, inoffensive, and as guileless as our first parents were in the beautiful garden before the fall." Other newcomers simply regarded the Indians as a wrong turn in the evolutionary

In 1869, several prospectors from Sitka felt the hostility of the coastal Tlingit. Led to a placer gold find by a Taku River Tlingit they began panning out the gold. When the Kake Tlingit from the nearby village discovered this, they forcibly stopped the men from working, took away their equipment, stripped one of them of his clothes and ordered them to leave, the while denouncing both General Davis, the American military governor, and the Taku River Tlingit who had brought the prospectors to their place.

• from the *Alaska Times*, September 25, 1869

The ice-laden *Alert,* one of many small steamers carrying miners and traders from Juneau to Dyea in the years before the gold rush.

Regional map of the Taiya Inlet prepared by the Presbyterian Mission Society. The society acknowledged the contributions of its staff and donors by freely naming geographic features after them. Miss Elizabeth L. Matthews of Monmouth, Illinois, had been the school marm at Haines since her arrival there in September, 1882. Mr. and Mrs. Walter B. Styles were missionaries at Hoonah down the coast. Mrs. Styles was the daughter of Alonzo E. Austin of New York who was in charge of the mission at Sitka in 1881. Sheldon Jackson was a leading Presbyterian missionary in the region. Point Langdon was named after Mrs. C.H. Langdon of Elizabeth, New Jersey who donated "the first Presbyterian bell in Alaska; and oh, how sweet it sounds! Just a perfect Presbyterian tone!" according to Mrs. Charlotte Willard. Not many of the Presbyterian place names on this map have survived to the present.

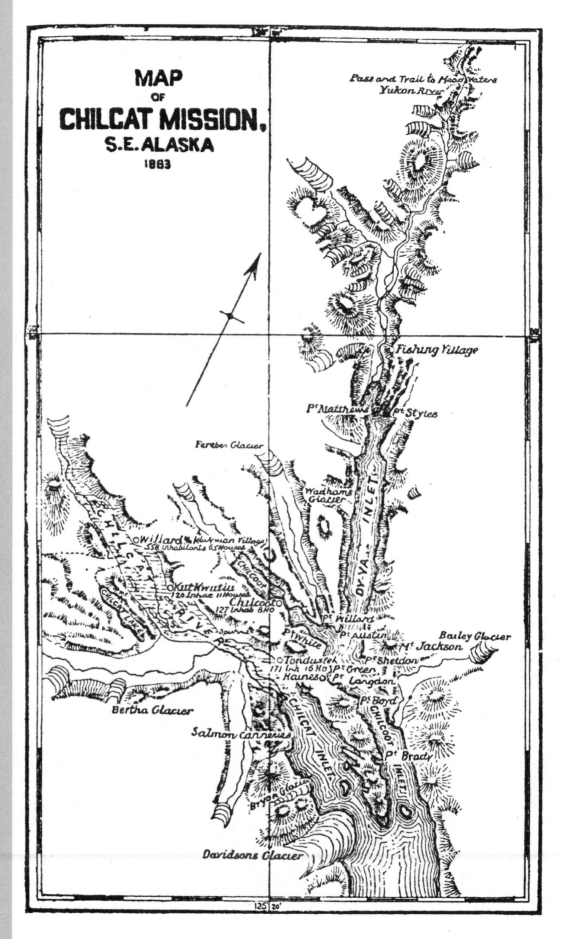

MAP OF CHILCAT MISSION, S.E. ALASKA 1883

process and destined to die out as they met with the more successful strains of the human race. These people took little care to respect and acknowledge First Nations claims.[31]

Most, however, believed native northerners were a savage, wild people incapable of saving themselves. The Presbyterians, who established a mission at present-day Haines, worked hard to educate the Indians, their objective being a people: "...virtuous, temperate, cleanly, industrious; a generation, in short, permeated with the alphabet and the ten commandments," and one completely separated from its past and the original character of its now ordered homeland.[32]

The missionaries at Haines had limited success in spite of their enthusiasm and dedication. Ivan Petroff, employed for the U.S. Census, noted that after nearly a decade of missionary effort, "The Chilcoot Indians never winter at the Mission, which was built in a romantic spot in the hope of getting the Indians to move, but the latter preferred salmon to scenery."[33]

Other newcomers preferred salmon as well. Commercial fishing began in the early 1880s at Taiya Inlet. Canneries were soon operating at Pyramid Harbor and at Chilkoot. Although

KEEPING CONTROL

EUGENE WILLARD, THE Presbyterian missionary at Chilkoot, purchased a ground-squirrel robe from a Yukon First Nations trader early in 1882. He paid the same price that he would have paid the Tlingit. His wife described the ensuing difficulties in a letter to her sister Eva:

You can scarcely imagine the hornet's nest that was stirred up; the people were ready to mob us. Early next morning, before we could get our breakfast, we were set upon by some of the headmen, of whom Kla-not was spokesman.... He charged us with having robbed them, for said he, the Sticks are our money, we and our fathers before us have gotten rich from them. They are only wild: they are not men; and now you have told them these things and taken away our riches.

Willard tried to defend his actions but Klanot, second chief of the Chilkoots, countered by accusing the missionaries of bringing nothing and now taking away their wealth. He threatened to have nothing further to do with the missionaries.[34]

The Presbyterian Church established a mission to the Tlingit in 1880.

the Tlingit initially complained about the harvesting of their fish, they were mollified by jobs at the canneries. The number and size of the canneries quickly increased. By the late 1880s, H.S. Bacon & Company of San Francisco was doubling its production each year, shipping some 15,000 cases of salmon from its two canneries near Chilkoot in 1888.[35] At the same time, the cannery operators began importing cheaper Chinese labourers for the seasonal cannery operations. Now the Tlingit found themselves without fish or wages.

In December, 1898, a group of Tlingit chiefs met with Governor John Green Brady in Juneau to present their grievances and appeal for some guarantees for their future.[36] Through their presentations they told of the losses of land, trade and animals they suffered by the arrival of the newcomers. They highlighted the challenges they faced as leaders of their communities and asked for fair treatment by the American authorities. Governor Brady responded with the advantages of American rule: the abolition of slavery, the reduction of clan warfare and the general increase in wealth available to all who would work. From his perspective there were only two options for the Tlingit: either assimilate into the American way of life and gain the benefits of full citizenship, or remain on reserves created to allow them to remain undisturbed and isolated in their old ways.

Opening the Chilkoot Trail

After the purchase of Alaska, the prospects for a major mine began to draw prospectors and miners into the Chilkoot region. For a decade, the searchers explored the coastal inlets and mountains. In the late 1870s, promising gold finds were located just south of the Lynn Canal Tlingit communities. Within a year, the mining community of Juneau was founded. As the mines at Juneau increased their output, the population grew, and the town became a base for the expanding hunt for gold and silver.

Tantalizing rumours of gold emerged from the Yukon interior.[37] Back in the 1850s, Robert Campbell had found gold near his post at Fort Selkirk. A dozen years later, in the mid-1860s, Reverend Robert McDonald of the Anglican Church Missionary Society located a creek where there was "so much gold...he could have gathered it with a spoon."

Prospectors in Juneau packed and ready for the trip through the Chilkoot, about 1895.

Henry Daw Banks of Springfield, Massachusetts took these photographs of Pyramid Harbor during a visit in August of 1898.

(*preceding page, top*) Chinese labourers cleaning salmon.
(*preceding page, middle*) Loading a barge with crates of tinned salmon.
(*bottom*) The salmon cannery at Pyramid Harbor.

The first prospectors in the Yukon River basin arrived in 1873. Since direct access to the interior was impossible because of the Tlingit blockade of their mountain trails, Yukon-bound prospectors spent almost a year following the old HBC route over the Mackenzie Mountains to Fort Yukon on the Yukon River. By 1880, there were probably fewer than a dozen prospectors sampling the sand bars of Yukon rivers for gold. Although the north seemed promising, it was just too hard to get to.

It seemed unlikely that the Tlingit, still profiting from their control of the fur trade, would acknowledge the demands of individual miners wanting access to the Yukon. However,

THE PROSPECTOR

An' its lonesome, lonesome, lonesome when the russet gold is shed,
And the naked world stands waiting for the Doom;
With the northern witch-fires dancing in the silence overhead,
An' my campfire just an island in the gloom.

I've been allus in the lead since I grew grass high
Since my father's prairie schooner left the Known,
For a port beyond the sky-line, never seen by human eye,
Where God and God's creation dwell alone.

A sweet voice kept calling from the Unexplored Beyond,
A wild voice in the mountains callin' "West"...
An' the voice that I have followed has not told me what it meant,
An' the eyes that sought a sign are nearly blind.

But I hear it callin' still, as I lay me down to rest,
An' I dream the Voice I love has never lied.
That I hear a people comin', the Great People of the West,
An' maybe 'twas His Voice callin' me to guide.

Mr. Clive Phillip-Wolley (from *Bennett Sun,* July 7, 1900)

Carcross-Tagish and Tlingit men stick gambling at Dyea in early 1897. They are likely between packing jobs.

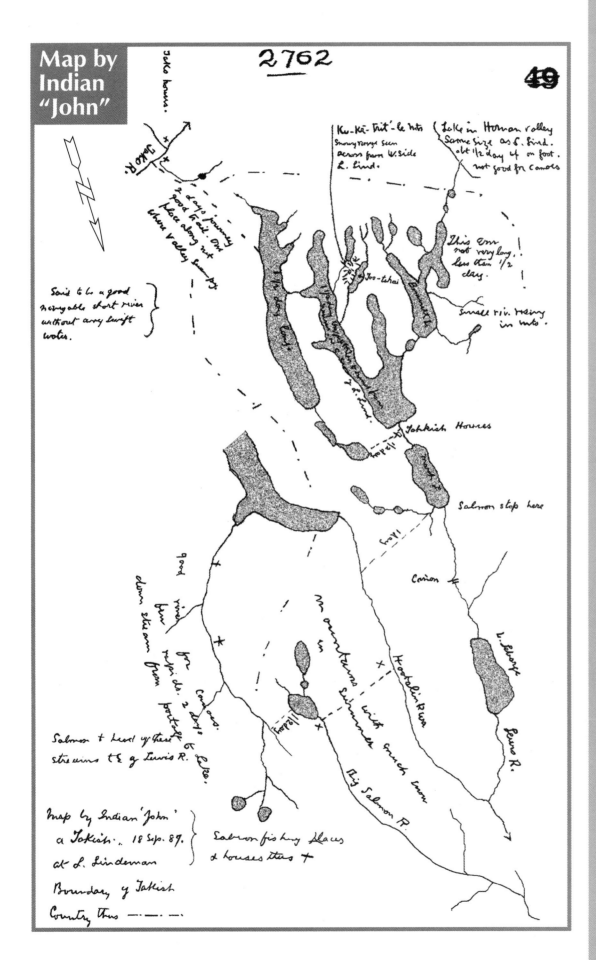

Map by Indian "John"

2762

49

[Handwritten annotations on the map include:]

Jaka house.

Jaka R.

Ku-Kā-Tūt'-le hts
Snowy range seen
across from W. side
L. Lind.

Lake in Hainan valley
Same size as L. Lind.
abt 1/2 day up on foot.
not good for canoes

a days journey
good trail. one
place along not
where valley from pt

This can
not very long!
less than 1/2
day.

Said to be a good
navigable short river
without any swift
water.

Small riv. rising
in mts.

Joo-tahai

Tahkish Houses

Portage

Salmon stop here

good
river
for
canoe

down stream from

Cañon

L. Surprise

good
river
for
canoe

Canoe
canoe 2 days of Lake.

Portage

Haatalinkwa

Swimmers with smooth snow

Lewis R.

Salmon + head of these
streams to q Lewis R.

Big Salmon R.

Map by Indian 'John'
a Takish. 18 Sep. 89.
at L. Lindeman
Boundary q Takish
Country thus ———

Salmon fishing places
+ houses there +

This map by Indian "John"
of Tagish is one of several
drawn by Yukon First
Nations people and
collected by George
Dawson during his 1887
trip. The map details the
area from the crest of the
Coast Mountains (top) and
follows the river drainages
north to the mouth of the
Big Salmon River. In his
diary, Dawson noted:[38]

*18. Sep. Still waiting [at
Lindeman]. Utilize part of
the day in getting of the
information I can
geographical & otherwise
from the one young Indian
here.*

Angela Sidney, in her book,
*Place Names of the Tagish
Region, Southern Yukon*
published in 1980, noted
place names of the Chilkoot
region.

Chilkoot Pass
Kwatese/over the mountain
(Tagish)
A Shakî/over it (Tlingit)

Log Cabin
Tū Ch'iłè' Tah Men/among
the small or ragged lakes
(Tagish)
Âx'w Sâni Xhù or
Hîn Kas'él'ti Xhù/among the
small or ragged lakes (Tlingit)

Lindeman Lake
Tl'ûxh'u Â/murky lake
(Tlingit)

Lindeman/Bennett portage
Ch'akhúxh Anaxh Duł.adi
Yé/place for packing skin
boats over (Tlingit)

through the fall and winter of 1879-80 a series of events amongst the Tlingit communities of the upper Lynn Canal opened a way for the miners.

The newcomers' arrival caused discord in these communities. The Tlingit were under pressure from miners wanting to travel through their lands. Many of the younger members of the Tlingit clans rebelled against new claims on their homeland and resources. The older leaders, however, especially Kohklux—headman of the Chilkat and one of the raiders on Fort Selkirk two decades earlier—suggested caution and warned of the dangers of direct opposition.[39]

These fractures split wide open in September of 1879. Kohklux attempted to make peace between the groups, but was seriously injured and a war between two clans seemed imminent. A large party of Chilkat Tlingit, then in Sitka, prepared to return home to settle the issue. Captain Lester A. Beardslee, commander of the U.S. Navy's patrol vessel in Sitka and the sole government enforcement agent in the region, was looking for an opportunity to come to friendly terms with the Tlingit in the Lynn Canal area. By assisting the outfitting and organization of the party supporting Kohklux, Beardslee gained his favour, correctly assuming the elder chief would be more willing to work with the whites. In return for this favour, Beardslee asked the Tlingit to allow miners to travel through their country into the Yukon.

Although the community disagreements continued well into the following year, in February, 1880, Kohklux and other regional Tlingit chiefs agreed to allow miners through. Passage was conditional on the miners' promise not to interfere with the fur trade. By May, a group of 19 prospectors was ready to travel to the interior. Accompanied by a well-armed

Klukwan, June, 1899.

naval vessel, the party reached Klukwan on May 27 and met with five chiefs of the local Tlingit.

Rather than allowing the miners to use the important Chilkat trail, running from Klukwan to Neskatahin, the main route for their fur trade, the Tlingit directed the miners towards the less important Chilkoot Pass. Tlingit guides accompanied the party to ensure no trading took place and slaves were made available to pack the miners' gear—for a fee. By mid-June, the miners were over the pass and building boats on the Yukon headwaters. The Chilkoot Trail was now open to miners and the foundations for a new Tlingit packing business were in place.

Packing: "We make our trail for our own use"

The Tlingit of Chilkoot village were hardened and skilled mountain travellers who adapted their skills to the packing business. The Raven clan there, led by second chief Klanot, quickly organized itself to take advantage of this new opportunity. Through the early 1880s, prices were established and small groups of prospectors were regularly accompanied through the pass as far as Lindeman Lake. But as the number of miners grew, problems started to develop.

The Chilkoots were firm in their statements of ownership of the pass. Chief Klanot expressed their rights in clear terms: "We make our trail for our own use, if others wish to use it should they not compensate us for our labor? The white man builds a wharf and all who lands goods over it must pay."

Other Native Americans—and even whites—trying to break into the commercial packing business were refused permission to pack goods on the trail. This was partially to keep as

Captain Beardslee explained his 1879 actions in the Chilkat country in his official report to his superior officers in 1882:[40]

The Indians [Chilkhats] fear[ed] that the whites would interfere with the trade with the Stich Indians who live in the interior, and whose trade the coast Indians monopolize. The Chilkhats were estimated as from two to four thousand in number, and considered to be the most warlike of all the tribes. The [Yukon] country was reported to be rich in minerals, and the miners were very desirous of penetrating it, and it seemed more than likely that sooner or later, bodies of them would undertake to force their way in which case serious trouble would probably have occurred.

much money as possible in Chilkoot hands, but also because of a question of liability. Under Tlingit law, an injury or death on the trail would be the responsibility of the owning clan. The Chilkoots, therefore, limited the packing trade to members and relatives of their families. By 1886, there were about 200 packers working at Dyea. Half of these were men from the Lynn Canal Tlingit clans, along with 13 Yukon packers and two Auk Tlingit from around Juneau, all probably related to the Chilkoot Tlingit by marriage. Eighty women and children of the district also packed over the trail.[41]

Prospectors, anxious to spend a long summer exploring the rivers and creeks of the Yukon basin, were often impatient. They bargained for better rates but the dangers of the trail and the difficulties of hauling their own outfits—averaging more than 180 kg (400 lbs.)—usually quickly persuaded them to hire packers. Miners who haggled too much found themselves boycotted altogether and forced to haul their own gear.[42]

All contracts were negotiated and personally supervised by the packing chief, Klanot. Prices through the 1880s for packing over the pass varied between $9 and $13 per hundred pounds. Packing was lucrative. It brought earnings of some six or seven thousand dollars annually to the Tlingit of Chilkoot village.

Itinerant traders quickly moved into the area to take advantage of this new wealth. In 1886, five seasonal posts popped up in Dyea and Chilkoot. They sold goods to the Tlingit and supplied the seasonal rush of miners from Juneau.[43]

In the early 1880s, only small parties of miners headed into the Yukon, and the Chilkoot accommodated them quite easily. By the mid-1880s, however, promising gold finds were drawing more and more miners to the Yukon. In 1886, over 100 miners went over the pass. The following year, after a major gold strike on the Fortymile River, the number more than doubled. Delays of up to two months became common.[44] In early May, 1886, while waiting for more packers, Captain H.E. Nichols wrote from Chilkoot:

The *Alaska Free Press*, February 26, 1887, in "More about the Yukon country" reported:

This little three miles of the whole route [the summit of the Chilkoot Pass] is the great stumbling block to the new Eldorado. It is the means of the miners now being charged the extortionate price of $13 per 100 lbs and up for the transportation of all articles necessary for the trip, which is done on the backs of the natives. If some man would only grasp the situation in its true light, he would forthwith blast out that little three miles, and establish a pack train there for the transportation of the large amount of merchandise that will necessarily have to be taken in during the coming summer and those to follow.

(preceding page, top) **Native American packers transporting stampeders' goods up the Chilkoot Trail near Sheep Camp, 1898.**

(preceding page, bottom) **Chilkoot chiefs Doniwak (left) and Isaac, Dyea, 1897.**

Packing up Long Hill beyond Sheep Camp, 1897.

Arrived here in three days after leaving Chilcoot inlet. The trail is fearfully bad from Summit to this place—soft snow to the hips. The Indians earn every dollar they get for packing—I paid $87.25 cheerfully.

• J.S.P. Robinson, letter from Lindeman Lake, May 17, 1886

Dyea just before the onslaught, summer of 1897. Indian village in the background. The Healy and Wilson store faces the river.

There are not Indians enough here now to pack in over twenty five men at a time, as the average is not less than six packs per man; of the present packers, nearly one half are interior or "Stick" Indians, many Chilcoots being out fishing or in the interior on their regular trading trips. Heretofore the Chilcoots have jealously guarded their hereditary privilege of packing, and trading over the Shasheki [Chilkoot] pass, not even allowing the Stick Indians to come out. With the small number of miners and others who have gone in they have been able to do this very satisfactorily, but with the sudden and unexpected increase they find themselves unequal to the task: I think too that they recognize the fact that the white man has come and submitting to the inevitable they are perfectly willing that all others shall come in and help and that this business shall be as free to all as is Juneau. It is expected that the Kakes and Auks [other Tlingit groups] will come up with the rest expected by the next Steamer.[45]

Miners, worried about the short mining season, were outraged by delays, especially those driven by Tlingit priorities. Mining in the Yukon was limited to early spring and late summer when the river water levels dropped, allowing panning of the sandbars. Backed by the vocal Juneau press, they began to work towards gaining control of transportation into the Yukon.

KLANOT AND THE PACKING BUSINESS

BORN IN 1850, Klanot was the nephew of Chief Kohklux. Klanot became second chief of the Chilkoots in the 1880s and was responsible for the trading and packing business through the Chilkoot Trail. Like his uncle, Klanot faced serious challenges to his clan's way of life. Unlike Kohklux, however, he did not live long enough to add an elder's wisdom to his community.

When Dyea merchant John Healy tried to take control of the miners' packing in 1887 and charge tolls for use of the trail, Klanot acted quickly. He refused to allow any white men to pack and asked the American government to clarify his clan's property rights:

I, Claanot, chief of the Chilkoot tribe, make the following statement: Mr. Haley [Healy] wishes to take away our road or trail to the Yukon, which my tribe does not like, as we made it long ago, and it has always been in my tribe. We fixed the road good, so that the miners would not get hurt, and Mr. Haley is putting sticks or logs on it, so he can get pay for people going in over our trail, and we do not want to see that....

I always treat the miners kindly, and when they do their own packing, I tell them that they had better let the Indians do their packing, so the miners will not hurt themselves on the trail, and some of the miners tell me that it is not my business, which hurts my feelings....

When the miners go in I would like them to arrange with me instead of the other men of my tribe, so as to save time and misunderstanding, as the Indians come to me anyhow as chief.

My tribe claims the winter trail over the Schkat-Quay [Skagway]. We have three trails to the Yukon, and we claim all of them....

I ask $10 for a half pack to pay me for my general supervision and responsibility of the packing, as I feel myself bound to see every man and packing through safe. I have never asked or demanded toll from any person and do not do so.[46]

The great demand for packers and the attractive wages had drawn many other Tlingit groups to Dyea. In early June, 1888, a large group of Sitka Tlingit arrived to pack. Klanot demanded the Sitkans either stop packing or pay the Chilkoots a percentage of their wages for the privilege of using the trail. Heated discussions led to a fight and Klanot was killed along with several others. He was succeeded as trading chief by his sister.

Klanot was a determined and proud man. Aware of his community's power and the grudging respect given by the newcomers, he appeared domineering and arrogant. He was conscious of his responsibility to protect his clan's rights in controlling and profiting from the interior trade. During the late 1880s, the erosion of these rights stiffened Klanot's resolve to keep control. However, by this time there were too many other factors shaping the Tlingit future for such direct action to be successful.

The Indians compel every miner to pay toll for going through their country. The second chief of the Chilkats [Chilkoots] is the one that makes the demands for toll, and all the miners pay rather than having trouble with the Indians, as this tribe is the strongest one in Alaska. Over 200 men have went in this spring, and combined they have paid one dirty, thieving, Indian about $300 for the privilege of travelling about thirty miles through the woods of Uncle Sam's domain.... If there is a class of men in Alaska who need the protection of the government, it is the miners, for it is they who go to the front and cut the first tree and roll the first stone out of the way.

• The *Alaska Free Press*,
May 14, 1887

Frederick Schwatka's Tlingit guide in 1883 denounced Schwatka for non-payment of guide services. Shown here in this formal portrait, he told Schwatka: "I will take your name and use it as long as I live." He was henceforth known as George Schwatka.

Losing control of the Chilkoot

The packing business was undermined as stampeders brought in horses and oxen and began the construction of roads and tramways.

High wages and a limited number of packers brought challenges to the Lynn Canal Tlingit monopoly. White miners demanded faster and cheaper passage and encouraged other Tlingit groups to come forward and pack. In the late 1880s, the American authorities also began to agitate for a more open packing business. The Tlingit definition of clan was broad, ensuring a large number of people were eligible to pack. By the time of the Klondike gold rush, Indians from all over southeast Alaska had come to Dyea for packing work.

At the same time, however, several Juneau business owners began planning more advanced transportation measures. In 1885, the Chilkoot Pass and Summit Railroad Company was organized to run a rail line through the pass to the interior.[47] Although the railway idea quickly faded, others sought more immediate solutions. Peter Peterson of Juneau designed a sled tramway for the pass; it was in operation by the spring of 1894.[48] In 1895, Healy brought in the first pack horses. By the middle of 1897, some 200 horses were hauling freight. In the following year, several companies also introduced wagon trains and aerial tramways. By the end of 1898, there was little for the packers on the Chilkoot Trail to carry.[49]

The Stampede Through the Chilkoot

"Label your luggage for Klondike" was a popular song in the Vancouver, British Columbia area during the gold rush.

Klondike, Klondike

"Label your luggage for Klondike,
For there ain't no luck in the town today,
There ain't no work down Moodyville way
Pack up your traps and be off, I say,
Off and away to the Klondike.

Oh, they scratches the earth and it tumbles out
More than your hands can hold,
For the hills above and plains beneath
Are cracking and busting with gold."[1]

(preceding page) The *Excelsior* leaves San Francisco to head back north.

For many Americans suffering through the economic depression of the 1890s, the Klondike stampede seemed an answer to their prayers.

Gold has always lured people. From ancient times gold has been a sign of wealth and prestige. In the early 19th century, it became even more important when the Bank of England set up an international gold standard to bring order and stability to the international economy.[2]

From the mid-1700s, the industrial revolution had transformed the economies of Europe and, later, North America. The new technologies and growing populations led to skyrocketing gains in agricultural, industrial and commercial productivity. The world supply of gold, however, grew much less quickly. With money supply limited to the amount of gold held by banks, cash soon became more and more difficult to borrow. By the end of the 19th century, countries tied to the gold standard began to feel the restraints of limited capital. In North America, the effect was especially dramatic. The rapidly growing economies of both the United States and Canada were held back by the tight money policies of the gold standard. The 1880s and 1890s brought tough times to working people; unemployment rose to new heights. To many of those without work, hunger was a grim reminder that the economic system was awry. The only way to free up the economy seemed to be by finding and mining gold. The world was primed for a new gold strike.

Prospectors filtered through the coastal mountains looking for the precious metal. By the early 1890s, some 300 to 500 prospectors were in the Yukon basin. Most of them had travelled through the Chilkoot Pass.[3] Some minor discoveries sparked interest but the real find came in the late summer of 1896. On the afternoon of August 16, a trio of prospectors—George Carmack, Skookum Jim, and Dawson Charlie—struck gold on Rabbit Creek, a small tributary of the Klondike River. By summer's end, news of the find had cascaded up and down the Yukon River. But because of the territory's geographic isolation, few confirmed reports reached the outside world until March of the following year.[4]

What finally set off "Klondike Fever" was the arrival of two gold-laden ships on the American west coast. On July 15, 1897, almost a year after the original discovery, the *Excelsior* steamed into San Francisco. The ship carried a score of Yukon miners and hundreds of kilograms of gold worth some $750,000. At first, these men were regarded as northern curiosities, but they became conquering heroes once people learned of their cargo. News spread like wildfire up and down the coast. Two

THE NEW NATIONAL GOLD PARTY.

days later, Seattle's Schwabacher Wharf was the scene of an even more dramatic event with the arrival of the *Portland*. Newspapers trumpeted the arrival of "more than a ton of solid gold." The phrase "a ton of gold" was soon on everyone's lips. Reality surpassed rumour: the *Portland* actually carried more than two tons of gold.[5] For the next three years, tens of thousands stampeded to the north in search of their fortunes.

While the promise of wealth drew many people, there was another reason for the mad rush to the Klondike—a dream of a better life. From the 17th through the 19th centuries, as Europeans explored and settled in new places, they perceived an opportunity to create a new and better world. The frontier became an important cultural component of this utopian new world. The promise of free, or practically free, land suitable for settlement, fired the dreams of millions.[6] The appeal of the frontier, especially in 19th century America, was powerful. Although the realities of the frontier demanded plenty of hard work, the apparent promise of relief from the unemployment and problems of the industrialized world was a compelling lure.

By the 1890s, the American frontier had passed from opportunity into history. The 1890 United States census noted the end of the continuous land frontier in the west; only isolated pockets of unsettled land remained. The loss of the frontier—of opportunity—was a blow to people's perception of their future. The sudden appearance of the Klondike seemed to be one last chance to get that opportunity.

Heading north

After hearing the reports about the gold-bearing ships, people began to make plans to head to the Klondike. Everyone talked of an area few had heard of before mid-July. There was a clamour for information about the Yukon. What was it like? What supplies did you need? And what was the fastest way to get there?

There were few published sources of accurate information. Government reports on the area were gleaned for relevant information. Guides began to appear. Some were fairly accurate, but

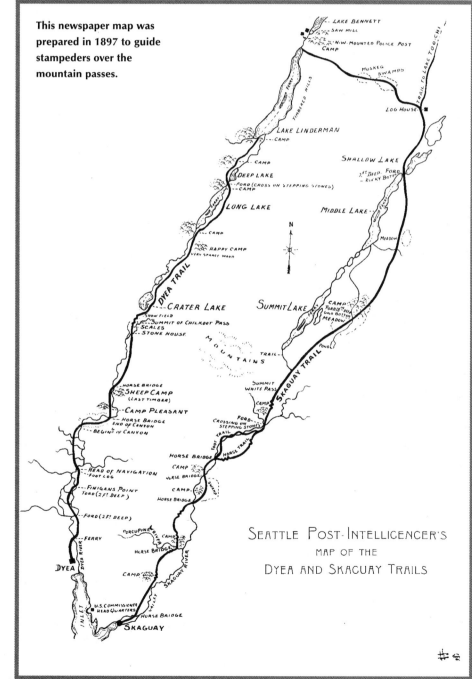

This newspaper map was prepared in 1897 to guide stampeders over the mountain passes.

SEATTLE POST-INTELLICENCER'S
MAP OF THE
DYEA AND SKACUAY TRAILS

OUTFITTING FOR THE KLONDIKE

ENTHUSIASM FOR THE Klondike spawned whole libraries of gold mining manuals, guidebooks full of advice on surviving in the northern wilds, and pamphlets and brochures offering suggestions on the quickest route and the necessary outfit. These suggestions were taken very seriously. Outfits became the measure of a person. A well-selected and tightly-packed outfit not only kept you from hunger and cold but also enhanced your reputation among your peers.

While there was considerable variation in the outfits prepared, stampeders shared a perception of what was needed. The prospective Klondike miner expected to get nothing from the surrounding environment but wood for heat and lumber, water for drinking and gold for spending. Everything else had to be carried in.

The *Manual for Gold Seekers* pointed out:

[At Dyea the gold seeker] bids farewell to hotels, restaurants, steamboats, and stores—in fact to civilization, and is a "free man" to pursue his course how and where he will; beyond all conventionalities of society.... Now for the first time the miner begins to realize that the proper outfit for a trip of this kind is the result of experience, and the longer he has been in the country, and the more thoroughly he knows it, just so much more care is used in the selection and packing of his outfit. A careful and thorough examination should be made to see that nothing has been lost or forgotten.[7]

Outfitting for the Klondike became a huge business and the west coast cities competed for the trade. Seattle was the major beneficiary of the Klondike trade, but Vancouver *(shown here)*, Victoria, Portland, San Francisco, and other port cities also reaped benefits from the boom.

others were full of fabrications, errors and misinformation, produced more with profit than knowledge in mind.

A major guidebook topic was a discussion of the various routes to the Klondike. Boosters of western Canada advocated all-Canadian routes favouring their own communities. Most of these routes, trumpeted by commercial interests, were long and dangerous, requiring hundreds of miles of overland travel. They were rough, unsurveyed and wildly impractical. Equally difficult were the all-American routes. Stampeders unlucky enough to follow any of these routes rued their choice. A group following one of the promoted routes out of Edmonton, Alberta took 14 months to reach Dawson, arriving well after the rush was over. The lucky ones turned around and limped home, but scores of others perished in their futile quest.[8]

There were three passable routes to the new goldfields. The longest but least difficult retraced the route of the miners from the *Excelsior* and *Portland*: by steamer to St. Michael, Alaska, at the mouth of the Yukon. From there, a shallow-draft riverboat provided transport up the Yukon River almost 2,400 km (1,500 mi.) to the Klondike. It was a lengthy and expensive journey, but didn't involve any hard travel. Many people, particularly the well-heeled, chose this route. However, there were problems. Few riverboats were available and the navigation season was very short. Most who took this route did not reach the goldfields until the summer of 1898.

The two overland routes were more direct and faster. The Chilkoot and White Pass trails were both difficult crossings. One writer called the Chilkoot route "the meanest 32 miles in history." The majority of Klondike-bound hopefuls used one or the other. Some even tried both before deciding. However, the Chilkoot, already familiar to the northern mining fraternity, was favoured, particularly in the first winter of the rush.

The Robinson brothers travelled the White Pass into the Yukon. This invoice served as a receipt for customs.

While guidebooks of the day stressed the importance of the right sled and clothing, transport companies made light of the trip. Offers to move stampeders quickly, and expensively, to the best jumping-off spots for the Yukon were everywhere. Riverboats were rushed north to St. Michael for the Yukon River run in 1898. Glossy printed schedules of service from the west coast to the new goldfields were distributed across North America. Reputable agents in San Francisco, Seattle, Vancouver, and Victoria took reservations and provided tickets to Dawson City on the same basis as a trip to Minneapolis or Winnipeg. It all seemed so easy. More than 100,000 people set aside their daily routines and started their trip north.

Typical of these Klondike stampeders was 20-year-old Walter Starr of Oakland, California.[9] Starr, a college student, decided in August, 1897 to head for the Klondike. After completing his studies in early February, 1898, he and a friend left Oakland on an evening train. A third partner joined them in Vancouver four days later. They bought an outfit of clothing, hardware, camp equipment and provisions, and arranged for passage to Skagway. On February 16, 1898, along with 500 other passengers and a host of howling dogs, they boarded the *S.S. Islander* and headed north.

Starr later gave two reasons for joining the stampede. The excitement of going to the wilderness drew him. Experience on long camping trips with pack animals in the High Sierras made Starr comfortable on the "frontier." Members of both sides of the family had been California pioneers, so "perhaps the urge was in my blood."

His second reason was the lack of anything else to do. The family business, Starr & Co., flour milling and wheat exporting, was bankrupt. Starr's future career had vanished in the depression of the 1890s.

Not all participants in the stampede were as well organized as Starr and his friends. Sailors on Royal Navy vessels stationed on Canada's west coast listened to the siren call of the Klondike and deserted their ships. The problem became so serious that Rear Admiral Palliser, commanding the naval squadron at Esquimault, British Columbia, expressed his concern about the strength of his command. In January, 1898, he complained:

Hordes of stampeders and their goods on the rocks at Dyea, 1897.

During the last 12 months some 40 seamen and marines have deserted my Squadron, mostly during the last few months, and all, I have reason to believe will find their way to the Klondyke country, and further in the spring I expect that more desertions will take place.[10]

News of the strike even reached the whalers over-wintering at Herschel Island off the Yukon's Arctic coast. They mutinied and headed south for Dawson.

Dyea: port town for the Chilkoot

Dyea, at the southern terminus of the Chilkoot, exploded into prominence soon after the celebrated "ton of gold" brought into Seattle touched off the Klondike gold rush. Dyea had been a seasonal hunting and fishing camp long before miners began to trickle through on their way to the Canadian interior. Outsiders, however, were scarcely aware of the area before 1880, and it was not until 1886 that the Healy and Wilson store was established there.

Interest in the Dyea area increased as greater numbers of miners crossed the Chilkoot. In 1895, two competing firms set up shop near Healy and Wilson's store: the Juneau-based partnership of Ed James and Karl Koehler, and partners Chester Johnson and John Williams. Competition for the packing trade came from Joseph T. Fields, who erected a store a mile up the trail and teamed up with tramway operator Peter Peterson to haul freight over the Chilkoot. Several hundred Native Americans, who flocked to Dyea from areas as distant as Juneau and Sitka, packed the majority of goods over the pass that year, as they had since the early 1880s.[11]

By the spring of 1897, word of the Klondike discovery had filtered out to the mining fraternity, particularly those living along the west coast. In response, more than a thousand stampeders came north to cross the Chilkoot Pass that summer.

Dyea's real boom began late that summer. Ships of every description converged on the area, and captains, intent on capitalizing on "gold fever," attempted to off-load merchandise as quickly as possible and return south. But the area's topography—a flat, sandy tidal zone

Wilson Mizner, who arrived in December, 1897, recalled the cacophony and near-anarchy of Dyea:

Here were no freight terminals, warehouses or docks, [and] there was no ceremony or delay about arrivals, either. The newcomers, bewildered by it all, were almost pushed off into waiting scows, rafts and rowboats. Horses, cattle, and dogs were run or pitched overboard to swim for shore, and vast masses of freight and baggage of every description was eventually piled onto a beach already crowded with the possessions of other arrivals who had found no place for shelter. Here was what was ever meant by chaos—and be careful what you touch! With people wrangling and fighting over freight, with confusion, great avalanches booming down the mountain sides all about us, and absolutely no one able to give us anything but abuse, my first view of Dyea was accompanied by one long and two thousand short blasts of profanity.[12]

Unloading a scow onto wagons at nearby Skagway.

bounded by rocky cliffs on either side—made such a task difficult. Chaos often resulted. As Robert C. Kirk, a stampeder who arrived in mid-August, noted:

> There were no wharves, of course, where our goods might land, so we dropped anchor, and made arrangements to discharge the cargo of men and horses and provisions on barges that had been previously towed north for that purpose. It would be difficult for one to imagine the confusion that existed when the tons and tons of boxes and sacks and barrels came ashore, where no steamship people were waiting to receive them, and where each one of the eight hundred passengers was hurrying about looking for the goods that bore his private brand.[13]

Compounding the problem was the large tidal range, which often exceeded 6 m (20 ft.). Addison Mizner recalled the experience:

> We dropped anchor three miles from the tiny village alongside a big flat boat. There was feverish haste. We all had to help unload from the steamer to the barge, amid shouts of "Hurry, the tide is turning." Everyone was making a panicky finish. The steamer pulled up her anchor and swung down the canal. We were standing still on the barge. Why? In an hour we

Scenes such as these were common in Dyea during the winter of 1897-98. Some had their outfits thrown onto the rocks *(below)*, while others carried their belongings onto the beach above the high tide line.

DYEA'S NEIGHBOURHOODS

THE CHILKOOT TRAIL, which had been used for hundreds of years before the miners and traders arrived, began on the west side of the Taiya River mouth. Before the gold rush, most settlement grouped around the site of the Healy and Wilson trading post.

The coming of the gold rush, however, considerably extended Dyea's settled area, both to the north and south. The platting of the downtown area, in October, 1897, was limited to a seven- by five-block area between the trading post and the high tide line, and it was here—particularly along Main Street—where the primary business district was located.

The town soon outgrew its platted area, and in addition, entrepreneurs recognized that the town's northern end—just before the trail crossed the Taiya River—offered additional commercial possibilities. North Dyea, long and narrow, wound along the western bank of the Taiya River for over a kilometre, and in this neighbourhood a large number of businesses—located in tents, log huts and frame buildings—catered to northbound travellers.

Though Dyea remained a viable community for less than a year, it attracted a wide range of businesses in that short time. The most common, by far, were hotels, restaurants, bars, and supply houses: more than forty of each of these have been identified. Other businesses thrived as well, including a bathhouse, attorneys, a reading room, a fire department, a dentist, an eye doctor, seamstresses, meat markets, a candy factory and two newspapers.[14]

Dyea was a long, narrow town sandwiched between the West Branch and the main stem of the Taiya River. During the gold rush, the Taiya River bed lay east of Trail Street; since then, as the map on the right shows, the river has meandered to the west and removed portions of downtown, the military reservation and the Native village.

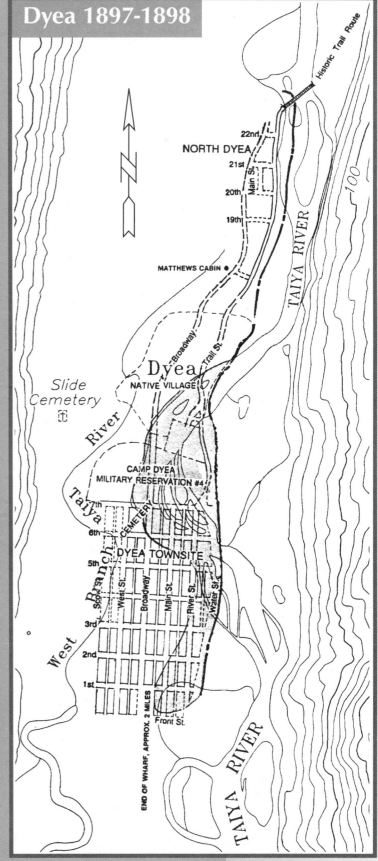

Dyea 1897-1898

were gently grating on the bottom. In twenty minutes we were high and dry, and wagons were coming out on the sandy bottom to get us. The tide had dropped thirty feet, and as far as the eye could see the Linn Canal was empty.[15]

The obvious solution to the problem was to construct a dock. Entrepreneurs, sensing an opportunity, wasted no time in staking claims on likely dock locations. In late September, 1897, the Skaguay Wharf and Improvement Company claimed a wharfsite on the west side of Taiya Inlet; the Dyea-Klondike Transportation Company made a similar claim a month later. However, deep water in the inlet was close to 2 km (1.2 mi.) south of the high tide line. Therefore, in order to have a workable dock, backers would have to construct either a long wharf, or build a road along the cliffside to a landing site adjacent to deep water.[16]

These difficulties, for the time being, proved insurmountable, so most of the Klondike ship captains avoided Dyea in favour of Skagway, where dock facilities allowed faster off-loading. Thousands of stampeders then continued on to Dyea by shuttling over on a barge or scow.

Those in the initial stages of the rush were in such a hurry to reach the Klondike before the interior rivers froze that few stayed in the port area for long. In August, 1897, Robert Kirk noted that "the town of Dyea is composed entirely of huts and hovels that belong to the

Dyea panorama, looking northeast, spring, 1898.

DYEA BUSINESSES, PEOPLE ON THE MOVE

THE MOST SUCCESSFUL people in the gold rush were those who mined the miners. The men and women operating Klondike businesses often saw handsome profits. To make money they had to be ready to seize the opportunities that came their way.

The most prominent business people along the trail—the owners of the large Dyea hotels and supply houses—migrated north from either Juneau or Seattle. Other business owners hailed from throughout the American and Canadian west, as evidenced by names like Skagit Saloon and Restaurant, Oregon Real Estate Company, Portland Hotel, Astoria-Dyea Trading Company and the Seattle Hotel.

Visitors were surprised at how rapidly businesses were established in the trail towns. Fred W. Hart captured the spirit of the business boom when he wrote:

My business in Vancouver was thriving, both retail and manufacturing, but when the Klondike gold discoveries were made my attention was turned to the north.... I wanted to make money faster than I could even in Vancouver.

I jumped into the building line and found plenty to do at big prices. Speed was the main thing that was demanded, for accommodation could be rented at fancy figures and with the northern winter coming on people were not in a humour to wait. For instance, one day I got an order for the building of a three-storey hotel of about forty rooms, with dining-room and bar-room, all furnished and the building heated throughout, the keys to be turned over to the owner in three days. I did it! It would be thought a tall order even in Vancouver. I also built a block of five stores in five days, and rented each one as it was finished! The first two were occupied and selling goods before the last one was completed.[17]

Most of those who succeeded in business also knew when to move on. By the late spring of 1898, Dyea entrepreneurs knew the town's prime was past. Many bailed out in favour of Skagway or headed over the pass. Businesses in the trail towns also moved north, and many later became established in Dawson, Atlin, Nome, Fairbanks, and other gold rush towns.

On January 12, 1898, in the *Dyea Trail,* the Pacific Hotel was described as:

...an imposing structure, three stories, and built in the very best manner. It will accommodate 300 guests. The manager of the Pacific will be Mr. J.J. Bell, of San Francisco, who says the cuisine will be the best in Alaska, bar none. All the essentials and delicacies of the season will be served, and the house will, he says, be a credit to Alaska's greatest city.

Ross Higgins store, Fourth and Main streets, Dyea.

A wagon train of freight leaves the Chilkoot Railroad and Transport Company warehouse at Dyea for the aerial tram at Canyon City, April 24, 1899.

tribe of Dyea Indians,"[18] and as late as September, the town was still nothing more than the Healy and Wilson post, a few saloons, a Native encampment and a motley assemblage of tents.[19]

A month later, the interior rivers and lakes began to freeze, and many of the same speculators who had profited from the off-loading in Skagway of the past two months moved en masse to Dyea. Harry Suydam, an eyewitness, recalled that people:

> ...went on shore in boats and started staking lots. There was a great crowd of people there who had heard of the large quantities of lumber being put ashore. When we commenced to stake out claims we told the bystanders of the merchants who were coming to Dyea. At this news the people ran about as if they had taken leave of their senses.
>
> A man would take off his coat and throw it on the ground, intending to hold a lot for him. Some men ran up the trail and brought back their tents. Hurriedly they pitched them on the lot of their choice. All hands paced back and forth and measure with a tape, if they happened to have one, from the stakes of the marked lot nearest them. Lots were all supposed to be fifty by one hundred feet. I staked a corner for myself on the principal street, called Broadway and carried several boards to it to indicate ownership. Hundreds of people were milling about and fighting over lots that only a few hours before nobody wanted or thought about. It was a full-fledged stampede. People came running from everywhere.[20]

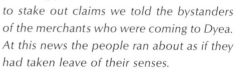

Dyea grew slowly for the next several months, largely because stampeders had little incentive to head north only to wait out the remainder of the winter. By December, though, the population started to increase, and in January, 1898, the *Dyea Trail* crowed:

> *A building boom is on in Dyea. No where in Uncle Sam's domain can its like be seen. Hotels, stores, business buildings of all kinds, residences, shops, manufactories, stables, warehouses, and storage houses are everywhere in course of erection. What a few weeks ago was a beautiful stretch of plain and timber is fast being covered with accommodations...and in thirty days Dyea will be one of the most metropolitan cities in the wide, wide world.... As sure as there was built a San Francisco, so surely there will be builded a Dyea.[21]*

Early 1898 also saw the construction of the two much-needed docks. The Dyea-Klondike Transportation Company (DKT) worked slowly through the winter. Having little capital, the company constructed a 5 km (3 mi.) wagon road along the western hill slope south of town. At its terminus, it erected a small dock. The facility opened on February 10. Three months later, the much larger Long Wharf—a 2,300 m (7,500 ft.) dock that reached from downtown south to deep water—was completed. This dock, far more convenient to use than the DKT wharf, finally surmounted Dyea's long-standing access problems. By the time it was completed, however, most of the gold rush tide had passed, and it was little used.[22]

Though less raucous than crime-ridden Skagway, Dyea was by no means tame. William Schooley, a December, 1897 visitor, wrote: "This is a mushroom town that you read about. One who has never been in the hot bed of a gold excitement cannot realize how crazy men get."[23] Pierre Berton, the popular historian of the gold rush, made a similar conclusion, noting that "a liquid stream of humanity gushed through Dyea's narrow streets day and night, so that the air was never still from animal cries and human curses."[24] Two murders, along with scores of lesser crimes, took place during Dyea's first winter. The town supported more than forty saloons, and it hosted its fair share of variety theatres, concert halls and bordellos. Ed Lung, who passed through in May, 1898, recalls the latter:

Some 300 gold rush businesses were established on the U.S. side of the Chilkoot Trail. About two-thirds of these were located in Dyea.

At Dyea, there was plenty of entertainment. Dance halls and saloon were going full blast! I stopped to see a show to kill time and saw the Cashey Sisters. Sewell of Dawson was there, too. Yes, Dyea was a typical gold-rush town. There was no doubt about it—even to its prostitutes, gamblers, and "sure thing" men! But it didn't have the sinister atmosphere of Skagway. It was mighty good to know that Soapy Smith didn't hold sway here!

I was hoping for a restful sleep that night of the 23rd, as I was leaving the following morning to tackle the big climb up Chilkoot. But, great Scott! It did not turn out that way! There was too much commotion going on in the next room and the thin partitions were like sounding boards. How many visitors that "daughter of joy" had during the night, I lost count! But, at close intervals, the squeaky door would open, there would be stealthy footsteps going down the hall and, in a moment more stealthy footsteps creaking up the hall and a woman's hoarse, grating voice called, "next!"[25]

The town's population, always shifting, rose from fewer than a 1,000 in the summer of 1897 to an estimated 8,000 in May, 1898, before dropping off again. Perhaps 30,000 to 40,000 people passed through during the winter of 1897-98.[26]

The Horseshoe Clothing House on Main Street, Dyea. It was operated by brothers Jack (behind the shovels) and Simon (on the first step) Hirsh and their brother-in-law Emanuel Hoeslech (behind the blankets), all of Seattle, Washington.

Tlingit canoes continued to be used extensively for carrying goods up the first stretch of the Taiya River.

THE GREAT DYEA MINING RUSH

SEVERAL THOUSAND STAMPEDERS lived in Dyea during the winter of 1897-98. All, in one way or another, had been attracted by gold. Most had prospecting equipment with them, most had idle time on their hands, and few could afford to pass up a chance for easy wealth. Given that state of affairs, it is not at all surprising that many prospected in the surrounding hills.

The first claims around Dyea were recorded on December 1, 1897 and less than a week later, new claims were staked on West Creek, northwest of town. News of the West Creek claims brought a rush of miners to the new "diggins," ten of whom filed new claims.[27]

Unseasonably cold weather slowed prospecting activity for the next several weeks. Miners, however, staked several new claims, both along West Creek and on the valley's eastern slope. The claimants apparently found few rewards for their efforts.[28]

Nevertheless, the local press hyped the rush, and nearly every issue featured Dyea-area mining developments. Particularly encouraging was a mid-April, front-page article in the *Dyea Trail*. "The outlook for mineral development around Dyea brightens with each week," it noted. "There will be discoveries made that will astonish the world and make Dyea the center of one of the richest and busiest populations in Alaska."[29]

Perhaps in response to the press blitz, prospecting continued, and in the early spring of 1898 more claims were staked.[30] In early May, a teamster provoked a new rush when he exhibited $400 in gold dust which he "positively asserted" had been found near Dyea. The claim, however, proved to be a "fairy tale," and "not a color could be raised anywhere."[31] By June, most of Dyea's population had headed north, and interest in area mining had faded.

Some might argue that the local "mining boom" was nothing more than a winter-time diversion for Dyea's residents and a desperate attempt for economic development on the part of local boosters. Geologists such as George Davidson, George M. Dawson, and Josiah Spurr had already passed through and described the area's limited mineral potential. But gold, after all, is where one finds it, and many could not resist taking part in the search for it.[32]

The *Dyea Trail* reported in March, 1898:

The probability that rich finds of gold-bearing quartz will be uncovered in the hills around Dyea continues to grow stronger. In truth, it is hardly any longer to be referred to as a probability for it has become almost a certainty.... There is now no question but that there will be considerable mining excitement in the Dyea district this summer. The beginning of it is near at hand. We may not have rich placer diggings, but quartz is here in abundance, and if a few discoveries develop into mines the future of Dyea is an established fact.

Taiya River valley, looking north. Most prospecting took place in the hills west of town.

Skagway and the White Pass

In the fall of 1887, Captain William Moore and his son Bernard (Ben) built a cabin and claimed a 160-acre homestead at the southern end of the White Pass. The elder Moore was a visionary who had rushed for gold up and down the west coast since the 1850s. In 1887, he had taken part in a Geological Survey of Canada expedition, travelling over the mountains and down the Yukon River. He was captivated by the dream of a major gold strike in the Yukon. To him, a route winding from Skagway Bay through the White Pass and beyond would be the easiest way for prospectors to reach the interior. For 10 years, Moore and his son bided their time, waiting and hoping for riches to come their way.

Most of those heading up the Inside Passage—the route connecting Wrangell, Sitka, Juneau and Glacier Bay—during the first few weeks of the rush were going to Dyea. Ship

Eager new arrivals for the gold rush trails disembark at Skagway.

Skagway harbour, with better deep water docks than Dyea, was always full of ships.

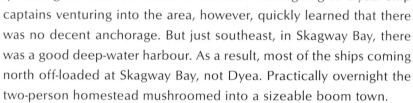

captains venturing into the area, however, quickly learned that there was no decent anchorage. But just southeast, in Skagway Bay, there was a good deep-water harbour. As a result, most of the ships coming north off-loaded at Skagway Bay, not Dyea. Practically overnight the two-person homestead mushroomed into a sizeable boom town.

On August 2, 1897, the self-appointed town fathers met and decided to survey a town, to be known as Skaguay. (The spelling changed to Skagway in late 1898.) Moore was allowed to carve out a small plot around his log cabin and sawmill. But his house, which was some distance from his homestead cabin, lay in the middle of a new street corner. The stampeders decided to move it. Moore fought a pitched, axe-swinging battle against them, but eventually, subdued, he withdrew and took up residence in a hotel.[33]

The scraggly tent town boomed through the late summer of 1897, catering to the never-ending flow of stampeders. Within weeks, however, snow began to fall around the passes. Soon the freezing of interior rivers prevented any further movement north. People on the trails then retreated to the relative comfort and warmth of Skagway, settling in for the winter. With more long-term residents in the town, wood-planked businesses and log cabins began to appear. In midwinter, the town boasted a population of 5,000. By spring, it was the largest town in Alaska.[34]

SOAPY SMITH

JEFFERSON RANDOLPH "SOAPY" Smith, perhaps the most well-known person connected with the gold rush, was an intelligent and skilled criminal. He controlled a well-organized underworld of thieves, thugs and con-men during the heyday of the gold rush. Skagway, a thousand miles away from law and order, attracted scores of society's outcasts. Smith organized this criminal element for his own purposes.

Born in Georgia in 1860, Smith came from a prosperous family fallen on hard times. As a young man he drifted west. Lured to dance halls and gambling dens, before long he was an expert at manipulating three walnut shells and a pea. For the next 20 years he perfected the con-man's trade in various Colorado towns. Upon hearing news of the Klondike rush, he joined the northbound migration.[35]

Smith settled in Skagway, where the larger population base offered greater rewards. By late January, 1898, he was the uncrowned king of the Skagway underworld. Six months later he was gunned down by surveyor Frank Reid on the Juneau Company Wharf in Skagway harbour.[36]

Soapy Smith in a dramatic pose on his white charger.

Skagway's law and order contingent gathers in front of the city hall after bringing Soapy Smith's gang to heel in July, 1898.

Smith's operations extended from the ships plying the Inside Passage to the summits of the White Pass and Chilkoot. His cohorts, posing as helpful fellow travellers, offered information and assistance to stampeders. Gang members quickly located those with the fattest wallets and steered them into Smith's bogus business operations. Along the Chilkoot Trail, the gang set up warm fires and sheltering tents to lure stampeders into thimblerig outfits, shell-game tables and phony poker games.[37]

Soapy's gang was at the height of its influence when Canada's North-West Mounted Police decided to transport $150,000 in gold dust and bank notes, collected as custom fees at the top of the passes, south to Victoria. Soapy's men controlled the White Pass Trail so completely it was foolhardy to attempt that route. Inspector Zachary T. Wood, using a ruse, made it safely to Dyea via the Chilkoot Trail. But Smith's men soon caught wind of the true purpose of his trip and confronted him in Skagway Bay. Wood held them off at gunpoint until he reached the *Tartar* at the Skagway dock. The captain of the *Tartar* was prepared for Smith's gang—the gangway was ringed with sailors brandishing rifles. Thus protected, Wood and the customs fees headed south, and Soapy returned to the easier pickings of Skagway.[38]

"A Plucky Little Woman," as reported in the *Dyea Trail*, February 18, 1898:

A handsome little woman dressed in a mackinaw suit and pulling a sled load of goods attracted considerable attention on the street this week. Each day she made a trip or two to the water front, returning with several hundred pounds on her sleigh. She asked assistance from no one and attended strictly to the business of getting her outfit up the trail to her cache. The woman is Mrs. Anna M. Smith, of Tacoma. She is thoroughly equipped and will endeavor to be one of the first to reach Dawson this spring.

Orderly camp above Dyea on the trail.

"THOROUGHLY EQUIPPED"

THE INEXPERIENCE OF the people pouring off the ships at Skagway and Dyea seemed to portend a disaster. Some of the first stampeders to enter the Yukon travelled very light, expecting to be able to buy their supplies along the way. Inspector Zachary T. Wood of the North-West Mounted Police, observing the chaos at Skagway in November of 1897, commented caustically:

People are beginning to flock in here, and some are preparing to proceed at once, little knowing what they have to go through.... They arrive here, think they know more about the country than anyone else, and start off across the pass. Supplies they think they can get at Bennett [at that time a few tents and one or two small log cabins], and imagine that four or five untrained dogs are going to pull all provisions for the party, camp equipment and dog feed through to Dawson [850 unsettled kilometres down the Yukon River].[39]

Despite Wood's misgivings there were few fatalities. This was largely due to the veritable explosion of entrepreneurs bringing supplies and services to the Klondike trails. By late spring, 1898, well-heeled travellers at the summit of the Chilkoot Pass could order an edible, if not elegant, dinner of fresh baked bread, potatoes and ham with coffee and apple pie, while they waited for one of the aerial tramways to deliver their goods to the summit. A customs broker was available to prepare a manifest to be reviewed by the Canadian customs officers stationed there. Other services at the summit included regular mail delivery, a blacksmith, feed for pack animals, hotels—open day and night—and even telephone service to Dyea. The Chilkoot summit was not a congenial place, with its howling blizzards, deep snow and frigid temperatures, but tired stampeders were able to enjoy most of the comforts of home. Services at this basic level were available all the way from Skagway and Dyea through to Bennett.

While far more people used the Chilkoot Trail than the White Pass during the winter of 1897-98, the population of Skagway remained consistently higher than Dyea's. Two factors accounted for this. First was the passengers who were unloaded at Skagway rather than Dyea. Second, the condition of the Chilkoot Trail, though rough, proved far superior to the so-called trail through the White Pass. Stampeders on the Chilkoot passed quickly through Dyea and up the trail, while those opting for the White Pass route were often forced to remain in Skagway or return there, discouraged, because of poor trail conditions.

The difficulties of the White Pass often meant long delays and slow progress.

A well-organized group pauses for lunch at their camp on the trail, spring, 1897.

Moving up the trail

Most of those reaching Lindeman or Bennett lakes during the first few months of the gold rush travelled by the Chilkoot Trail. People typically assembled their gear just above the high tide line in Dyea before winding along Trail Street, the town's main thoroughfare. At the crossing of the Taiya River, those on foot proceeded up the river valley on the trail, while those with canoes poled their boats along the riverbank.

Soon after the rush began, Dan Finnegan and his sons built up a low part of the trail. They also constructed a rickety bridge, charging stampeders a dollar apiece to take advantage of their improvements. A tent camp of other services, called Finnegan's Point, soon surrounded the crossing.

Five kilometres (3 mi.) farther north, beyond Canyon City, the trail followed a series of switchbacks to a high perch overlooking the steep, narrow canyon of the Taiya River. The trail clung precariously to the canyon wall, before gradually descending to the river, where stampeders crossed on a log to the west side of the valley. From there, the trail continued up the valley before crossing the river yet again at Sheep Camp. The original Palmer House Hotel there

BLOCKADE WHITE PASS

There are several women in camp, among them one doctor. I would not want my wife out on such a trip, it is too rough and in many other ways not a trip for a woman.

• Louie B. May of Anaconda, Montana, March 31, 1898[40]

Still on the easy part of the Chilkoot Trail—horses drawing sleighs of freight through the canyon.

Street scene at Sheep Camp.

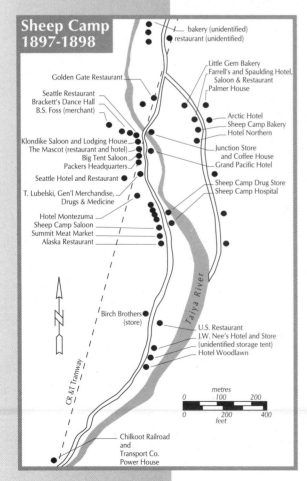

Sheep Camp 1897-1898

bakery (unidentified)
restaurant (unidentified)

Little Gem Bakery
Farrell's and Spaulding Hotel, Saloon & Restaurant
Palmer House

Golden Gate Restaurant

Seattle Restaurant
Brackett's Dance Hall
B.S. Foss (merchant)

Arctic Hotel
Sheep Camp Bakery
Hotel Northern

Klondike Saloon and Lodging House
The Mascot (restaurant and hotel)
Big Tent Saloon
Packers Headquarters

Junction Store and Coffee House
Grand Pacific Hotel

Seattle Hotel and Restaurant

T. Lubelski, Gen'l Merchandise, Drugs & Medicine

Sheep Camp Drug Store
Sheep Camp Hospital

Hotel Montezuma
Sheep Camp Saloon
Summit Meat Market
Alaska Restaurant

Taiya River

Birch Brothers (store)

U.S. Restaurant
J.W. Nee's Hotel and Store
(unidentified storage tent)
Hotel Woodlawn

CR &T Tramway

metres
0   100   200
0   200   400
feet

Chilkoot Railroad and Transport Co. Power House

was able to advertise running water, inasmuch as a corner of the building dangled directly over the river bed.

The trail then climbed Long Hill on the east side of the river—by now only a rivulet—and ascended the steep slope from the Scales—the point where packers weighed and assessed final fees—to the top of Chilkoot Pass. After crossing the summit into the interior, the trail descended to Crater Lake. It followed the east side of the valley to the mouth of Long Lake, forded the creek, passing on the west side of Deep Lake. It then crossed a ridge before descending to the camp at Lindeman Lake.

For travellers carrying hundreds, if not thousands, of kilograms of equipment and supplies, traversing the trail was an ordeal. It lasted anywhere from three weeks to three months, as they moved their freight in short stages over the summit. Inga Sjolseth, a young Norwegian housemaid from Latona, Washington, reached Dyea in mid-March, 1898, with a group of friends. Travelling with another young woman, Ida Bodin, and three young men—Anderson, Sandvig, and Kolloon—the group's progress over the trail can be followed in Inga's diary:[41]

> *Fri. March 18—Today we have taken all our supplies from the dock to the City of Dyea. Have now set up our tent on a sand bank near the river. It rained this afternoon. The tent is full of wet things—boxes and clothes.*
>
> *Mon. March 21—We got up at five this morning, had a little coffee first and then Sandvig and Anderson went for a load of supplies. When they got back, we prepared breakfast and the men went after another load. I pulled three sacks on my sled, and it went pretty well. There are hundreds of people here dragging or carrying their supplies, all striving to reach the Klondike. Some have horses and still others have dog teams. I have baked bread and biscuits and cake and yellow peas, the only thing I had. We had chicken for dinner, a luxury here in Alaska.*
>
> *Tues. March 22—We were up early and dragged a load of our supplies to the next*

Sheep Camp had more than 60 businesses during the spring of 1898.

The entire lower part of the trail was lined with tents and freight as groups staged their goods from Dyea up to Sheep Camp in preparation for the final climb to the summit.

stopping place. I dragged one sack this time because I was so weak. When we got home I was very tired. I went to bed at six o'clock, but did not go to sleep until nine o'clock. The others played and sang for Ida and me which I thought was delightful and uplifting, especially the songs to Jesus Christ which turned our thoughts toward Heaven.

This gruelling daily round continued for a week as the group moved their supplies from Dyea to Canyon City—some 12.5 km (8 mi.). They then moved their main camp to Canyon City, where the whole process was repeated on the next stage of the trip to Sheep Camp.

Tues. March 29—Today we moved from Canyon City. The trail in from Canyon is narrow and crowded, lying between two steep mountains. If we look up only mountains tower above our heads. The snow has turned to water, so progress has been very difficult. Ida and I pulled a loaded sled together through the canyon. We heard one man say he wished he had such a

Finally, the stampeders reached the Scales and beheld the final climb up the pass. Peterson's Pass is the trail at the right.

"tram." Some of the men took off their packs and laughed at us. We have now set up our tent here in Sheep Camp. The snow is thick under our tent. A little rice, then we are ready to sleep.

Wed. March 30—It has snowed and rained all day and the water has come through our tent so many of our provisions are wet. It is uncomfortable and unhealthy to live in a tent like this. We hope that this will get better very soon. The snow has melted, and I fear the tent may fall down any minute. It leans to one side. I visited Miss Knudsen today, also Mr. and Mrs. Drange. I also visited Mr. Waldal, Mr. Knudsen and Mr. Molseth. Mr. Paulson was here with us.

Thurs. March 31—The weather has been pretty good today and we have moved our tent to a place lower down, away from the snow. He has shovelled away much of the snow so now we are living on bare ground again and quite comfortable. The town of Sheep Camp consists for the most part of tents. The place is so full of people that one can barely breathe. There are many restaurants here, where a meal costs 50 cents. A dozen eggs cost 62 cents. Mr. Sandvig and Mr. Anderson have lost a box of sardines. Someone must have taken it.

Over the next 10 days, while the men hauled more gear up the trail, the two women visited with friends, did laundry, and baked bread and pies, the whole time watching the unceasing activity of the trail. For Easter, they prepared a special meal including bacon and eggs and a lemon pie.

The men continued hauling goods up the trail. Sjolseth also tried to make a trip to the summit but was turned back by a blizzard. Stuck in camp by bad weather, ill and unable to see any progress, she grew restless.

I am bored and weary with this place, and wish I could get away from this dirty Sheep Camp!

Bad weather and slow progress in the freighting kept her in Sheep Camp until the end of the month. Finally, on April 27, she hiked over the summit.

Louie B. May, in a party of 12 (along with 13 dogs), wrote this account of his attempt to cross the pass:

March 22, 1898 (at Sheep Camp). Very stormy and I was not in favor of going up at all but the rest think it is not stormy on summit so away we go and the further we go the worse it gets and when we get to the scales we find one of those storms which you read about, raging over and around the summit. We find it just as I predicted and out of the question to try to work, so the rest turn back for camp. Such a storm. I staid in a Restaurant for 3 or 4 hours and had 2 cups of coffee + 2 sandwich and as the storm got no better I started home and got 2 or 3 hundred yds + found I had left my creepers, went back + got warm + started again + got lost, as I had started for the summit instead of Sheep camp. Turned and got home just in time for supper—we eat fresh meat and potatoes.

Many stampeders hauled their goods up the Golden Stairs on their backs, making dozens of trips. Others, like T.R. Lane (left) in late spring, 1898, paid the tramway companies to deliver their goods to Lindeman and Bennett lakes and enjoyed a pleasant hike over the pass carrying only their lunch.

Death on the trail

Bad weather was always a danger. In 1898, a Carcross-Tagish woman, Nadagât Tlâ, and her young daughter died of exposure on the pass. Mrs. Lucy Wren tells the story:[42]

This time she say she don't want to wear her skin pants, my grandma, 'cause she say she gets sweaty all time when they walking...just as soon as they come out to that open place [above treeline], boy north wind start blowing....

Well Grandma, she got that little girl with her, and she pack that baby, too. Well, that little girl is getting cold.... [Grandma] got warm blankets and everything on, you know, so they sit down behind a big rock....

When her party got to Sheep Camp, they told about those still on the trail.

So these three white men...they went back. They find them...behind that big rock. She say...I'm just about frozen...and that little girl too.

The only one that kept warm, she say, is the one she pack. She give that little one to that white man.... So that white man, he just pack that baby, and then he went down really fast from there... Just that little one they pack, that's the one is safe, that's all.

The Palm Sunday avalanche

Sjolseth witnessed the worst disaster of the Chilkoot stampede. On Palm Sunday, April 3, 1898, an avalanche descended on the trail, less than an hour's walk above her camp. The massive wall of snow thundered down the eastern slope of the valley and engulfed scores of stampeders. About 70 died; many others barely escaped with their lives. A few days later, Sjolseth went up to the site of the slide:

> *Wed. April 6—This afternoon Ida and I went up to Hans Summer's and saw the snowslide. On the way there we saw a dead man being pulled on a sleigh. It was a shock to us and I went home much discouraged and depressed, but at the same time grateful to God for his goodness toward me, for he has spared me and my friends here from this dreadful accident.*

The Palm Sunday avalanche of 1898 between Sheep Camp and the Scales was the deadliest event of the Klondike gold rush. Deep, heavy snow became unstable in early April as warm winds blew in from the south. First Nations packers, knowledgeable of local conditions, refused to pack above Sheep Camp.[43]

Saturday evening, avalanches had begun to tumble down the slopes above the Scales. At 2:00 the next morning, a slide buried 20 stampeders; another, at about 9:30, buried three more. These people were rescued, but the impending danger convinced everyone at the Scales to evacuate. Workers for the tramway went first. It was snowing heavily, and visibility was cut to almost zero.[44]

Between 10:00 a.m. and noon, three more snowslides cascaded down onto Long Hill from the eastern escarpment. The first crushed three campers to death in their tents. Sometime later, as the party of tramway workers was passing through a narrow gorge, the second avalanche buried the entire party. All were killed.[45]

The largest and most destructive slide came soon afterwards. The remaining 200 people at the Scales retreated to Sheep Camp, just before 11:00 a.m., marching in a sinuous line. Due to the low visibility, they kept together by lining up on alternate sides of a 60-metre (200-foot) rope.[46] Totally unaware of the fate of the tramway crew, they stumbled down Long Hill. When

Digging out after the Palm Sunday avalanche.

they reached the site of the second avalanche, the mountainside again gave way. The rear of the party was untouched, but those holding the front end of the rope were buried, some to a depth of between 6 and 15 m (20 and 50 ft.).

The roar of the third avalanche, louder than the others, alarmed campers all the way to Sheep Camp. An eyewitness to the event—possibly one of those that had been holding the rear portion of the rope—soon staggered into camp bearing news of the disaster. Gunshots summoned help, and 1,500 stampeders immediately responded.

In a display of unanimity and selflessness, the stampeders interrupted their trek for four days in order to rescue the victims. Estimates of the number of lives saved ranged widely, from a mere handful to more than one hundred.[47]

A tent in Sheep Camp was donated for use as a morgue, and a committee, appointed at a miners' meeting, presided over the processing of the bodies for shipment and burial.[48] Eyewitness accounts indicate that most or all of the victims were identified and claimed, and death certificates were issued.[49]

There is little agreement regarding the number of victims. At first, wild reports suggested 200 to 300 lives had been lost.[50] More realistic estimates were later published in four newspapers. Significantly, all the lists had different numbers and few names appeared on all four lists. To further confuse the issue, several of the names in Dyea's Slide Cemetery (where some of the victims were buried) did not match those found on any of the four lists.[51]

Avalanches were not the only danger on the trail. Other notable disasters during the stampede took place in September, 1897, when a flood swept through Sheep Camp, and in December, 1898, when a snowslide killed six tramway workers at Stone Crib, just north of the Chilkoot summit.[52] Avalanche remains one of the most dangerous aspects of winter and spring activity on the Chilkoot.

A romantic episode related to the snowslide concerned Arthur Jappe, who was buried by the cascading snow. Jappe had been laid on the floor of the tramway powerhouse with other victims and left for dead. However, a packer named Vernie Woodward happened by. According to a report from the *Dyea Trail*, she:[53]

...discovered in the row of dead the body of Mr. Joppe [sic], who she had known for a long time, and was very much attached to. When she recognized him her grief was unbounded. She cried and begged for him to come back to life to look at her. She unfastened his shirt, and in frenzied grief began to rub him. She worked upon him as only a true woman will—moving his arms this way and that; pressing his chest and breathing into his lungs until three-o-clock in the morning. She was then rewarded by his opening his eyes and speaking her name, "Vernie." Everyone shed tears of rejoicing. The little heroine and hero were at once taken to Sheep Camp. Mr. Joppe is out of danger and Miss Woodward is the heroine of the hour.

The story of the angelic "Lady of the Chilkoot" spread far and wide. Jappe himself, however, admitted in a 1962 letter to the *Alaska Sportsman* that the story was, in part, a fabrication; he had not known the woman before and never saw her again.

An estimated 70 people died in the avalanches. Here, a body is being removed.

THE DYEA-KLONDIKE TRANSPORTATION COMPANY

THE STAMPEDE INTO the Chilkoot stalled in the shallow flats of the Taiya River mouth and the steep rocky canyons just up the river. Many schemes for overcoming the difficulties of the Chilkoot route were quickly hatched. Proposals included docks jutting out into the Lynn Canal, toll bridges, tramways, wagon roads and even railways. Promoters of all stripes converged on the upper Lynn Canal, hoping to reap a bonanza from the gold rush.

The intensity of gold rush excitement spawned grand dreams, and emptied deep pockets. One group of investors—F.C. Hammond, E.F. Cassel, and T.I. Nowell—founded the Dyea-Klondike Transportation (DKT) Company in late September, 1897. The trio were old hands in Alaska development. They announced their intention to construct an electrically-powered transportation system to haul freight from a wharf in Dyea right through to Lindeman Lake. A "narrow gauge tramroad with cars like those used in the mines" would travel to the foot of the pass; from there an aerial tramway would haul goods over to Lindeman.[34]

The company installed a boiler and an electric dynamo for the tramway at Canyon City. Planning for both the tramroad and the aerial tramway moved ahead. By spring, 1898, two other tramways—the Chilkoot Railroad and Transport Company (CR&T) and the Alaska Railroad and Transportation Company—were also being constructed. As a result, the DKT abandoned efforts along the lower trail and concentrated on completing its aerial tramway. The modest two-bucket tramway, running from the Scales to the summit of the pass, opened on March 14, 1898.[55]

The DKT dock was isolated from Dyea and saw little traffic. Their tramway was more successful, operating through the height of the Klondike stampede. However, it was no match for the CR&T's longer, more sophisticated aerial tramway. In the summer, most freight and passengers to the Klondike were using the Yukon River steamers via St. Michael, Alaska. This reduced traffic on the aerial tramways in the Chilkoot, to the point where the companies agreed to merge their operations. The DKT tramway, its small capacity no longer required, shut down soon afterward.[56]

Today, little is left to tell the visitor of the once-vaunted DKT system. Only a few pilings of the dock remain. The wagon road between the dock and Dyea can be traced for most of its length, and the tramway steam boiler can still be seen in Canyon City. But the only reminders of the tramway itself are the steel cables snaking up the rocks of the Scales and the Golden Stairs.

Martha Kelsey of Dorchester, Massachusetts claimed to be the first person to ride the aerial tramway over the summit of the Chilkoot:

They tucked me into a little box, only 2 feet wide and 3 feet long and about 2 feet deep. It was made only for carrying freight, so they tied and strapped and bound me in as they would a load of groceries.... The [overhead] cables attached to the box I was in started with a creaking, grinding sound. Straight up the mountain side and into the dark canyon I went as if I were a bird.... I whirled just around the edge [of a cliff], and then had the awfulest sensation, for I was suspended over a great chasm, hundreds of feet above a glacial torrent, and it appeared to be a mile from one side of the canyon to another, where the spiderlike cable lines were suspended from towers.... The rest of the way was straight up the rocky pass... it seemed as if the north pole must be right ahead of me. Then came the intense relief as the summit of the pass was reached...the car slowed up. It was the end of the line, and a group of rough but kind hearted men cheered me as the car was lowered...and I was unstrapped.

• Redwood City [California] *Times-Gazette*, March 5, 1898

A fanciful press sketch of a Chilkoot aerial tramway. Although similar in appearance, the actual trams carried only freight and no passengers.

Freight services past the summit

During the first months of the stampede, freight services expanded quickly. The network of roads and aerial tramways from the Dyea waterfront carried goods away from the beaches only to dump them at the icy summit of the Chilkoot. Then, the many thousands of tons of material—from tinned hams to grand pianos—were pushed, pulled or dragged from there down to Lindeman Lake. Soon, freighters extended their lines over the summit of the pass.

From the summit north to Lindeman, difficult terrain and uneven ground made for rough travel. Pack horses were the only effective way to move the huge volume of freight beyond the Chilkoot summit to the commercial boat services on the lakes. Heavily-burdened horses trudged up and down the crude roadways in the high alpine sections of the valley. Eventually, wagons and sleighs were added but they did little to ease the life of a pack pony. While the lakes were free of ice, usually only from June to September, commercial freighters offered a combination of colourful wagons, rugged packhorses and small boats to carry goods.

In winter, arrangements were much simpler. Convoys of horse-drawn sleighs picked up freight from the aerial tramways at the summit and moved it north over the dark, churned-up snow road to Lindeman and Bennett. However, wild weather and accidents frequently interrupted the flow. And during spring break-up and fall freeze-up, freight traffic sloshed to a halt in the soft snow and uncertain ice.

Ferry services profited from the through transportation system established by the Chilkoot tramway companies in the spring of 1898. One family operated a boat service and restaurant on the rocky shores of Crater Lake. Arriving early in 1898, a Mr. Johnson found his small knockdown boat in great demand for freighting. He spent the next two or three months at Crater Lake and made $100 a day. At the same time, his wife broke open their supplies and baked pies for the passing horde. Later in the year, Johnson sold his boat, and he and his wife continued on to Dawson.[57]

Tappan Adney described his boat travels in the Chilkoot in the fall of 1897:[58]

[At] Crater Lake, a body of pure green water, of irregular outline, a mile or more in length, lying in a great, rough, crater-like basin of rock...[there are three boatmen] ferrying goods to the foot of the lake at 1 cent a pound. Forty dollars a day was paid for the use of one rowboat, but the men are making more than that....

[A few days later] the ferry man at Long Lake refuses to go out in the storm, so we pay him full price, 1 cent a pound, for his boat, a large double-ender, load our goods in it, rig a small square-sail in the bow, and scud to the other end, leaving the owner to get his boat when the storm eases up. A portage of a few hundred yards to Deep Lake, and another ferryman takes us to the foot, a mile distant, where we set up our tent.

Boat services at Crater Lake in September, 1898.

In winter, boats were replaced with sleighs. The steady winds through the pass helped push the sleighs across Crater Lake.

From Crater Lake, freight was packed over a rough wagon road to the end of Long Lake. After being shipped across to Deep Lake camp, it was once again transferred to horses.

Many people brought their own horses with them to the trail. However, the difficulties of wrangling in the coastal mountains meant hardships for horses and a clear field for professional companies. The experience of three Ontario men in Skagway in August, 1897 was typical. Split up in the chaos of arrival, two of the party were dropped off in Skagway with their outfit, while the third landed in Dyea with the horses and some of the feed. The remainder of their hay was dumped into Skagway harbour by the departing ship's captain. The two in Skagway built a boat to get themselves and their outfit over to Dyea, where they found their partner in despair. American customs officials had seized their horses in lieu of a duty payment of $290 on their Canadian goods. After futile arguments they paid the duty and retrieved their horses. Only now were they able to start the real challenge of moving up the trail.[59]

Most of the freighting on the trail was done by commercial companies. One of the larger firms was Orr & Tukey from Tacoma, Washington.[60] Edward S. Orr and William V. Tukey set up their company early in the rush. They invested in the Chilkoot aerial tramway and brought in horses, harness and pack equipment. The company was based at Lindeman and operated with some 150 animals, hauling freight from the summit to Bennett. Ward Hall, a teenager from San Francisco, worked for Orr & Tukey in the spring of 1899. His first job was on a shovel gang, digging through snow drifts 3 to 4 m (10 to 13 ft.) deep to open up a pack trail to the summit. He was then assigned to the company's camp at Deep Lake:

The first camp was established at an old tent roadhouse at [Deep Lake], about midway between Chilcoot Summit and Lake Linderman[61].... I was transferred to the kitchen as dish washer, flunky, horse wrangler, and what not. It fell to my lot to have to get up about 3:00 a.m. and start the fires, feed the horses and mules, and wake up the cook.

Breakfast was over about 5:00 a.m. and the packers off for the day, many times not returning for supper until nine or ten at night. The packers would take the pack train up to the Summit, load their animals, pack down to Lake Linderman, and there unload on a barge...

It took a considerable number of animals to pack forage for themselves and supplies for the men at the [Deep Lake] Camp, and as soon as the snow melted from the flats east of the Chilcoot Summit, camp was moved to that point so as to eliminate the long pack of camp supplies.

There was no timber at the Summit with which to make tent poles, so that it was necessary to pack these poles on mule back to the new location. What a time we had lashing them

on the animals; they would not stay put and the mules, becoming frightened, would run, shaking the poles loose and leave them behind. The packers almost exhausted their vocabularies by the time camp was moved....

It was quite a sight to see the pack animals, some 150 in all, led by a bell male, and strung out one behind the other down the trail; the animals knew they must follow the tinkle of the bell. Many unwieldy things were sent over the Summit for us to

Thomas Scott, an Ontario stampeder, described the morning ritual of packing animals:[62]

The pack-saddles are generally put on before breakfast, and then one is able to get a second and tighter cinch when ready to load. Some ponies one has to take with great subtlety, drawing the cinch suddenly when they are intent on something else—for instance ruminating on the state of the trail, or their final chance for life with oats at twelve dollars a sack.

Firewood was an expensive necessity at the summit. It was hauled up from the Alaskan forests.

Tappan Adney's horse struggles back to its feet on the Chilkoot Trail, fall, 1897.

Florence Hartshorn, living in Log Cabin during the stampede, recalled watching pack trains:[63]

The pack trains afforded much amusement for me, as everything one could imagine went over the...trail on horseback. Some of the burros that went by were loaded so that all one could see would be the ears and tail.

pack down to the lake. One day a big French range came along, weighing about 300 pounds, which had to be packed on the mule's back. Our packers were able to load this so that it did not fall off or get one-sided on the animal.

One time a 24-foot canoe showed up, and another time two barrels of whiskey, both weighing about 400 pounds. This whiskey was loaded on a big, strong, mule one barrel on

Transfer camp at the north end of Long Lake.

Loaded with live turkeys, this pack train rested briefly at Log Cabin, summer, 1898.

each side of him. This load was so great that two of the packers stayed with him throughout the trip, and when the mule returned we had to leave him in camp for a week to rest up.[64]

Archaeologists have studied the remains of the transport camp at Deep Lake. In addition to the quays and docks built into the lakes, there is evidence of a large camp. A blacksmith and harness repair shop, many tents housing the packers and a hotel offering commercial accommodations were all located here.

Julius Price travelled through the Chilkoot in the spring of 1898. He recorded his arrival, late one evening, at the Happy Camp restaurant:[65]

[After ploughing through deep snow we were disappointed] to find only a tent lighted dimly by a candle. Inside was a long sort of counter spread with iron cups and plates, and behind it a man was standing over a wretched little stove making coffee. The aspect was wretched in the extreme, the thin tent merely serving to keep out the wind, not the cold. We were, however, glad to get even a cup of so-called coffee, for it was at any rate hot, and to a certain extent comforting. This and a slice or two of coarse bread and butter, and a plate of tinned beef, made up a supper that was perhaps more filling than satisfying, but as this was more than we had expected to find on the way, we could not grumble.... One wondered at the strange fascination of gold that it could reconcile a man, and, for the matter of that, his wife also, to come out and eke out a miserable existence in such an awful place as this.

Opening a trail restaurant was as simple as stopping and breaking open your outfit. Crater Lake, about 1895.

The interior of a restaurant near Crater Lake in September, 1898.

WOMEN ALONG THE TRAIL

On our way...we were overtaken by an ox-team, the owner of which lifted little Emily and placed her on the loaded wagon, which gave her quite a rest.

There were so few children on the trail that our little girl attracted a great deal of attention and every one had a smile for her. One day a man said: "God bless you dear, you are just the size of my little girl at home," and tears sprang to his eyes as he pathetically spoke of his child.

- Louella Craig diary, February, 1898[66]

At Bennett, spring, 1900.

THERE WERE MANY instances where men were amazed to see non-aboriginal women on the trail, dressed in men's clothing and living a hard life. William Haskell noted:

Sheep Camp is a favorable place to...see what some women are made of.... It was a revelation, almost a mystery. But after awhile I began to account for it as the natural result of an escape from the multitude of social customs and restraints which in a civilized society hedge about a woman's life. Hardened miners enter on the Alaskan trail as a sort of grim business, something a little worse than they have been accustomed to, and yet much the same. The stimulus received from the novelty of the situation is much less than in the case of a woman, especially one who has not been used to roughing it. She steps out of her dress into trousers in a region where nobody cares. Her nature suddenly becomes aware of a freedom which is in a way exhilarating. She has, as it were, thrown off the fetters which civilized society imposes, and while retaining her womanliness she becomes something more than a mere woman. Her sensitive nature is charmed with the new conditions, and her husband, who has had the advantage of no such metamorphosis, sits down, tired and disheartened by the obstacles in his path, and marvels at his wife as she drags her heavy rubber boots through the snow and climbs with a light heart the precipices of mighty mountains.[67]

Lindeman: tent city

At last, on reaching the top of a long hill, there lay stretched at our feet, though some distance below, a large placid sheet of water, looking like a huge piece of rose-coloured silk spread between the mountains. At the point nearest us on a promontory of flat shore was a huge conglomeration of white tents, looking like a flock of seagulls on a distant beach. This was Linderman. Dotted in and about the tents and along the shore were numerous strange-looking yellow objects. As we got nearer these took definite shape and I saw they were boats in various stages of construction. It certainly was a curious and withal weird sight, this sleeping city of tents.... Many hopes lay dormant in that confused mass of white canvas. How many were to be realized?[68]

Lindeman camp was built on the first good campsite beyond the summit. Well-drained, except for swampy areas near the point reaching out into the lake, and, sheltered by a high ridge, it enjoys markedly better weather than sites just a few kilometres back up the trail.[69] Lindeman Lake is a major water access to the Yukon River and—before the rush, at least—was surrounded with good timber for shelter, heat and boats. In late summer, 1897, the first of a huge wave of people reached Lindeman, changing it completely.

By early September, Lindeman consisted of some 200 tents scattered through the trees along the upper lakeshore where the trail first reached level ground. Over 400 men and

Lindeman as seen from the high trail in the early summer of 1898.

LAKE LINDEMAN
AND CITY.
J.M.B.
2-7

women were "busy cutting wood and sawing timber, building boats, packing them and starting off on the sail...to the Klondike." By the end of the month, six saw pits had been erected and 60 boats were under construction. Up to 10 boats, each carrying five to 10 people, left Lindeman daily in a desperate bid to reach Dawson before freeze-up.[70]

By mid-October, ice on the lakes closed all river travel farther north into the Yukon. However, the rush from the coast continued unabated, leaving newcomers trapped along the shores of Lindeman Lake for the winter. With a long stay ahead of them, the citizens of the new community began to organize themselves.

Even before the gold rush, Yukon miners had looked after their group interests in a loosely organized fashion. Miners' meetings were community gatherings where disputes were settled by a vote after both parties presented their case. They administered a rough justice.[71]

Banging boats together at Lindeman.

Pack train arrives in Lindeman. The main trail passes before the NWMP post.

In spring, 1897, NWMP officer W.H. Scarth reported on a miners' meeting along the trail. After catching a thief, a committee confiscated and sold his outfit, the proceeds "for the benefit of a 'miners library' to be established at Clondyke." The thief was given 50 cents and told to keep clear of Canadian territory "if he valued his health."[72] As trail camps were established, the powers of the miners' meeting expanded to regulate community affairs.

At least 1,000 people were camped at Lindeman by freeze-up and the population continued to grow through the winter of 1897. To cope with the organization of the new town, the people at Lindeman elected a mayor and a justice of the peace.

Following hard on the heels of the stampeders was the Flowers, Smith & Co. land development and transportation company. By December, 1897, John Flowers had built a warehouse and was preparing a dock for his proposed launch service on Lindeman Lake. He also began to import collapsible canvas and sectional metal boats to sell to stampeders. Some of these boats are still piled up at the Chilkoot summit.

Flowers filed a town plat for "Lake Linderman, Alaska" in Dyea, in January, 1898. This charter, a flagrant attempt to usurp land north of the pass, proved to be the company's undoing.[73] When the NWMP arrived at Lindeman Lake in the following month, Flowers and his Alaskan company were evicted from Lindeman and his property confiscated.[74]

Despite this company's setback, however, Lindeman grew. At its height in the spring of 1898, Lindeman was a noisy community of 4,000 people. A steady stream of stampeders and horse-packed freight coursed through its main street between the canvas walls of hotels, bakeries, and saloons. Along the shores of the lake, people feverishly hammered together boats for their trip downriver to the Klondike.[75]

In the spring of 1898, the community busily awaited the break-up of the frozen rivers and lakes. Many stampeders, Harley Tuck among them, continued their preparations for the trip downriver. Tuck was one of a group of four men from Seattle staying at Lindeman. His diaries, written for his wife and regularly sent back to her, describe the scene:

Sketch of a camp at Lindeman, June 6, 1898.

The Courtney family supplemented their store's profits by running an unofficial mail service between Dyea, where the U.S. postal service stopped, and the many camps along the trail as far as Bennett.

Lindeman June 6th 1898

April 20, 1898[76]

Got your letter on Thursday last. The P.O. delivers our mail to Sheep Camp, from there a private carrier brings it to Lake Linderman for which we pay 15¢ per letter, and am glad to get them at that price.

Another day of hauling from the Summit. Been four days already, and seems like we've hardly dented our pile of stuff. The trail down to Linderman is busy, we meet dog trains, horses, goats, to say nothing of the men hauling their sleds. One can hear dogs yelping and men swearing all the time.

Our fellow travellers proved to be very pleasant companions. Rogers the Chicago man, being quite well educated and not used to roughing it. He is disgusted with the trip already and it is only his pride that keeps him from turning back. He told me one of his troubles, seemed trivial, also very funny to me. He did not seem to think it a laughing matter. He said he had got the itch a few days before and he had been taking sulphur and rubbing himself with carbolic

BEDDING DOWN

HOTEL FACILITIES ALONG the trail were plentiful but the level of service varied widely. Trail bunkhouses were usually filthy, rag-tag affairs offering only primitive accommodation. One stampeder, Leon Boillot, travelling in early April, 1898, described an evening at his lodgings at Bennett:

Enter now, if you please, the Lake Bennett Hotel, a rough log cabin. The main floor is one room with a single window allowing in a little daylight while the door is always open allowing in lots of people. Along the wall under the window is a long table flanked by rough benches. An immense stove covered with pots, cans, and frying pans occupies the middle of the room, around which the cook and his man fill plates, pour tea, and run from one end of the room to the other never satisfying the hungry crowds sitting around the table.

Others, forced to wait, stand at the back of the room, talking in husky voices, warming their hands on the stove pipe glowing red, while others thaw their supply of tobacco or sip drinks at the bar over there, all watched over by an old bearded swindler wearing glasses and cap. The menu, it is always the same: you can order what you want and you will receive what you do not expect, the only thing you can be certain of is the increase in the price, but you shouldn't pay too much attention to that. After a candle stuck in the neck of a bottle is placed on the table, the door is closed and the hotel keeper leads the way up the ladder to the loft where everyone ends their day by finding a pigeon-hole, some with blankets, some without. Latecomers remain below discussing the latest rumours of the goldfields over a mug of grog. Eventually they go to bed as well and soon all is quiet in the hotel. Outside 25 degrees of frost freezes everything.[77]

However, there were a select few hotels attempting to provide service to a clientele that valued amenities and were willing to pay for them. The Olympic, reputed to be the finest hotel in all Alaska, graced downtown Dyea during the gold rush. It was constructed as Dyea was nearing the height of its prominence. The *Dyea Trail*, in August, 1898, called it:

...one of the most modern buildings in Dyea. It is the largest and most complete hotel in Alaska, and would be a credit to any of the Coast cities. It is three stories, 75x100 feet; contains 115 large and elegantly furnished rooms; spacious dining room; handsomely fitted office and barrooms, and is conducted on a truly metropolitan plan. The house is becoming very popular under the management of one of the owners, R.A. Crothers.[78]

Stampeder at Lindeman bunkhouse.

The interior of the White Pass Hotel.

Guests at the hotel were equally impressed. Stampeder William E. Patterson, who hiked back to Dyea from his camp at Bennett Lake, provided the following description:

April 10, Easter. Left Sheep Camp early, got into Dyea in time to do my shopping. Got a bath and shave, whisker trim $1.00, then bot my stuff, stayed all night at Olympic, 112 rooms, largest hotel in Alaska, elegant accommodations, $3 paid, had an elegant Easter dinner. April 11. Slept last night on a real spring bed & real feather pillow, could hardly tear myself away.[79]

Dyea lost much of its population during the summer of 1898, and never really recovered. Even so, the hotel hung on, closing in early 1900. In the following April, an enterprising hotel keeper, R.J. Hilts, hit upon the idea of moving the structure south to Douglas City, near Juneau. C.W. Young, a Juneau businessman, cut the building into sections and barged them south. By early June, it reopened as the Hotel Northern in downtown Douglas City. On March 9, 1911, it and several other buildings were destroyed by a fire that swept through the downtown area.[80]

Rev. R.M. Dickey describes a hotel at Lindeman in the spring of 1898:[81]

Filthy, stuffy, overcrowded bunk-houses on the trail, where, tier above tier, in closely packed rows, weary men sleep and snore and cough and swear through the wearisome nights.

The British Hostelry at Log Cabin, summer, 1899.

Tugwell's Hotel
. . . Log Cabin, B. C.

The Oldest and Best Place in Cabin. Only Wooden Building With Rooms. Opposite Custom House.

The Olympic Hotel, located at the corner of Third and River streets, was Dyea's finest hotel.

solution but it did not seem to do any good. And this morning he discovered he and his crowd was lousy. He thought that was enough to disgust any on the trip. He said it made him feel like the lepers of old, unclean.

Tonight we are camped on the ice on Linderman having brought down two sled loads from the summit. The camp is full, some people have been here all winter. We will have to go a mile or so down the lake shore to find a place to pitch our tent.

May 15, 1898[82]

Here it is the middle of May and we are walking around in two feet of snow although on the hillsides the snow is just about all gone but around the edge of the lake it seems to hang on like grim death. The weather has been good, that is all we can brag about here for a more desolate place to stop in could hardly be found.

Life flows along in about the same groove these days. Boat-building is not a very interesting subject to write about. We have made a very good start but we are not rushing matters as it is not the kind of work that one can rush at, especially when one has to stop and think what his next move will be and how one is to do it. Ed has taken the lead in planning the boat so far. While he is not as handy with tents as I am, still he has a better idea how to go at it. We will build a boat but what it will be like the future alone will tell.

This country is policed by the North-West Mounted Police. They are not mounted in this country but use dog-teams and Peterborough canoes. There was one came by and notified everyone was to stop at Bennett and register their boat and get a number. When asked what the charge would be replied there would be none, but most of us took that with a grain of salt, for we have found that whenever one has any business with any of these Canadian officials one never gets away without leaving some good Americans $s behind.

I have been making furniture this p.m. Have made a rack of four shelves to sit my dishes on, made it of the slabs which we took off from the logs as lumber is too precious to use in that way. Lester is making a saw horse to edge up our boards on, and so we get away with the time for long days has been the order of the day ever since we started up the trail.

For many stampeders, like this man baking his first loaf of bread, the trip was their first camping experience. Despite the frontier ideal driving the rush, very few of the people involved had actually lived on the land.

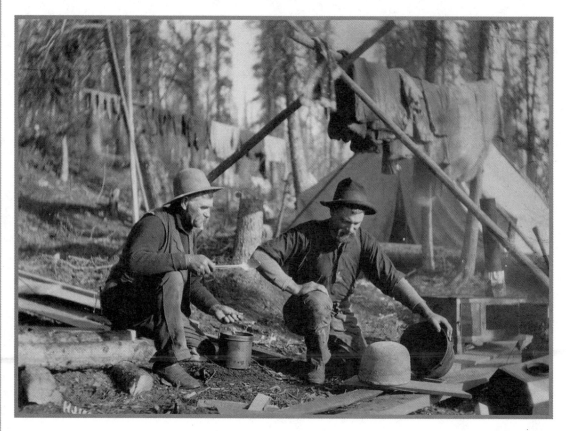

It seems as though there is no darkness at all now. We are usually in bed by or before 10 o'clock and it is broad day light at 2 am although the sun does not rise till about 4. Suppose that will cease to be a novelty before the summer is over.

Before closing this letter I will tell you about my first attempt at pie making. After had got my clothes washed started in to make an apple pie having had my apple on to cook for some time, got out Miss Suzy to see how it was done. In getting my crust dough ready had trouble in getting it rolled thin enough as had to use the baking powder can for a rolling pin and had to use a cloth on top of the grub box for my cake board. In consequence the lower crust was thick and thin but got the top one fairly good. Seasoned it with cinnamon and put it in oven. I watched that pie mighty close you can bet. It reminded me of the old song Where is My Wandering

FOREST CHANGE AROUND LINDEMAN

THE FORESTS OF the Chilkoot Trail corridor underwent dramatic change during the gold rush.[83] Timber had been cut for rafts and boats around Lindeman Lake even before the rush started. During the winters when Lindeman boomed, the forests were also cut for firewood. In the summer, forest fires raged through the area. William B. Haskell wrote about the forest at Lindeman in 1895:

Around Lindeman could be found a few fair-sized trees, though few were over thirty feet high. They are mainly confined to varieties of spruce, hemlock, and balsam fir, but spruce everywhere predominates, and its lumber resembles that of southern or pitch pine. The hemlock is less plentiful. White spruce is the staple timber, and though in some places near running streams it attains the height of from fifty to one hundred feet, it is most commonly found below forty, and averaging about fifteen inches at the butt. It is a fairly clear white wood, straight grained, and easily worked, light, and yet very tough. It endures the weather well, and a log house built of it is good for over twenty years. It abounds in a light and delicate looking gum, and those addicted to the chewing-gum habit can always be sure of a supply.[84]

A year later, Omar Maris reported that the largest tree available for their raft was only 20 cm (8 in.) in diameter. And in the spring of 1897, one party gave up the idea of building a boat at Lindeman when they found most of the timber at the site burned off. Over the next two years, thousands of people and two commercial sawmills operated at Lindeman, clearing both sides of the lake well back from the water. The Kerry Canadian Company alone cut 75,000 board feet in 1898.

Before the rush, the Lindeman forest was a mature old growth forest. Today, the predominant tree species around the lake is lodgepole pine. Subalpine fir survives from the pre-rush forest on higher slopes and in wet areas not cut over by the stampeders. Barring other disturbances or fires, white spruce will gradually succeed the pine and re-establish the climax forest, probably by the 300th anniversary of the rush.

The woods along Lindeman Lake are still littered with the stumps of trees cut during the gold rush.

Boy Tonight? The child of my tenderest care for it was with great care that I watched that pie, but it came out browned to a turn. I cooled that pie and kept it out of sight till the boys got through eating, then brought it forth in all its splendor. Ed and Lester voted it first class.

The group started downriver at the end of May. They spent two weeks up the Stewart River on the way to Dawson, prospecting and cutting timber. On July 12, they arrived in Dawson with a large lumber raft. Tuck spent the summer working at a sawmill in Dawson, and had a few unsuccessful prospecting trips into the goldfields. He began his return trip to Seattle in late September.

October 9, 1898[85]

Reached Bennett at 1:30 pm when everyone began making ready to take the trail. Myself and some thirty others decided to go over the mountains via Chilcoot Pass although most of the crowd was going via White pass as the R.R. was operating trains from the summit into Skagway. With our packs on our backs we was soon hitting the trail for the foot of Lake Linderman where we boarded a little steamer. The town of Linderman, at the present time consists of about three tents and a few wooden buildings.

Through the winter and spring of 1898-99, Lindeman once again experienced a steady stream of travellers, although most of them continued on to the more established community of Bennett. After spring break-up, there was little traffic through Lindeman. By the fall of 1899, only the few who couldn't afford the train fare hiked out the Chilkoot. The following summer, a NWMP constable reported that: "Lindeman is at present deserted, no one living here with the exception of myself." Six weeks later, the police abandoned their post and Lindeman was empty.[86]

A winter trail ran the length of Lindeman Lake, spring, 1899.

Miners' boats

Once stampeders reached the lakes, they devoted their efforts to building a boat to take them to Dawson. The journey beyond the trail, with only one or two exciting interruptions, was a placid, flat-water trip on lakes and the broad waters of the Yukon River. Vessels built by the stampeders came in a wide variety of shapes, sizes, and styles. All, however, had to be able to carry the stampeders' goods, up to four tons of freight. Julius Price reached Lindeman in spring, 1898. His description of the town emphasizes the importance of boat building:

> I certainly was prepared for a busy scene, but certainly nothing to equal what was before me. It almost baffles description. All along the shore and to some distance up the side hills, boat-building was being carried on with quite feverish activity, and the sound of a steam sawmill, whipsaws, and hammering and planing, resounded on all sides. Boats there were in all imaginable shapes and sizes, from big unwieldy barges to tiny craft that reminded one of the paper boat dear to childhood. It was, indeed, a wonderful sight. Many of the boats were constructed with great skill, and were evidently the production of practical boat-builders, whilst others were little better than flat open boxes.... Apart from these home-made craft, there were Peterborough and Strickland canoes, steel boats built in sections, collapsible boats, punts, and, in fact, almost anything fit for the long river journey.... The animation of the scene can be more easily imagined than described.[87]

Lumber for boats was highly valued. A few stampeders even hauled boat lumber over the Chilkoot Pass. Tappan Adney describes the difficulty he experienced in this venture: "A

Our neighbor who is going alone had built a boat that was more like a floating coffin.... [He] loaded his stuff in and pushed it out to see how it would float. It turned bottom up and spilled his goods into about four feet of water.

• Harley Tuck diary, Monday, May 30, 1898

Busy waterfront at Lindeman in 1898. One of the sawmills is just visible at the back left of the photo.

Inga Sjolseth watched the boaters running the One Mile Rapids between Lindeman and Bennett lakes on a sunny Wednesday afternoon in early June, 1898:

Today there are many boats going down the One Mile River. Some of them go through the canyon safely, but many have a dangerous ride. I saw one of them run into a large rock and be broken into two pieces. Another one capsized and went under the water with all its cargo. However, no one was drowned.

Running One Mile River.

dozen packers take my outfit across the pass to Crater Lake, but will not touch the boat lumber. Flour is a packer's first choice, lumber last."[88]

Most people used local timber for their boats, cutting their own trees and erecting saw pits or whipsaw frames to cut the tree trunks into planks. Walter Starr's party set up their boat-building camp on the shores of a lake in early April, 1898 and began felling the stand of fine fir trees there. On April 14, they built a saw pit and began sawing boards. The next four weeks consisted of the same tasks, interrupted only by Sundays, an unsuccessful hunting trip and the search for more good trees. One week of practice with the whipsaw and the party established a record, sawing a log into five boards 7.5 m (25 ft.) long in two hours. After three weeks, however, familiarity bred carelessness and on Monday, April 26, Starr:

> *...took a dive off the scaffold while marking a log to vary the monotony and escaped with only a bruised knee and some lost breath. The next day, a log rolled off the scaffold and hit Gil on the head. Luckily his skull is very thick, and he was only stunned for a while.*

On May 2, two of the party began assembling the prepared lumber into a boat. The others did the cooking and continued to haul in additional logs and whipsaw them into boards. By mid-May:

> *...all hands are anxious to get going down the lake so we work twelve or thirteen hours a day.... Bowman and I caulk the seams in the boats. Billy made sails and Gil oars. The pitch to cover the seams gave out but I collected enough in the woods to make out. The lake is opening along the shore. Our boat is a beauty, twenty-seven feet in length, from four to six feet wide and with three foot sides. Her capacity is three tons. With her natural bow stem and fine lines I dare say she is a peer of all boats on the lakes, handmade.... [On May 20] about*

TAPPAN ADNEY BUILDS A BOAT

EVERY ONE IS in a rush to get away. Six to ten boats are leaving daily. They are large boats, with a load of five to ten men each. The boats are of several kinds. A fleet of seven large bateaux got off as we arrived, but the favorite and typical boat is a great flat-bottomed skiff, holding two or three tons; in length over all, twenty-two to twenty-five feet; beam, six or seven feet; sides somewhat flared; the stern wide and square; drawing two feet of water when loaded, with six to ten inches freeboard; rigged for four oars, with steering-oar behind. Some of this type were thirty-five feet in length. There are several huge scows. Well forward, a stout mast is stepped, upon which is rigged, sometimes, a sprit-sail, but usually a large square-sail made generally from a large canvas tarpaulin.

A party usually sends two men ahead to build the boats [at Lindeman]. They must go either five miles up and raft the logs down here, and construct saw-pits, or else to a patch of timber two miles back, and carry the lumber all that distance on their shoulders. A saw-pit is a sort of elevated platform, ten or twelve feet high. On this the log to be sawn is laid, and a man stands above with the whip-saw, while another works the lower end, and in this way they saw the logs into boards. The boards are small, rarely more than nine or ten inches in width. It is a poor quality of spruce, soft and punky, and easily broken. There is some pine.

The boards are an inch thick, and planed on the edges. After the boat is built the seams are caulked with oakum and pitched. The green lumber shrinks before its gets into the water, so that the boats as a rule leak like sieves, but the goods rest upon slabs laid upon the bottom cross-ribs.

Everybody is happy, singing at his work. When a boat is ready to be launched everyone turns in to help, for some have to be carried some distance to water. And when a boat departs it is with shouts of good wishes and a fusillade of revolver-shots. Nails are in great demand, bringing $1 or more per pound; likewise pitch which commands the same. A few days ago, in order to finish a boat, a man gave $15 for two pounds of pitch. No one will sell lumber at all.[89]

Tappan Adney launches his boat at Lindeman in September, 1897.

Cutting planks on a saw pit at Bennett in 1898.

fifteen of us carried our boat and the Whalley's party two scows to the lake shore and launched them. I made a grub chest for our boat.... [The next day we] loaded our camp and outfit in the boat. Bowman went through the ice and Billy pulled him out.[90]

In late May, 1898, the NWMP counted 778 boats under construction at Lindeman Lake, 850 in Bennett and the surrounding area, and a further 198 at Caribou Crossing and Tagish Lake. Inspector Samuel Steele estimated at least 1,200 more boats were built in the subsequent three weeks.[91]

The extraordinary market for boats attracted several commercial manufacturers. The first operation had arrived in 1896 from Juneau when Messrs. Rudolph, Markus, and Rocco brought in a two-horsepower engine and boiler over the Chilkoot and set up a 35-centimetre (14-inch) saw at Bennett. During the sudden rush in 1897, they ran short of raw materials but the partners continued to make money sawing up logs brought in by stampeders. A

SCOWS

In Arthur T. Walden's *A Dog-Puncher on the Yukon*, he describes his freight scow as:

...made of two inch planking, forty-two feet long, and twelve feet wide, with straight sides. They were square at both ends, but sheered up like a barge, with pointed outriggers running about eight feet at the bow and stern, and a long heavy sweep at the end. They were decked fore and aft for eight feet, with the middle open, and a plank around the sides to walk on.

Each scow had a mast about twenty feet high, rigged with a square sail. The mast was set about eight feet back of the bow, so that a man could work the sweep in front of it. Sails were used only when crossing the lakes. Usually a tent was placed over the cockpit in the middle. After the cargo was loaded, this was where the crew lived, cooking on a little sheet iron stove. The scows were unpainted, capable of carrying twenty tons, and drew from 24 to 26 inches.[92]

Floating down the river on a scow, June 19, 1899.

sawmill was also set up in Lindeman that same year and operated for at least two seasons. Another, King's Mill, started up near Bennett and ran for about two years before being moved to Carcross.[93] Most of these mills also made boats and scows for stampeders.

Boat transportation during the gold rush was one-way. From Lindeman Lake, boats had to run the treacherous rapids of the One Mile River to reach Bennett Lake. Josiah Spurr, the leader of a United States Geological Survey party, described lining the rapids in the spring of 1896:

> [We] began the task of "lining" [the boat] down. With a long pole shod with iron, especially brought along for such work, Pete stood in the bow or stern as the emergency called for, planting the pole on the rocks which stuck out of the water and so shoving and steering the boat through an open narrow channel, while we three held a long line and scrambled along the bank or waded in the shallow water. We had put on long rubber boots reaching to the hip and strapped to our belts, so at first our wading was not uncomfortable. On account of the roar of the water we could not hear Pete's orders, but could see his signals to haul in, or let her go ahead. On one difficult little place he manoeuvred quite awhile, getting stuck on a rock, signalling us to pull back, and then trying again. Finally he struck the right channel, and motioned energetically to us to go ahead. We spurted forward, waddling clumsily, and the foremost man stepped suddenly into a groove where the water was above his waist. Ugh! It was icy, but he floundered through, half swimming, half wading, dragging his great water-filled boots behind him like iron weights; and the rest followed. We felt quite triumphant and heroic when we emerged, deeming this something of a trial: we did not know that the time would come when it would become so monotonous that all feelings of novelty would be lost in a general neutral tint of bad temper and rheumatism.[94]

In the spring of 1898, high water made the run through this stretch fairly easy, although there were several reports of wrecked scows. In the first week of June, the Mounted Police noted 10 scows lost in the rapids.[95]

Some short-lived commercial boat services operated on Lindeman Lake during the rush. Several vessels hauled freight and passengers. In May, 1898, the *Lindeman*, a sternwheeler with a 40-ton capacity, began carrying freight from Lindeman to the Bennett portage. For a dollar, passengers were also carried to the portage. The *Lindeman* was moved onto the upper river system later in the year. It eventually sank in the White Horse Rapids.[96] By the summer of 1899, with train service direct to Bennett, commercial shipping on Lindeman Lake ended.

Not everyone had an easy trip to Dawson. High winds on Bennett Lake sank many scows.

Boom Towns & the Railway

The echoes of the blastings roll hither and thither among the mountain peaks, repeating to them ever in reverberating tones that eternity is no longer theirs. The solitude of nature here is forever undone, and the absolute reign of the monarchs is over. Alas for the giants! Are they grieving beneath their icy crests that their haughty heads must yield to the demands of the universe. The irresistible power of progress opens the way for the traveller and adventurer, cleaving the massive boulders, levelling the mountains and bridging the chasms, that it may girdle the globe with its bands of iron, and plant its standard with its watchword "Excelsior," upon hitherto inaccessible summits.[1]

Charles Taylor, the Chicago newspaper editor, recorded his exhilaration while watching the construction of the White Pass and Yukon Railway at Bennett in 1899. He enjoyed a comfortable train ride through the White Pass but also remembered the trials of the travellers of only the previous year and marvelled at the amazing changes that had taken place.

The stampede through the Chilkoot and White Pass was far more than a colourful camping trip into the mountains. The masses of newcomers demanded, and received, more and better services along the trail. Boom towns sprang up along the Klondike route offering accommodations, meals and a host of other services. And as the importance of the northern gold strikes grew in the public eye, so did the amount of money invested. Whether in tramways, towns, or eventually a railway, these investments had the effect of tying the north into the rest of the world.

Log Cabin and the White Pass

While many of the first stampeders in 1897 headed up the Chilkoot Trail, some chose the rough trail over the White Pass starting at Skagway and promoted by William Moore. Though the lack of a real trail prevented any great number of stampeders from making it through to Bennett Lake in the fall of 1897, the White Pass soon became an important parallel route to the Chilkoot.[2]

Winter freeze-up and heavy snowfall actually improved the trail because the snow and ice made the trail surface more even. In the spring, rough areas and sections of the trail subject to thaw were corduroyed—tree trunks laid side-by-side on the ground as a rough roadway—or bridged by commercial packers. (Some of this corduroy is still visible on both the U.S. and Canadian sides of the White Pass Trail.) Even with these improvements, spring storms often closed sections of the trail for days at a time.[3]

Finally, by early March, 1898, the White Pass Trail was in good shape. A mounted rider could travel from Skagway to Bennett in a day. Pack horses, generally loaded with about 90 kg (200 lbs.), were slower, but were able to travel over rougher ground. However, the trail wasn't open for long. By May, the spring thaw effectively closed it down again. About that time, though, plans for a railway through the pass came to fruition.

(preceding page) **Looking south over Bennett, 1900. Bennett Lake and slough are in the foreground, One Mile River is in the right background and Lindeman Lake is to the left, in the distance. Mount Harvey—named after the first Parks Canada superintendent in the Yukon—looms behind the town.**

Corduroy trails were laid down over the wet areas between Log Cabin and Bennett.

Log Cabin, a day's walk from Bennett, developed as a major settlement in the first winter of the rush. In the fall of 1897, Thomas Tugwell and his son erected the grandly-named "British Hostelry" there. The pair of squat log buildings faced the trail, hugging the rocky ground and providing only minimal head room; patrons were clearly expected to remain seated during meals. The British Hostelry offered rooms and meals to travellers, and office space to a variety of entrepreneurs.

A collection of tents sprang up on both sides of Tugwell's buildings. Storage, a general store, several suppliers of feed and outfits, even a bakery, were housed here. By spring, 1898, the community stretched haphazardly across a low ridge and boasted a large number of tent hotels, almost all with restaurants. Accommodation was basic, usually just a rough lumber cot. Log Cabin became a designated customs point that summer. Railway construction further increased the community's already booming businesses.

Traffic, like a wide, muddy stream in flood, flowed past the front of these establishments day and night. A well-travelled path meandered across the ridge among the huge stacks of

Log Cabin in April, 1899. The North-West Mounted Police post is on the left while, on the right, Tugwell's British Hostelry (with the flag) faces the trail.

hay bales, outfits awaiting customs clearance, piles of cordwood and building materials, and heaps of sacks containing everything from flour to roulette wheels. People on the move, amid yelping and barking dogs, haggled for a good price on new outfits or additional feed, while heavily-loaded sleighs pulled by straining horses crunched through the frozen mud of the trail. The noise, smells, and activities made for a lively scene.

The rapid movement of people northwards on the trail meant constant change in the face of the community. In one of the few descriptions of Log Cabin from that busy spring of 1898, Leon Boillot describes his visit:

> As it is Sunday, and the tent is up, we are resting. Log Cabin consists of a half-dozen log huts and hundreds of tents randomly scattered along a ridge covered with pine and fir trees. This provides an effective barrier to the violent winds savaging the area; it is sort of an oasis.
>
> On the ridge a few log cabins rise here and there from amongst the tents which are of various shapes and sizes. Some serve as stables, with as many as 50 horses. Others contain hundreds of tons of baled hay, sacks of oats and barley, while still others, even smaller, pompously proclaim themselves to be hotels, restaurants, saloons, and so on.

A most excellent and easy grade roadway is now open from Bennett to Log Cabin at which point are now located the police post and custom house. Here are piled up load after load of freight. Some marked Dawson, more to Atlin.

• *Klondike Semi-weekly Nugget, March 25, 1899*

FAMILY LIFE AT LOG CABIN: THE HARTSHORNS

Florence Hartshorn's first impression of the Kittitas Restaurant was mixed:

[T]he eaves were so low one could sit on them when standing on the ground. It had no windows, only a small glass in the door. Mud roof with a tarpaulin over the top, mud floor, and the door was so low we had to stoop to get inside. Inside there was a long table covered with a dark oil cloth and all tin dishes. Also a dandy large Yukon range, which was a very good baker, as I soon learned.

Florence Hartshorn on her arrival at Log Cabin.

FLORENCE (DAVIS) HARTSHORN grew up on a Michigan farm.[4] She married Albert Hartshorn, a neighbour's son, in 1889. The young couple briefly tried farming, but soon sold out and headed west to the coast. However, the economic depression of the mid-90s left them destitute. Albert continued to work as a blacksmith and mechanic when he could while Florence apprenticed with a photographer, and gave birth to their daughter, Hazel. In 1897, the excitement of the Klondike swirled down the Pacific coast and once again their lives turned upside down.

Albert went north in April of 1898. He blacksmithed on the White Pass Trail. His friend, Clarence Crane, started a restaurant, the Kittitas. Prospects were good so Albert returned south and picked up his wife to return to Log Cabin. After a harrowing trip over the White Pass Trail, Florence arrived at Log Cabin on July 4, 1898, just before a forest fire swept through the community.

Although the roof caught fire a number of times, the Kittitas Restaurant survived and Florence started work. Hearing rumours of a new gold strike, Albert dropped his tools and with many others rushed to the new strike at Atlin. Florence later recalled her feelings:

My, that was a cloudy day for me, all alone on the trail.... All the cooks in Log Cabin went to the new diggings, so I was the only one who could feed the rushers, and I did the best I could as I had only

bread and butter and beans to give them (while they lasted).... When Clarence returned I was so glad and pleased to show him all the money I had made, over two hundred dollars clear, and I felt very rich.

Albert and Florence headed south that fall to see their daughter and settle down. By spring, 1899, however, Albert got a job as second engineer aboard one of the new Bennett Lake steamers and returned north. Florence and Hazel followed in October. Through the winter of 1899-1900, the family lived aboard the *S.S. Gleaner*, acting as caretakers. The dark, cold days of winter at Bennett were made even more dreary by the need to nurse an acquaintance through a spell of typhoid.

In spring, mother and daughter settled into a house in Bennett. Florence opened a photo studio there while Albert sailed aboard the *S.S. Gleaner* on the run to Taku Inlet near Atlin. For the next five years, the family moved throughout the southern Yukon as Albert worked for mining companies at Atlin, serviced the electric light plant in Whitehorse, and for one summer ran the *Duchess*, the small locomotive on the Taku portage. (This locomotive is still preserved in Carcross.) In 1907, the family moved north and settled near Dawson where Albert held a job with the Yukon Gold Company.

Albert Hartshorn at his forge at Log Cabin, summer, 1898.

Hazel Hartshorn and her friend Goldie playing in a dog sled before the Hartshorn winter home, the *S.S. Gleaner,* at Bennett.

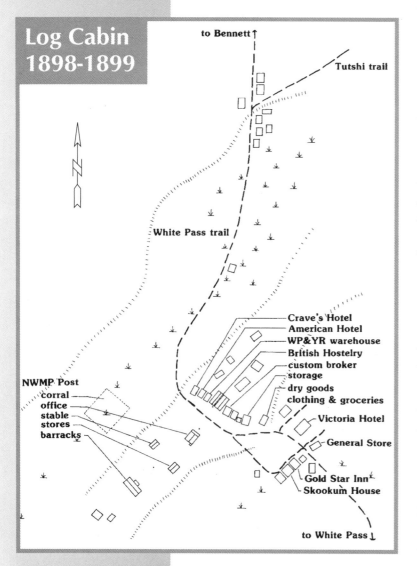

Log Cabin 1898-1899

to Bennett ↑

Tutshi trail

White Pass trail

Crave's Hotel
American Hotel
WP&YR warehouse
British Hostelry
custom broker
storage
dry goods
clothing & groceries

Victoria Hotel

General Store

Gold Star Inn
Skookum House

NWMP Post
corral
office
stable
stores
barracks

to White Pass ↓

For 2 francs 50 you can enjoy a cup of coffee and a slice of meat, or, for a more substantial sum, a nondescript kind of ratatouille decorated with shrivelled accoutrements which might have been potatoes, turnips, or onions at one time. A so-called dessert of prunes or baked apples, and you have spent 5 francs or better.

Several professionals, doctors, clockmakers, shoemakers, have set up shop in small tents beside the trail and are desperately trying to earn enough money to pay their way into the interior. For those interested in probing the deeper mysteries of this journey, it is likely that the doctor is a charlatan, the clockmaker a blacksmith, and the shoemaker a true disciple of Saint Crepin.[5]

As trail conditions deteriorated in the spring thaw, traffic through the White Pass ground to a halt. Freight hauling was limited to nighttime, when frost firmed the trail surface. With supplies cut off from the coast and outfits broken up for transport and storage, anxious stampeders began stealing from each other. Petty theft of flour, pork, and staple groceries in the Log Cabin area reached serious proportions in the early summer of 1898.

This situation posed a problem for Boillot and his group. After struggling over the trail and transporting their goods to Log Cabin, they found they had left their flour behind. Too exhausted to retrieve it, they visited restaurants, hotels, and the bakery to try to purchase some bread or flour. No one had either. Eventually a woman provided them with two fistfuls of bread for five gold francs (roughly equivalent to a dollar). Bread was literally worth its weight in gold.[6]

The spring thaw altered Log Cabin's oasis-like nature. Many people found their previously comfortable camps inundated with murky ice-cold water as the snow melted into an unsanitary swamp. John A. Sinclair, a Presbyterian minister on his way to Bennett, felt that, between the miserable terrain and the unsavoury local population, Log Cabin was the dirtiest place on earth:

Such a filthy hole I never have seen as that group of shacks and tents at Log Cabin. Loathsome looking dogs slunk around the tents. They were red-eyed and diseased-looking through gorging themselves on decayed horse-flesh. Greasy and slatternly women, begrimed and ragged children and rough, shifty-eyed men wallowed in a sea of mud and filth. All this, plus the terrible stench of dead horses, more noticeable in the warmer temperature, spurred us on and fired us with renewed energy to get away from there with all haste.[7]

Bennett: "A good camping ground"

Lightly burdened and living off the land, early prospectors and First Nations traders traditionally used Lindeman as the starting point for their trip downriver. However, gold rush stampeders travelling with a ton of goods found the rapids of the One Mile River between Lindeman and Bennett lakes a serious obstacle. Despite river improvements and the construction of a portage tramway (remnants of the tracks are still visible where they cross the trail), most travellers preferred to start their river journey from Bennett. Furthermore, as traffic over the White Pass Trail increased, its junction with the Chilkoot Trail at the foot of Lindeman Lake also favoured Bennett as the terminus of both trails. Originally just a "good camping ground, perfectly dry, and lots of firewood," Bennett changed radically in the winter of 1897-98. That fall, few stampeders made it past Bennett before freeze-up. The latecomers at first set up winter camps at Lindeman. By January, 1898, Bennett still consisted of "only 3 or 4 log buildings and a few tents."[8]

(preceding page, bottom) **This pack train is just leaving Log Cabin on its way to Bennett. The Kittitas Restaurant is in the background.**

Boat builders on the Homan River near Bennett.

There was a sawmill at Bennett even before the gold rush had begun. Esther Lyons, exhausted after her trip over the Chilkoot in May, 1897, wrote: "To hear the buzz of the sawmill and the whistle blow was indeed cheerful, and relieved greatly the intense loneliness of the situation, making us feel as though we were once more near to civilization." During 1898, as many as six sawmills buzzed and whistled along the shores of Bennett Lake, most churning out lumber for boat construction.[9]

Completed boats were also available from companies like Abbot and Gillis. Ranging from "roughly put together" for $80, to 9-metre (30-foot) vessels for $600, boats were valuable and hard to obtain. By spring, 1898, stampeders were building hundreds of boats, scows, and canoes. In early June, more than 1,000 small craft were ready to sail down Bennett Lake.[10]

Freighting was a major business in this gold rush town. While some people carried or hauled their own goods, thousands of horses were also imported to pack and haul freight. Although the main corrals were placed away from the townsite, large storage tents and freight offices mushroomed in Bennett. Hay and horse feed were also available in vast quantities;

Down the main trail into Bennett, spring, 1898.

the site of Lilly Brothers' provisions tent still spouts hay today. Lilly—popular because of his skill with the violin—and his daughter ran provisions stores in both Bennett and Log Cabin.[11]

The trail was the spine of Bennett. Although it provided a hard surface in winter, once the spring thaw began, it turned into a foul mass of muddy sand, waste, and manure. Henry Cryder thought "Bennett City smelled pretty badly" in the spring of 1898. Nevertheless, soon there were hotels, warehouses, and stores jostling for space along both sides of the trail. Most early businesses were in tents. Some, like Bartlett's Hotel, appeared to serve both

The Pack Train Inn at Bennett, one of a chain owned by a Juneau saloon keeper.

Main Street, Bennett, 1898.

"man and beast." The tents were spread along the shore to the Dawson Hotel. There the trail finally left the land and headed across the lake ice to the many individual camps scattered along the shores of Bennett Lake, continuing on to Carcross and Tagish.[12]

Log buildings also appeared. Among the first was the Hotel Portland, a squat single-storey log cabin facing the trail. Run by J.D. Puter and his partner, the Portland later expanded into a large two-storey frame building, eventually billing itself as the "Family Hotel" in Bennett. Hotel chains of a sort also reached Bennett. The Pack Train Inn and Restaurant was built by George Rice right at the entrance to Bennett. Rice was the owner of a Front Street saloon in Juneau and he expanded his operations into the Yukon following the rush. He also started the Pack Train Saloon and Rice's Restaurant in Skagway, the Pack Train in Circle City, and later the Grand Hotel and Cafe in Atlin.[13]

In the spring of 1898, Bennett grew dramatically as more stampeders left their winter quarters to get ready for their trip downriver.[14] In May, about 1,000 tents and 40 wooden buildings covered the sandy hills of the town, spread down the riverbank to the shores of Bennett Lake. The community bustled with activity. While about 2,500 people actually lived in Bennett, thousands of others who camped

Partners who toughed out a winter at close quarters often fell out when the ice broke. W.R. Rant, the Bennett Magistrate, was busiest in April and May:[15]

June 4, 1898—Arthur Morgan charged on the information of Wm. John Henderson with stealing one pot of jam. Accused Discharged.

St. Andrew's Presbyterian Church, Bennett, 1899.

Departure for the goldfields, Bennett, May 30, 1898.

nearby came to Bennett for everything from nails to watch repairs. "A city of tents" stretched along the trail as it followed the One Mile River into Bennett Lake.[16] A prospector noted: "This entire distance [between Lindeman and Bennett lakes] and for a mile deep is one mass of tents—looks as large as San Francisco from a distance—that is built up so solid with streets, etc."[17]

As Bennett grew through the first winter of the rush, the need for some organization was soon apparent. The crowds along the One Mile River began fighting over the limited number of sites for cabins and space for boat building. In August, 1898, Presbyterian minister Sinclair reserved a lot for his church at Bennett. When he was ready to build two months later, the site was already occupied. He was granted another site in the Government Reserve. Working with labour volunteered by the winter-bound stampeders, Sinclair erected a fine looking church clad in the barked slabs discarded by the sawmills.[18]

At a series of miners' meetings in January and early February, 1898, residents demanded that Bennett be recognized as a town. A week later, Captain W.J. Rant, in his mid-40s and

retired from the British military, arrived to take over local administration for the British Columbia government. Rant and his son Norman (later the Atlin mining recorder), worked closely with the NWMP. The British Columbia government made a townsite grant to two men, J. McLeod and E.H. Sullivan. In June, 1898, these two had the town surveyed and divided into lots for sale. By early summer, Bennett—and Lindeman—were both reasonably orderly communities.[19]

With orderliness came growth, confidence and an air of permanence. Bennett, as the head of river navigation, quickly became an important shipbuilding and transfer point. Several companies began building steamers. The Upper Yukon Co. packed two 15-metre (50-foot) steamers, the *F.H. Kilbourne* and *H.A. Goddard*, over the White Pass in March, 1898. The boats were launched in May as soon

THE NWMP AT BENNETT: "It tastes like weeds"

THE NORTH-WEST Mounted Police had a reputation for honesty and fairness in bringing order along the trails. Although the police were a respected force on the Canadian prairies, their entry into the Yukon in the fall of 1897 was less than successful. Their initial travel and supply arrangements were inadequate and ridiculed by experienced Yukoners.[20]

Although the regular uniform was "most striking to foreigners...[and the] men...keep themselves braced up and smart looking," the uniforms supplied were too small—"I defy any 15 year old boy...to get into [one]"—and they shrank. Winter clothing was poorly designed for trail work. The mackinaw was "most useless" while the fur coats, too long for running alongside dog teams, had to be shortened and have hoods added to be serviceable. Supply difficulties meant that even these items were hard to come by. By the fall of 1898, NWMP officers complained: "It is impossible for the men to have a creditable appearance as there is next to no clothing in store here."[21]

Police accommodation was also abysmal. For almost a year, the Bennett detachment was housed in a single 4.9 m by 9.2 m (16 ft. by 30 ft.) log building. (The foundations of this building are still visible in the Bennett campground.) As many as 14 constables and their officers crowded into the combined kitchen, office, mess room and bedroom. They struggled to carry out their duties under a constant stream of dirt or rain from the leaky sod roof.[22]

The food supplied to the force was equally bad. The biscuits were "sticky and nauseating to the taste," canned meats provided "neither taste nor nourishment," and bacon was so fatty no one could eat it. Even the tea "tastes like weeds." Coffee was "dark and muddy," while sugar and tobacco were equally unappreciated. The police at Bennett often bought fresh meat, vegetables, and tobacco at their own expense rather than draw goods from their stores. Only the regular whiskey ration passed without criticism.[23]

This bland and limited diet and the poor living conditions made the police, like many at Bennett, susceptible to disease. Through the spring and summer of 1898, dysentery and typhoid fever raged through the camp. By fall, so many of the police were sick that additional housing had to be rented. On August 31, 1898, Constable E.E. Pearson died of typhoid.[24]

It was late 1898 before better supplies began to arrive. By then most of the posts also had decent accommodation. After a year of near chaos, when only the strength of the men and the character of their officers had carried the force along, the NWMP was finally equipped to carry out its duties.

At ease, NWMP constables in their ill-fitting uniforms at Tagish Post.

Tent store at Bennett in the summer of 1898. Surrounded by thick forests and unmapped mountains, the stampeders often felt lost. Nevertheless, they were still able to drink their favourite British ale, munch on apples from Washington, and even enjoy bananas from Central America.

A letter in the *Canadian Mining Review* of June 3, 1898 noted:

I have seen Linderman and Bennett contain about 5,000 people each, and have not seen a drunken man in them; all is orderly; the rule of the Mounted Police is splendid. I have never seen such order in any town.

The *Australian* under construction at Bennett, May 19, 1899.

as the ice was off Bennett Lake. The Bennett Lake and Klondike Navigation Company established a dock and warehouse at the mouth of the One Mile River. The company's three steamers, the *Nora, Ora,* and *Flora,* ran regularly scheduled trips to Canyon City, just above Miles Canyon and White Horse Rapids. By late summer, 10 steamboats, the largest carrying upwards of 63 tonnes (70 tons) of freight, had been built at Bennett, and at least four shipping companies operated vessels on the upper Yukon River.[25]

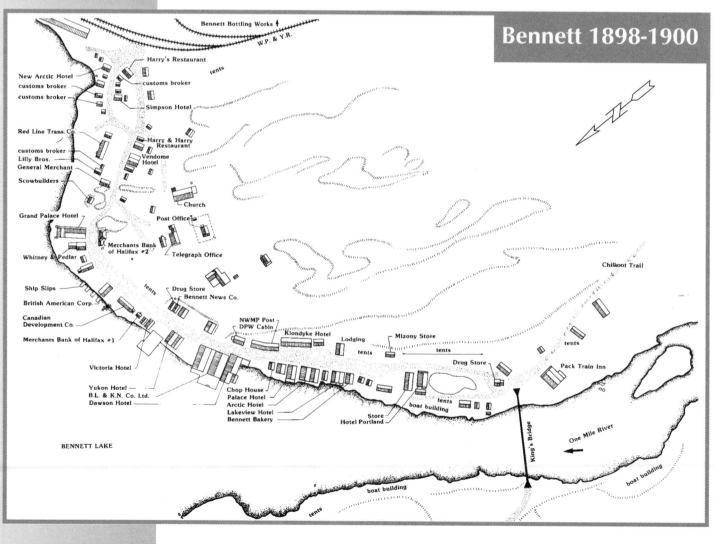

Bennett 1898-1900

The White Pass and Yukon Railway

In late May, 1898, construction of the White Pass and Yukon Railway (WP&YR) started in Skagway. Financed by an English syndicate, the line was to extend through the White Pass at least as far as Bennett Lake. Few could have predicted it at the time, but this project would change the face of the gold rush and turn the trail camps into ghost towns.[26]

Talk of railway proposals had been heard by Skagway residents ever since the first stampeders swarmed ashore the previous summer. Some promoters pushed for the White Pass; others favoured the Chilkoot. Still others wanted to start from Haines Mission, 24 km (15 mi.) to the south. These efforts were high on expectations, but low on cash; some were out-and-out swindles. The most serious railway bid, the Mackenzie & Mann scheme for an all-Canadian route, from Glenora, British Columbia on the Stikine River, to Teslin Lake in the Yukon River drainage, evaporated in one of the regular railway scandals then plaguing the Canadian parliament.[27]

The WR&YR, unlike previous efforts, was well-financed and showed every sign of completing its goals. Within days of ground-breaking, its labour force numbered in the hundreds, and work on the line proceeded quickly. During a three-day period in mid-June, workers constructed almost two kilometres (over one mile) of line, and by late July, more than 11 km (7 mi.) of rail were in place for the first passenger train.[28]

After this early promise, however, the promoters ran up against difficulties which would have challenged even the most stalwart backers. In August, 1898, word of a gold strike in nearby Atlin, British Columbia reached the construction camps. More than half the workers quit and headed off to the new diggings, most with the railway's shovels and picks. In November, a strike against wage cuts paralysed work on the line. Construction was also slowed by the route's steep canyons and granite slopes. Despite ingenious engineering efforts and dangerous rock work, construction barely kept

White Pass and Yukon Railway cooks in their tent kitchen/bunkhouse at Camp 10, Caribou division, July, 1898.

The start of construction on Broadway in Skagway, May, 1898.

going. Last, but not least, the autumn of 1898 brought the onset of a winter long and bitterly cold enough to try the endurance of everyone involved.[29]

Until freeze-up, the rough trail conditions limited supply efforts. Although the trail was

frozen solid by December, two weeks of fierce storms then made travel in the summit area almost impossible. Huge stores of both goods and railway construction material started to stockpile at White Pass City, 16 km (10 mi.) north of Skagway. At the summit, the trail simply ended in mountains of snow. In spite of all this, workers were able to push the end of track to the summit of the White Pass on February 20, 1899. Railway officials gathered there to celebrate their progress. The skies were clear and sunny and the temperature was -20°C (-4°F).[30]

Railway construction past the summit was impossible; most workers simply shovelled snow. In January, 1899, Michael

Working on the railway provided many stampeders with the cash needed to continue their trip north.

Blasting the grade through solid rock near Rocky Point, August, 1898.

Laying tracks in close quarters, just north of Skagway, September, 1898.

Heney, the railway's construction contractor, split his work force. One group remained in Alaska, keeping the right-of-way free of snow, while a second crew began work on the road-bed between Log Cabin and Bennett on the Canadian side.

The crew in Canada was housed in a large camp at Log Cabin. There was accommodation for the 350 labourers, a well-equipped field hospital, and extensive—but never extensive enough—storage tents. Largely made up of tents, the camp remained until late summer, 1899. (Its exact location is still unknown.)

The workers' large tents offered only basic creature comforts. A mess tent was also put up. Common labourers were paid 30 cents an hour for a 10-hour day. They spent $1.00 a day for room and board and $1.00 a month for medical care. Many of the workers on the WP&YR construction crew stayed only long enough to earn a grubstake before heading farther north. Some 35,000 people eventually worked on the railway, though the largest labour force at any one time was about 2,000, and usually much less than that.

The field hospitals at White Pass City and Log Cabin became very important facilities. Previously, medical care had been limited to a police surgeon at the Tagish NWMP post and private facilities in Skagway. The railway hospitals not only served company workers but

Shovelling snow from the railway tracks at the White Pass summit, March, 1899.

treated others for a fee. At Bennett, Reverend Sinclair maintained a special church fund to cover the medical care for those unable to pay.[31]

At the summit, winter brought high winds, six-metre (20-foot) snowdrifts, and brutally cold temperatures that temporarily slowed construction. But by April, 1899, workers were moving north again. Progress was rapid. On July 1, rail finally reached Log Cabin, 19 km (12 mi.) beyond the summit; just five days later, the line extended all the way to Bennett Lake.[32]

The Chilkoot Trail is bypassed

The completion of the railway to Bennett in the summer of 1899, and to Whitehorse a year later, effectively overwhelmed competing routes and forms of transportation into the Yukon River watershed. Although the facilities at Log Cabin had been an integral part of the

Damage to freight during transit was common until the spring of 1899, when the WP&YR completed its warehouses at the summit, Log Cabin and Bennett.

The railway camp hospital at Log Cabin. The cold, wet weather caused many respiratory problems while the unbalanced diet led to stomach and digestive ailments. Construction accidents were a less frequent cause of hospitalization.

gold rush, the trail camp lost much of its importance as traffic moved onto the railway. Residents moved to either Bennett or Atlin. The NWMP post there withdrew to Bennett in the fall of 1899, while the customs post remained behind only until the following spring.

As late as July, 1898, two months after work started on the railway, the *Dyea Trail* had crowed that almost all traffic was coming by way of the Chilkoot Trail.[33] As the rails advanced up the Skagway River valley, traffic shifted to the White Pass corridor and the Chilkoot's popularity plummeted.

By February, 1899, a passerby noted that the population of once-boisterous Sheep Camp had shrunk to 18; by the end of June, 1899, the camp was all but deserted. The tramways combined their operations in the summer of 1898, though, and remained in service during the following winter. Competition with the WP&YR was futile. In July, 1899, the tramway owners sold out to the railway and the trams were shut down and disassembled.[34] By the following March, Dyea still had a population of about 250, but by the spring of 1903, fewer than a half-dozen inhabitants remained. One of these, Emil Klatt, made his livelihood growing vegetables at the old townsite and dismantling the buildings for reuse in Skagway and other places.[35]

A White Pass and Yukon Railway train at the White Pass summit.

Bennett booms

When the WP&YR reached Bennett in July, 1899, the town boomed. For an entire year, it was the end of steel. More buildings went up and a broad range of services were added. The Yukon Hotel, operating out of a tent as early as the summer of 1898, moved into a fine new two-storey frame building. Featuring baths, toilets (draining into the lake behind it) and gas lights, the 25 rooms were among the best in town. By the end of the summer, the hotel attracted clients to its "extensive barroom and fine card tables" with piano concerts every evening. Merchants also profited from the growth of the town. J. West—vendor of liquor, cigars, and general merchandise—moved from his tent on the Bennett waterfront into a large new two-storey building. The Department of Public Works also erected two large buildings on the hillside for the crew building the Yukon telegraph line. (The attractive view from the large verandah of the main building makes the site of this structure one of the more popular camping sites at Bennett.)

By the spring of 1900, Bennett had a population of 2,000.[36] As Joseph Near noted:

> The houses are most all built of timber, log cabins and tents, there are Hotels, shops, saloons, offices, Theatre, and there is also a good Presbyterian church.... Scores of men are arriving daily as work on the railway has started again...all day long we hear the blasting and booming of the dynamite, the clanging of picks and shovels making the old mountains echo again and again as civilization forces her way through the solid rocks.[37]

Life in Bennett was full of energy; accounts reveal a busy, invigorated community. Most of the town's residents were young people fired with ideas of wealth and dreams for the future.

Convention was often disregarded. For many the stampede was their first experience of the north, of the wilderness, and of people from other countries and cultures. The new

Bennett, June 1, 1899. One Mile River (foreground) splits the community as it runs into Bennett Lake (seen on the right).

experiences challenged their attitudes and assumptions. Inga Sjolseth, at Bennett in the spring of 1898, noted:

> There are many people who are camping here now, and wherever one goes there are crowds. They are from all countries and wear many different kinds of clothes. I saw an old woman dressed in men's clothing. She wore a yellow coat. Another woman who was dressed in black, walked arm in arm with her. It was a comical pair. Many turned and stared at them.[38]

The mixing forced people to recognize other groups and ways of living. For some the freedom from ordinary constraint meant trouble. Many "loose characters" came into Bennett along with gambling, prostitution, and drinking. A winter's confinement in "about as miserable a looking place as one could imagine" often brought out the worst in people. The Bennett police court was busiest in the spring just before break-up. The majority of cases were brawls, thefts from outfits, and arguments over the division of goods. Cruelty to animals, both dogs and horses, and the avoidance of customs or liquor license dues were also common. The high-spirited nature of life offended some. Reverend Sinclair threatened to report one bank clerk to his superiors if he didn't stop racing around town on his dog sled with "fast women."[39]

Not everyone lived the fast life. Sinclair worked hard to offer "the better things" to Bennett through his church. Although his services were initially conducted in hotel dining rooms, he soon had his large church under construction. When completed in the summer of 1899, it became a focus of community life. In addition to two Sunday services there was also a Thursday night service. Up to 120 people attended. The Ladies Auxiliary of the church also organized socials every Tuesday. There were debates and lectures on capital punishment, the war in South Africa, and the enduring friendship between the United States and the British Empire, usually accompanied by musical programs. Local performers sang, played

Joseph Near wrote about the church at Bennett in April, 1900:

...the church is used as a free reading and writing room, in the evening prayer meetings, socials and the like are held, if it was not for this church life at Bennett in the winter would hardly be bearable.[40]

Abandoned after completion, the church was kept up by the WP&YR as a tourist icon.

BENNETT N.W.T. JUNE 1

Charles Taylor, visiting Bennett in June, 1900, wrote:[41]

A score or more of wooden houses of primitive structure meet the eyes, and dozens of tents, in which miners and railroad employees dwell temporarily.... In the distance are indications of a Christian settlement, for a large church with tall belfry, from its elevated position, overlooks its congregation, as they pursue their weekly avocations.

By February, 1900, the railway tracks at Bennett were lined with tent warehouses.

banjo, violin, mandolin and bagpipes, and recited poetry. William Cullin, a police constable, even performed whistling solos. On other evenings the church was open as a public reading room. Equipped with a phonograph, magazines and free writing paper, it was an alternative to the bars.[42]

Other organizations helped fill the time. The Arctic Brotherhood, Bennett Camp No. 2, held regular meetings on Monday evenings. Many people from the Bennett business community were members. Winter sports included dog sledding and, for the less active, checkers:

> *The 327th inning of the Great Inland Checker Carnival at the Bennett Bakery closed last night [December 8, 1899] after one of the most exciting sessions of the series.... This championship contest is one of the longest on record: lasting from the close of navigation to the opening of the same, and the interest, like the cold weather, is beginning to get intense.*[43]

A tent post office had been an early fixture in Bennett. By the late spring of 1899, a larger log post office was completed on the hillside, among the other government buildings. In December, 1898, a telegraph line from Skagway reached Bennett, making more rapid communications possible. A year later, the telegraph line was extended north to Dawson City. Remains of the original line can still be seen along sections of the White Pass Trail.[44]

CELEBRATING VICTORIA DAY AT BENNETT

VICTORIA DAY, QUEEN Victoria's birthday and a Canadian national holiday, provided a break from the pursuit of personal wealth. Rampant nationalism made a patriot of everyone, and after a long winter confined to small cabins and tents the stampeders were ready for some activity.

Just as the sky began to lighten on May 24, 1898, an early rising bugler played "God Save the Queen." Rubbing the sleep from his eyes, Archie Bain of Montreal joined the crowds and enjoyed the day's events:

> We had a big time at Lake Bennett on the Twenty-fourth of May. The North-West Mounted Police got up games, baseball in the morning, and athletic sports in the afternoon, open to the public, with good prizes. In the evening there was a regatta. A tug-of-war, Scots against the Australians, was won by the Scots, to be beaten by the North-West Mounted Police after a very hard pull. On the previous evening, at a concert, an American was called upon to speak, and he started to say that he believed he was addressing Americans almost entirely, and when the audience shouted "No" to this he took a United States flag from his pocket and commenced a comparison of his country with Great Britain in such terms that I thought it would end in a free fight. However, they made him get off the platform.[45]

Tug-of-war on the main street of Bennett, Queen's Birthday celebration, May 24, 1899. The steamboat crew competition was won by the Canadian Development Company's men, while the Victoria-Yukon Transport Co. team beat the All Comers.

Bennett was a hive of activity in the spring as parties readied themselves for the trip downriver.

P.F. Scharschmidt, a customs broker operating at the summit of the Chilkoot earlier in the rush, gained support for the publication of a newspaper. The *Bennett Sun* began "casting its beams" in May, 1899. *Sun* readers obtained a full diet of local news, events, and advertisements. News from the outside world was less common but was closely followed.[46]

The transition from pack trail to railway meant a dramatic change for the transportation business. Freight traffic through the Chilkoot disappeared overnight. A month after the first train came into town, Orr & Tukey—the Chilkoot packers—pulled up stakes. For a week their outfit of some 100 horses and mules wandered around Bennett while wagons, harness, and feed piled up as the Chilkoot freight system coiled up at the end of the trail. In early August, the whole works were loaded onto nine large scows, floated downriver to Dawson, and uncoiled again, this time for use in the Klondike goldfields.[47]

Bennett turned its back on the old trail and the One Mile River. Instead, the marshy flat beside the new railway tracks filled with buildings. Most businesses simply moved from one side of town to the other. Several new restaurants, hotels and saloons opened to serve railway travellers.[48]

Transferring freight from railway to boats was a major part of town life. Through the winter, trains of freight sleighs moved down the frozen lakes and river to Lake Laberge for an early start to the goldfields the following spring. Docks were built beside the newly-erected White Pass warehouses. In spring, the whistles of the steamboats announced the break-up of lake ice.[49]

The summer of 1900 brought a demand for construction lumber in Dawson. The sawmills at Bennett entered the vigorous and profitable trade in the construction of freight scows. The *Atlin Claim* noted:

> All the sawmills, and private parties besides, are building scows with feverish energy. They find a ready and profitable sale at Bennett and White Horse whence they go down the Yukon never to return.

One company had two large scows, 13.5 m by 3.7 m (44 ft. by 12 ft.), launched within a month of break-up. At least three other companies, and many private individuals, were involved in the scow business, and they kept the sawmills and carpenters busy.[50]

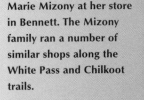

Marie Mizony at her store in Bennett. The Mizony family ran a number of similar shops along the White Pass and Chilkoot trails.

Mr. and Mrs. Moor and child on the street at Bennett, winter, 1898.

Along with this steady growth in business came a change in the character of the town. Bennett, always a way station, for a brief time had aspirations of becoming a permanent community. Several families settled there to run businesses. The Merchants Bank of Halifax and the Bank of British North America both set up branches.[51] There were even plans for a chamber of commerce.[52]

Ghost town

When the railway line continued along Bennett Lake and was completed to Whitehorse it was soon obvious that Bennett's future was limited. Reverend Sinclair wrote to his wife early in 1900: "There is only one family here now that was here a year ago. And out of from 50 to 120 who attend our services I do not think half a dozen were here six months ago." According to Sinclair, the saloons, growing desperate as their clientele diminished, began holding dances, "where prostitutes are kept as decoys to draw men to drink at bars!" on the same nights as the church socials.[53]

The economic profile also changed. By the spring of 1900, businesses began to leave. The Bennett Lake and Klondike Navigation Co. sawmill shut down in April, moving its equipment to a new timber berth on the West Arm of the lake. King's Mill abandoned Bennett for Carcross, where the railway crossed Nares Lake. There it gained lucrative contracts for railway ties and trestle timber. The banks moved on and hotels began shutting down. By midsummer, the Pack Train Inn had closed its doors and the Hotel Portland was offering its furniture for sale "cheap."

Not all businesses were leaving, however. The Canadian Development Company, one of the larger freighting companies, amalgamated with the aggressive WP&YR, expanding the

The *Bennett Sun* on a party in mid-January, 1900, noted:

Last evening saw the good steamer Clifford Sifton in gay attire. The most largely attended dance of the season.... It was no light matter to transform a steamboat, which has been laid up for weeks, into a palatial ball room, but this stupendous task proved no obstacle to these estimable ladies. The long saloon of the boat furnished ample room for all the dancers, while the entrance lobby was patronized by the lovers of the fragrant weed, and ample accommodations by side tables was provided for those inclined to card playing.

The *Clifford Sifton*, *Bailey* and another vessel about to depart the WP&YR docks for Whitehorse and Dawson.

THE ARCTIC RESTAURANT & HOTEL

THE TOWN SEEMS to consist almost entirely of saloons, restaurants, and hotels.... It appears as though the people here do nothing but eat and sleep.[54]

Most stampeders travelled with a complete camp outfit; both Lindeman and Bennett were tent cities. Many, however, were prepared to pay for hotel accommodation or for the privilege of eating a hot—or at least lukewarm—meal under a roof that didn't flap in the wind. The Lake View, Savoy, Northern, Vendome and, of course, the Klondyke, among many other hotels, were established in Bennett during the rush. Most started as tents. The successful, or perhaps determined operators, put up more substantial wooden structures as they prospered. When the rush ended, the need for the services passed and the operators disappeared.

Fred Trump, grandfather of the well-known Donald, and his partner, Ernest Levin, arrived in Bennett in the spring of 1899. They ran a small restaurant on the trail. Aware of the opportunities in Bennett, they obtained a lot beside the trail—quickly becoming the main street—and erected a large tent. The Arctic Restaurant was in business, with a respectable wooden front, large windows, and a welcome length of boardwalk.[55] Before the end of their first year they replaced their tent with a two-storey wooden building.

The Arctic Restaurant & Hotel was located on the main street in Bennett, spring, 1900.

The Arctic was part of a busy jumble of hotels, stores, and other restaurants. From the stable or railway station visitors strode down the muddy main street, kicking or stepping over sleeping dogs. In April, 1900, a local journalist, "The Pirate," provided a review of the Arctic:

I would advise respectable women travelling alone, or with an escort, to be careful in their selection of hotels at Bennett.... For single men the Arctic has excellent accommodation as well as the best restaurant in Bennett, but I would not advise respectable women to go there to sleep as they are liable to hear that which would be repugnant to their feelings and uttered, too, by the depraved of their own sex.[56]

The completion of the WP&YR meant the end of trade at the old trail location. The partners overcame this problem by simply moving the hotel to a better spot. By the time the trains began running to Carcross, Trump and Levin were in business at a new site on WP&YR land across from the Bennett railway station. The trend was clear, however, and they eventually gave up in Bennett, opening a new hotel in Whitehorse early in 1901.[57] The original hotel was later burned down by the WP&YR.

In the summer of 1900, the Arctic Hotel was floated to a new site across from the railway station.

capacity of the latter company and solidifying its domination of the Yukon freight business.[58] Within a decade, the WP&YR had a monopoly of Yukon traffic that rankled local people for years.

People left Bennett too. By early summer, 1900, the town was practically deserted; only about 80 people remained, hammering together scows, running the few remaining hotels, and dismantling the railway warehouses. In late July, the railway was completed to Whitehorse and by 1902 everyone had gone—even the church was abandoned.[59]

By the early 1920s, First Nations families began moving back into the Bennett area; they cleaned up much of the rest of the town. Elders recalled trips to either Lindeman or Bennett

Scow traffic from Bennett remained an important part of freighting to Dawson. Even after the railway reached Whitehorse, differential freight rates favoured shipping from Bennett, but only for a short while.

A new Bennett railway station was built as a lunch stop for train passengers in the early 1900s.

to pick up supplies or replacement parts amongst the abandoned goods. William Atlin still keeps an eye out for useful pieces of hardware when he visits Bennett. First Nations people were conscious of the momentous events of the recent past. Children avoided the stampeders' graveyard at Bennett and Winnie Atlin remembered: "In between Bennett and Lake Lindeman, there's the trail there. You can see it, all those dead horses there, with their harness and everything on them." Atlin was also impressed with the ghostly buildings of the town: "There was so many, there was quite a few houses when we first moved here, you know. [We] went around tearing them down for wood; burn them for wood, that lumber. Yeah, there was lots of houses."[60]

Skagway and the White Pass route were the undisputed winners in the traffic war with Dyea and the Chilkoot Trail. When the railway reached Whitehorse in July, 1900, Skagway's position as a transfer point for Yukon freight was assured. Even so, the town lost much of its population and commercial importance during the years following the turn of the century. In March, 1900, the census recorded 3,117 residents in Skagway. Four months later, the completion of railway construction hit the community hard and the population began to drop. By 1910, Skagway had less than 1,000 residents and the town was almost completely dependent on the railway and associated port operations.[61]

Hudson Stuck remarked in 1917:

The town of Bennett stands on the shore of the lake, completely deserted, a church with a tower and spire amongst the abandoned buildings. The railway killed this place.

The Lake View Hotel at Bennett in 1924.

Politics & Justice

Here begins the last and really only hard climb on this pass.... For about six hundred feet we cut every foot of the way in the ice, and so steep is it that I had to bend forward constantly to maintain my equilibrium. It is very hard on one's lungs and legs...from Stone House to the summit, we made in five hours. I am obliged here to confess that it is a real hard climb, but there is never any real danger....

But what a satisfaction after reaching the summit! I had accomplished that which strong men had left undone because of cowardice or timidity. What pen can describe that hour on the summit of the Chilkoot? Behind us civilization; before us vastness, silence, grandeur. What a place to think, to dream! What grandeur! As I gazed I saw the ocean only twenty miles away, and as I turned I saw the descending slope melting away into the great valley of the Yukon. I then began to realize that our journey had fairly begun. In order to feel your own smallness and insignificance, stand alone on the summit...and realize what an atom in this great universe you are. The loneliness, the awfulness of all this largeness and sublimity! How a poet's soul would swell!.... But there is but little time here for resting, and none for dreaming.[1]

I n the spring of 1897, a vigorous young woman named Esther Lyons travelled into the Yukon with a small party. Her experience of the summit was not unusual. Swept by bitter winds and regularly sluiced with rain, snow, or both at once, the summit is no

(preceding page) Looking south toward the coast from the summit of the Chilkoot Pass.

Looking north from the Chilkoot summit in April, 1898. The aerial tramway terminus unloads freight on the hillside while the trail winds down to and across the frozen surface of Crater Lake below.

At 3 o'clock in the morning of February 13, 1898, the NWMP began construction of a small cabin at the Chilkoot summit. On the 26th, the Union Jack was raised and the collection of customs duties began. The cabin was fitted out with a 12" plank as a customs desk, and two bunks. Julius Price described the quarters as "a rough canvas shanty [equipped with] a big jar of Canadian whiskey...to keep out the cold."

The custom house at the Chilkoot summit is the building behind the flag.

place to linger. Nevertheless, it remains a place to take away one's breath. After struggling to the summit of the pass, the traveller is greeted by an open vista of lakes and rocky mountains, an obvious route into the Yukon basin.

This powerful image was not lost on those stampeders storming through the pass during the gold rush. Escaping from the pressures of economic depression, unemployment and the loss of the western frontier, these eager individuals headed for the promise of Klondike gold. However, gold and riches eluded most of them. For many, the most exciting part of their trip was the moment on the Chilkoot summit. Joaquin Miller expressed the deep emotional impact of his trip through the pass:

> A stately peak, communing with heaven. This wonderful white scenery!... One constantly thinks of the Transfiguration all along this land of whiteness and blue. Heavens! had I but years to live here and lay my hand upon the color! This fearful and wonderful garment of the Most High God.[2]

During the stampede, the summit became a symbol of the rush, and later the Yukon. The struggle to climb to it, the beauty of the view from it and the exhilaration of success are common in the reminiscences. However, the stampeders' journals indicate that they were

primarily occupied with the day-to-day process of moving their outfits over the pass. The summit became a snowy freight yard, thronging with people and animals. Huge piles of supplies, almost buried in the swirling snows, were gradually relayed down the hills and over the lakes to the north. At times, the action became so frantic that the Mounties assigned a "traffic cop" to keep the sleds and toboggans, heading down to Crater Lake, from crashing into one another. George Coffey, a mining engineer, was at the summit in May, 1898. His record of an early morning is probably typical:

> From the Summit...supplies are transported by sleighs. Here may be seen some very peculiar outfits. Some of the sleighs being drawn by men, some by dogs (2 to 10 to a sleigh driven tandem), some by horses, some by goats and some even being drawn by women. In the early morning hours this place reminds one of Bedlam turned loose—men all cursing and yelling as though their very lives depended there on.[3]

In this bedlam, only one thing remained constant—the lively body of people, animals and freight continued to stream northwards onto the lakes, bringing with them their civilization and its politics. In the midst of it all, in February, 1898, the North-West Mounted Police set up a boundary post that effectively—and, as it happened, permanently—established the boundary between Canada and the United States.

Summit caches, spring, 1898. Every cache was inspected and duties assessed by the Mounties before freight was allowed beyond the summit.

From the 1825 treaty
between Great Britain and
Russia:[4]

*That whenever the summit of
the mountains which extend in
a direction parallel to the
coast, from the 56th degree of
north latitude to the point of
intersection of the 141st
degree of west longitude, shall
prove to be at the distance of
more than 10 marine leagues
from the ocean, the limit
between the British
possessions and the line of
coast which is to belong to
Russia...shall be formed by a
line parallel to the windings of
the coast, and which shall
never exceed the distance of
10 marine leagues therefrom.*

Establishing the boundary

The boundary between what would become Canadian and American territory was established by a treaty between Russia and Great Britain in 1825. At the time, few were interested in the ramifications of the treaty; even after the U.S. purchased Russian America in 1867, little attention was paid to the boundary. The issue lay dormant until the mid-1880s, when white settlement in the area began.

Miners were starting to find gold in the Fortymile watershed, not far from where Dawson City was later established. They knew the boundary lay along the 141st meridian, but were ignorant as to where that line actually was. Because the meridian was thought to be close to the gold outcrops, the miners were not even sure what country they were in. To resolve this situation, residents along the Fortymile River demanded surveys and legal protection for

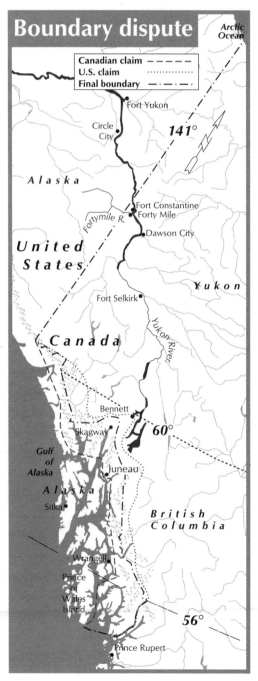

Boundary dispute

Canadian claim — — — —
U.S. claim ....
Final boundary — · — · —

their claims. Local traders, assuming they were located in Canada, called on the Canadian government to enforce customs regulations in the area. Bishop Bompas, working at his nearby Anglican Indian mission and concerned about the bad influence of the miners on the Indian population, also asked the government to assert control over the region.[5]

In order to clear up the sovereignty issue, Canadian surveyor William Ogilvie arrived at Forty Mile in 1887. Soon afterward, he and his crew surveyed the 141st meridian, both north and south of the Yukon River. Their investigations revealed that, as expected, the Forty Mile townsite lay in Canada but that some of the territory staked by miners was in Alaska.

In the summer of 1894, the Canadian government sent two North-West Mounted Police officers to assess the situation in the Yukon. Inspector Charles Constantine and Staff Sergeant Charles Brown hiked into the Yukon over the Chilkoot Pass and spent the summer at Forty Mile. They imposed mining regulations, collected $3,200 in customs duties and recommended a permanent police force for the Yukon. The following summer, Constantine returned to Forty Mile with a detachment of 20 officers and men. By the winter of 1895, they had completed the barracks and a stockade for their first post in the Yukon. It was known as Fort Constantine.[6]

Determining where the boundary lay through the Alaska Panhandle was not so simple. In the 1825 boundary negotiations, geographical knowledge of the Panhandle area was vague. The boundary treaty, as a result, was inexact and open to various interpretations.[7] As with the Yukon River basin, few cared about the boundary location for most of the 19th century. However, the Klondike gold rush made the Alaska boundary dispute the focus of a protracted and heated diplomatic tug-of-war, with each side claiming a significantly different boundary.

Some newspapers, both in England and the United States, worried that disagreements over the boundary would lead to war. This situation was indicative of the world-wide clashes between the major powers in the late 19th century. The Alaskan boundary dispute illustrates both the American and Canadian perceptions of their role in world politics.[8]

World affairs

In the latter half of the 1800s, Great Britain followed a policy of "splendid isolation." Britain used its powerful navy to avoid diplomatic entanglements with European powers and to build a large world empire. The British Empire's primary focus in the 1890s was the broad band of colonies, protectorates, and trading partners stretching from South Africa, through Egypt and India, to China. However, the growing pressures from other world powers challenged Britain's ability to stand alone.

From 1899 until 1902, the British army was fully engaged in a vicious guerilla war with the Boer settlers in South Africa, who were being encouraged by Germany. Through the rest of Africa, the expanding colonial empires of France and Germany challenged Britain in Nigeria (1897-98), on the Nile (1898), and in Egypt. Dervish resistance to a British army in the Sudan in 1898 ensured that British attention remained focused on Africa.

Russian threats to British imperial interests in the Middle East, and the unstable rule of the British over the Indian sub-continent, were perhaps the most serious problems facing the Empire at this time. Farther east, the slow disintegration of the Chinese Empire drew in all the major powers as they jockeyed amongst themselves to gain concessions and areas of interest in the Far East.

All of these events were of two-fold significance for the Alaskan boundary dispute. First, with the focus of British attention in Africa and Asia, there was limited interest in the issues of the western hemisphere. Canada, and Canadian issues, were not a priority. Second, the British were no longer able to maintain their empire alone. With the burgeoning power of other European countries, "splendid isolation" was no longer possible. Alliances, or at least agreements, with other world powers were needed to protect British interests.

Canadian politicians, however, had a different set of priorities and were under different pressures. Prime Minister Wilfrid Laurier claimed the 20th century belonged to Canada. His opinion was based upon the obvious national strength developing in the northern half of North American, and upon Canada's central location between the British Empire's Atlantic and Pacific territories. Canada saw itself as the new centre of the British Empire.

Although Canada had no independent foreign policy, the Dominion government's strong, protectionist National Policy

Many Englishmen fear that the proximity of the Alaskan boundary, the sensational wealth of the mines and the mad rush now being made will end in war between England and the United States.

> • Sitka *Alaskan,*
> September 11, 1897

Great Britain's foreign policy choices in the late 1890s: Britannia considers alliances with Japan (left), the United States and Germany.

DISENGAGED.

Miss Britannia (meditatively). "I THINK UNCLE SAM WOULD BE A GOOD PARTNER; AND SO WOULD LITTLE JAP! I WONDER IF MY 'COUSIN-GERMAN,' WILLIAM, WILL ASK ME TOO!"

Not everyone thought the establishment of a boundary was a good idea. The Sitka *Alaskan* reported in December 22, 1894 that Alaskan Lieutenant Governor Charles D. Rogers threatened to "utterly destroy" everything of a British nature in the Yukon if Canadians "lay claim to a single inch of our territory."

was chiefly an anti-American program. The end of a free trade agreement with the United States in 1866 led Canada to increase restrictions on the export of raw materials and on imports of manufactured goods. This policy was designed to build up its industrial base. The economic prosperity in parts of Canada during the 1870s and 1880s seemed to justify this policy. For politicians, however, the growing strength of U.S. nationalism and the need for economic progress left little room for political manoeuvring. The conflict over the Alaskan boundary became a popular rallying cry in Canada. The Canadian government had little choice but to try and face down the United States.

In the U.S., a combination of factors also shaped their response to the Alaskan boundary dispute. The closing of the western land frontier in the 1890s caused concern about the future growth of the nation. Economic need for continuously expanding markets, the underlying desire for American political domination over the western hemisphere, and a prevailing belief in the superiority of their own democratic institutions, all supported an aggressive American approach to foreign affairs.

The late-century, deep depression in the United States was blamed on overproduction and the glut of the national markets. Americans, searching for new markets, looked overseas. Hawaiian sugar plantations, nitrate deposits in Chile, and trade with Latin American countries all attracted investment. To protect these investments the United States extended an "informal empire" through the western hemisphere.

The United States also had been pursuing the extension of a "formal empire" with the purchase of Alaska in 1867 and the capture of the Spanish Empire in the Pacific and Caribbean at the turn of the century. America's desire to expand their influence was built upon a wish to exclude European power politics from the new world and a humanitarian, if somewhat arrogant, desire to extend the benefits of their own republican democracy. However, through the 1890s, the United States found itself increasingly dependent upon British goodwill. The American support of a successful Panamanian revolt against Colombia (1903), seen as necessary for the building of the Panama Canal, and the war with Spain (1898) were both possible only with British consent.

Miners at a temporary boundary marker in 1895.

The economics of the Panhandle boundary

Before the Klondike excitement, both the United States and Britain were well aware of the need to establish a boundary in the Alaska Panhandle. In 1893, the two countries created a boundary commission to further this effort. The United States interpreted the 1825 treaty to claim territory extending 16 to 19 km (10 to 12 mi.) inland of the Chilkoot and White Pass summits. Canada, however, felt that the treaty gave them sovereignty over Skagway, Dyea, the entire length of both trails, and most of the territory between Skagway and Juneau. Because the sides disagreed on so many issues, nothing came of the commission's effort.

One contentious aspect of the boundary question was the collection of customs duties. Those familiar with conditions in the Yukon basin were well aware that miners and prospectors needed almost a ton of food, clothing, and mining equipment to sustain them for a year. These supplies cost at least $500 per person. Considering the tens of thousands of stampeders who poured into the Yukon during the rush, the value of those outfits has been estimated at between $40 and $100 million. This amount is especially significant when compared to the 1900 Klondike peak gold production of about $25 million.[9]

The country that collected customs duties stood to receive a huge financial windfall. Furthermore, customs duties were collected only on "foreign" goods, that is, goods not purchased in the country in question. This meant that the country collecting customs duties could influence miners to buy the vast mountain of needed supplies in their country's stores. There was no income tax in the 1890s; the bulk of government revenues in both Canada and the United States came from customs duties, excise taxes and licence fees. Therefore, the Klondike stampede was potentially a huge money-maker for governments as well as businesses.

The Alaskan coastal towns soon felt the effect of the Mounted Police presence at Forty Mile. In 1896, U.S. Treasury officials noted miners heading into the Yukon no longer purchased supplies at Juneau, their usual jumping-off point. The high duties paid on American goods, and improved supplies in the Yukon, encouraged miners to purchase their outfits from Canadian suppliers.[10]

The Mountie order for adequate supplies required to survive a Yukon winter.

Inspector Charles Constantine and his command erected the impressive Fort Constantine at Forty Mile in 1895.

N. W. M. P.

DAWSON, Nov. 18, 1898.

THE Commissioner of the Yukon Territory orders that no person will be permitted to enter the Territory without satisfying the N. W. M. Police Officers at Tagish and White Horse Rapids that they have with them two months' assorted provisions and at least $500 in cash, or six months' assorted provisions and not less than $200 in cash, over and above the money required to pay expenses from the border to Dawson.

N. B.—This order will not apply to residents of the Yukon Territory returning, if they are identified and prove their competence to pay their way into the country.

By order,

(Signed), **S. B. STEELE,** Supt.,
Commanding N.W.M. Police, Yukon Territory.

With more than a score of Mounted Police already in the region, the Canadian government had a distinct advantage. However, the overwhelming number of Americans in the rush and the tenuous supply lines through American territory made the Mounties very aware of the weakness of their position.

A calendar of action

July, 1897

☞ Dyea, Alaska is made an American customs sub-port of entry. This allows Canadian goods to be shipped in bond through U.S. territory to the Yukon without payment of U.S. customs duties. Suppliers in Juneau, Seattle, and other American west coast cities are outraged that their favoured trading position has been lost to the Canadian ports of Victoria and Vancouver.

August, 1897

☞ The growing rush of people and supplies into Skagway and Dyea overwhelms the few U.S. customs officials there. American officials express concern about a Canadian syndicate under Captain Moore that controls and charges a toll on the White Pass Trail in U.S. territory.

☞ Canadian customs officers in Victoria are also worried. Concerned about possible violence in the passes, one official telegraphs the NWMP headquarters: *Rush unprecedented. Steamers continue crowded rough American element going forward menacing regarding payment of duties at Tagish. Advise Mounted Police be pushed forward.*[11]

September, 1897

☞ A combined NWMP and Canadian customs post is established at Tagish. The Tagish Narrows, a comfortable location some 100 km (60 mi.) from Dyea, funnels all the gold rush traffic from the Chilkoot, White Pass and Taku River trails right past the post. Tagish becomes the main base for the Mounted Police and customs activities in the southern Yukon during the rush.[12]

Canadian customs collector John Godson, his wife, two daughters and their nurse pictured in front of their cabin, near the Kittitas Restaurant, at Log Cabin, in July, 1898.

October, 1897

☞ After many months of increasingly desperate requests from officers on the scene, the NWMP secretly ship two Maxim machine guns to the police in the Yukon.

☞ A Mounted Police post is established at Bennett.[13]

November, 1897

☞ Canadian customs collector John Godson travels from Tagish to the Bennett area and collects duties from stampeders camped there. Three American cattle merchants question the Canadian government's right to collect customs duty on disputed territory and two of them refuse to pay. Godson orders the cattle seized to the amount of the duty owing.[14]

December, 1897

☞ Juneau newspapers react violently to Godson's actions and fuel a popular demand for a U.S. government response. George Brackett in Skagway also requests the presence of American troops to maintain order at the trail heads, exercise U.S. sovereignty over Skagway and forestall any future Canadian moves. By the middle of the month, U.S. customs officials institute a convoy system on Canadian goods travelling in bond through U.S. territory. The related costs equal the duty charged on American goods at the Canadian boundary.

☞ NWMP Inspector Zachary T. Wood at Tagish Post requests advice from the Canadian government regarding the seizure of cattle at Bennett for customs duty.

☞ The British Columbia government establishes its claim to Bennett by appointing a government agent to administer the area.

☞ The two crated Maxim machine guns shipped in October arrive at the coast and are moved on to Bennett. The crates are placed in a snowbank behind the Bennett police post.[15]

The NWMP post at Tagish was established in the fall of 1897. It became the southern police headquarters during the gold rush.

U.S. Commissioner John U. Smith.

The Mounted Police post and customs tent at the Chilkoot summit, late spring, 1898.

January, 1898

☛ American newspapers report that the NWMP are seizing cattle at Bennett to pay customs duty. Inspector Wood notes: "The real object of the merchants of Juneau is to force the trade to the U.S. cities, or to compel Canada to allow miners to take their outfit in free if bought in the United States." He feels that control of trade, not boundaries, is the issue in the passes.

☛ The Alaskan government extends a U.S. claim over Lindeman and part of Bennett. At Skagway, U.S. Commissioner John U. Smith attempts to formalize this claim by registering an official Lindeman town plan with the U.S. government. Stampeders with American goods at Bennett hold a public meeting and decide not to pay duties except under protest.

☛ The Canadian government awards the contract to build an all-Canadian railroad through British Columbia and southern Yukon.

☛ The NWMP, outnumbered and feeling vulnerable on the trails, comes to an arrangement with the U.S. Commissioner to forestall violence. They agree to establish a temporary boundary at the north end of Lindeman Lake. This accommodation is reported to Ottawa.

☞ The Canadian Minister of the Interior, Clifford Sifton, responds immediately by telegraph: *Boundary is at the Summit or further seaward. Instruct your officers that provisionally the boundary is at the summit + to act accordingly.* A symbolic force of two or three men at each summit is suggested. Mounted Police reinforcements from the south are to be rushed forward as quickly as possible.[16]

February, 1898

☞ Well-armed detachments of the NWMP move to the summits of both the White Pass and Chilkoot and establish camps. By the end of the month, they are collecting customs duties and enforcing Canadian law.

☞ American stampeders and local officials are outraged at the Canadian move seaward and fear the Mounties may come down and take over both Skagway and Dyea. Several groups organize to drive the police back to Bennett. However, foul weather and cooler heads on both trails keep everyone in their tents.

☞ Alaska Governor John G. Brady formally requests army troops for the Taiya Inlet to maintain order and raise the U.S. flag. The possibility of a violent confrontation alarms local officials on both sides of the passes.[17]

March, 1898

☞ Discussions between newly arrived U.S. Army and NWMP officers result in recognition of the summits as a temporary boundary.

☞ In a show of goodwill, U.S. customs officials provide the Chilkoot Railroad and Transport Company—the largest of the Chilkoot tramway systems—with bonds allowing for the transfer of Canadian goods through U.S. territory without inspection or charges.[18]

BLOCKHOUSE OF THE CANADIAN POLICE AT LAKE BENNETT.

The *Dyea Trail* responded to John Godson's actions at Bennett on January 12, 1898:

Reports have time and again reached Dyea that the Canadian customs officials were collecting duties on American territory. The reports state that this has been done at Lakes Linderman and Bennett. This should not be permitted. These rumors may have no substantial foundation, but they are increasing in number. The Canadian officials have no right to collect duties this side of Tagish, and Americans should resist all attempts to make them pay. Captain Strickland, of the Canadian service, denies that he has been responsible for any such attempts, but he may not know. Some of the Canadian mounted police may be making a private snap of the affair. Pay no duties this side of Tagish. They cannot be collected on American territory by any Canadian mounted police. Americans, insist upon this. Do nothing that will lend a shadow of color to the Canadian claim that they have rights on territory we have always assumed to be ours.

This blockhouse is seven miles this side of Bennett Lake and is the headquarters of the Canadian customs and police forces in that district. Since the establishment of Canadian stations at the summits of the Chilkoot and White passes the force of men at the blockhouse has been greatly reduced.
· Seattle Post-Intelligencer,
March 11, 1898

GUNS ON THE PASSES: "Our only strength is moral strength"

ON FEBRUARY 13, 1898, acting on orders from Ottawa, a contingent of NWMP moved forward to secure the summit of the Chilkoot Pass. They were armed with Lee Metford carbines and a Maxim machine gun. The men managed to set up a tent camp and a small plank hut before a blizzard swirled into the pass. On February 26, they raised the Union Jack and began collecting custom duties from travellers entering Canadian territory.[19]

The move was not popular with the police officers on the trail. Although they were an organized force of armed men, their numbers were pathetically small compared to the potential number of attackers. Nevertheless, it was their duty to exercise Canadian sovereignty in the Yukon and extend the rule of law. They were expected to introduce order to the perceived chaos of wilderness.

Inspector Charles Constantine was preoccupied with the need to balance these heavy responsibilities with the limited possibilities allowed by his small force. As early as spring, 1896, Constantine requested a Maxim machine gun to reinforce his command. Machine guns were a recent development. Their ability to make up for large discrepancies in numbers made them an obvious weapon in dealing with mobs. Constantine's request highlights the extremely dangerous position he felt the police were in.

Constantine had two fears: that the miners would challenge his authority, and that his men would abandon their duty. NWMP officers responded by maintaining absolute power over their men and presenting a brave front to the miners.

Constantine worried about the reaction of miners, who were mostly American. Most of them, however, were reassured by the guarantee of property rights. Although sovereignty was an issue at the White Pass and Chilkoot summits, the immediate threat was from the troublesome armed rabble controlling Skagway. Loud threats rumbled up to the summits but no body of armed men followed them.

The NWMP played a delicate balancing game in the Yukon during the gold rush. Commissioner James Walsh emphasized the situation in a report to Ottawa:

> The Officials in this district should be made to remember that they are now on a foreign frontier and.... They now have a foreign population in front of them and foreign population in rear of them and wisdom and caution should be exercised in every decision and move they make. They should never forget the weak and helpless position they are in here.

It was a lesson taken to heart. The Mounties in the Yukon recognized both their own limits and those of the stampeders. Their reputation for fairness was built on an ability to effect a compromise between the demands of southern Canadian law and their ability to enforce it.

There are not sufficient Police here. Should anything of a serious nature turn up in which there was a strong public feeling, and the law had to be carried out in the face of it, I should be powerless. No maxim gun was sent us.

• Inspector Charles Constantine at Forty Mile to Commissioner L.W. Herchmer, September 2, 1896

The famous machine guns at Whitehorse in 1900. The Nordenfeldt Maxim gun on the left is displayed at the MacBride Museum in Whitehorse.

April, 1898

☞ A U.S. Army exploration party is sent out to explore an all-American route, via the Copper River, to the goldfields at Fortymile.

☞ The railway contract for the all-Canadian route is cancelled by the Canadian parliament and all construction work on the route stops.

May, 1898

☞ The U.S. customs convoy system is shut down. American customs officials are posted to the summits to check bonded goods. As tensions cool and the traffic over the trails diminishes, the NWMP recommends the withdrawal of the summit detachments to Log Cabin and

One NWMP officer described the summits:

As points for the collection of duty [they] are practically useless, as no one with a spark of humanity would keep people waiting in those dreadful places, with the danger of perishing from cold, while their goods, exposed to the inclement weather + blowing snow, are spoiled before their eyes.[20]

The NWMP bunk tent at the summit of the White Pass, 1898.

A military parade on Main Street, Dyea, summer, 1898.

THE NWMP AT LOG CABIN: "a decent, civilized set of barracks"

AFTER A DIFFICULT spring guarding the summits of the passes under the most inhospitable conditions, the Mounties were withdrawn to more congenial surroundings at Log Cabin and Lindeman. Log Cabin had several advantages over the White Pass summit. It was well supplied with firewood, sheltered by the forest and was located at a trail junction.

Construction of the detachment buildings began in mid-July, 1898. The post consisted of four log buildings in a square. An office, initially used for customs collection and later as an officers' quarters, opened onto the trail. A guard room and storehouse made up one side of the square; an eight-horse stable formed the north side. The base of the square was closed by a large barracks building with a mess, kitchen, sergeant's quarters and men's accommodation. It was completed and occupied on October 9 and was described as "a very comfortable and neat looking detachment."[21]

The police commander was Inspector F.L. Cartwright, assisted by a sergeant and four constables. They worked almost around the clock fulfilling their many duties. In addition to constructing their post, the detachment continued to staff the White Pass summit. Only in November, 1898 was the summit post finally abandoned; even then they maintained daily patrols to check the boundary and ensure that the Union Jack was still flying. While undertaking these patrols the Mounties also carried the mail and visited the construction camps of the White Pass and Yukon Railway. One of their main tasks was the prevention of cruelty to animals by the hurrying stampeders. All of this was in addition to the continuing assistance given to customs and the regular routine of the detachment.[22]

The police post at Log Cabin was described as "near a model as was possible under the circumstances of a decent, civilized set of barracks," and the rigorous enforcement of regulations reflect the important role of the NWMP in creating order and maintaining Canadian sovereignty on the frontier.[23]

This stove lies near the foundation remains of the NWMP post barracks at Log Cabin, spring, 1990.

NWMP post at Log Cabin, spring, 1898.

Lindeman with daily patrols to the boundary. The Maxim machine guns are withdrawn from the summits and sent downriver to Dawson.

☞ At Skagway and Dyea the number of American soldiers is reduced.

☞ The U.S. and British governments formally agree to submit the boundary dispute to a commission of arbitration.[24]

The boundary issue in the Chilkoot and White Pass areas was effectively solved by the late spring of 1898. The involvement of the national governments ended the danger of conflict and in October, 1899, the summits were made the provisional boundary between the two countries.

Negotiations on the Panhandle boundary continued for another four years. At one point the American government offered Pyramid Harbor to the Canadians as an ocean port for the Yukon. However, this was leaked to the newspapers and the outraged American public forced a retraction. Finally, in 1903, a six-member tribunal with three Americans, two Canadians and the British chief justice, Lord Richard E.W. Alverstone, was set up to settle the boundary. Lord Alverstone eventually broke the deadlock by siding with the Americans. The two Canadians refused to sign the boundary award.

The boundary was surveyed and marked in 1905 and 1906. Canada, a minor partner in the negotiations, felt betrayed and began working to gain more control over its foreign policy.[25]

North-West Mounted Police by the Union Jack and the Stars and Stripes on the White Pass summit, April 9, 1899.

Canadians were generally unhappy with the results of the boundary decision in 1903.

PUNCH, OR THE LONDON CHARIVARI.—October 28, 1903.

THE ALASKA CRACKER.

Uncle Sam. "WHAT'S THE MATTER WITH THIS?"
Miss Canada. "ROTTEN, I SAY."

Law enforcement in Alaska

Law enforcement on the U.S. side of the passes was rudimentary at first.[26] When the gold rush began, the closest U.S. law officers to the Chilkoot were in Juneau, almost 160 km (100 mi.) to the south. By early August, 1897, the first in a series of marshals was assigned to the area. Some served in Dyea; others in Skagway. As Governor John G. Brady noted, however, a marshal was so poorly paid that "his earnings will hardly pay for the salt that goes in his mush." Marshals tended to stay for only a short time; by the end of 1898, nine deputies had come and gone.[27]

To judge by some accounts, criminal activity in gold rush Skagway was the norm rather than the exception, and crime was seldom punished. Alexander Macdonald, an Englishman who passed through in the fall of 1897, noted:

> I have stumbled upon a few tough corners of the globe during my wanderings beyond the outposts of civilization, but I think the most outrageously lawless quarter I ever struck was Skagway.... It seemed to me as if the scum of the earth had hastened here to fleece and rob, or...to murder. There was no law whatsoever; might was right, the dead shot only was immune to danger.[28]

On the trails, which were beyond the reach of the marshals, the worst crime was theft. On February 15, 1898, three men were tried in a Sheep Camp miners' meeting for stealing cached goods left by a group of Californians. One of the accused, a man named Dean, was quickly absolved of all wrongdoing. But both William Wellington and Edward Hansen were found guilty. Wellington, fearing he was to be sentenced to death, bolted from the tent

U.S. Army soldiers patrol the stampeders' camp at Dyea.

saloon and broke free. As his pursuers caught up with him, he whipped out a pistol and blew his brains out. Soon afterward the meeting reconvened. Those who had passed judgment recognized that one man had already paid the ultimate price; the other was sentenced to 50 lashes. Billy Onions, an ex-muleskinner, laid on 15 well-directed blows before the crowd intervened. Hansen was released, then marched down the trail with a placard reading "THIEF" for all to see. He was never seen again.[29]

Local law enforcement could barely deal with local crime, let alone the escalating boundary tensions. Plagued by the criminal chaos of the towns and the perceived threat of the Mounties moving down to the coast, influential Skagway citizens began to lobby for American troops.

In response, in February, 1898, the U.S. government sent two companies of soldiers, headed by Colonel Thomas M. Anderson, to a Skagway base camp. Two more companies, under the command of Captain Richard T. Yeatman, arrived in Dyea a month later.[30]

Although the presence of American troops and Canadian Mounties caused tension along the vaguely-defined border, neither side provoked the other. The Mounties, situated at the top of the passes, were preoccupied with the overwhelming task of processing the flood of northbound stampeders. In contrast, the U.S. Army troops had little to do. Their efforts were limited to stand-by duty during an altercation at the Skagway dock, deflecting a threat to the security of the Brackett Wagon Road (a toll road from Skagway up the White Pass valley), and rescue work after the Palm Sunday avalanche.

The two companies stationed in Dyea carried on much the same role as Colonel Anderson's troops in Skagway. Most of the time the soldiers' lives were filled with the pedestrian concerns of camp life. In October, 1898, the soldiers' routine at Dyea was interrupted when the camp moved from central Dyea to a site near the Dyea-Klondike Transportation Company dock, 5 km (3 mi.) south of town. The area proved isolated and inhospitable, however, and they prepared to evacuate the camp in favour of a site in Skagway. The removal of the camp, in July, 1899, was well underway when a forest fire bore down on the camp and forced all personnel to flee across the inlet to Skagway. Within hours, the site of the camp was incinerated.[31]

In May, 1898, two of the four companies left the area. At the time, the commander reported cordial relations with Canadian officials and no friction with local civil authorities.[32]

Although seldom called upon, the other two companies remained on the upper Lynn Canal. The camp in Skagway, staffed either by infantry or artillery companies, continued until the summer of 1904, when it was moved south to Port Chilkoot, near Haines. That camp, at times Alaska's only military presence, remained active until 1940.[33]

On August 4, 1898, William Zimmer wrote about the challenges of being a U.S. customs agent on the Chilkoot:[34]

Dear Sir:

You will see that I am still on the summit as I cannot go to Lindeman as I have no quarters to go to or a cent in my pocket. I have been here now over two months and nothing has been done for my comfort. I of course have a corner of a tent to sleep in through the courtesy of a Mr. Steel [NWMP Inspector Samuel Steele] but no place to write on only my knee. My clothes are in Skaguay because there is no room here for anything. Here on the summit we have had about seven days clear weather since the 17th of May…. I have no books or supplies with me outside of a few certificates of exportation. Would have no place to keep them if I had, and have to keep them between my blankets.

Children at a military parade in Dyea.

Justice issues between newcomers and First Nations

Although overshadowed in the gold rush corridor by thousands of newcomers, the First Nations did not disappear. Difficulties arising from cross-cultural misunderstandings grew in number and significance through the 1880s and 1890s. One observer noted: "The great trouble about the [Tlingit] Indians is their utter lack of any sense of morality *as we understand it.*"[35]

In crimes among Native Americans on the Alaskan coast there was at first only minimal interference by American officials. The long-established arbitration system governing crimes between clans continued to be the accepted form of conflict resolution well into the 1890s.[36] Clans accepted responsibility for the crimes of their members and, to settle differences, provided compensation either in blankets or the lives of individuals of equivalent status. European law, focused upon the responsibility of individuals for their actions, had a completely different way of adjudicating guilt and establishing punishments. Murder across the cultural line in the north was unusual, but when it did occur the character and operation of justice, by both sides, was fraught with misunderstandings and confusion.

One case in the southern Yukon, the shooting of two stampeders near Marsh Lake at the height of the gold rush, illustrates this difference.[37] The story began some years earlier. Some miners left behind a small tin of arsenic, used for refining gold, at an old camp. Kitty Smith, whose uncle became involved, retells the first part of the story:

> Well, whitemen are just bad friends for Indians. They don't want Indians to come close, I guess. They try to do things [to keep them away], I guess. I don't know.... I don't know what they were doing....
>
> Somebody found that can, some white-man place. A little baking-powder can. An old lady found it—an old lady just like me. People have got flour. A young fellow was staying with

Sketch by Leon Boillot of the miner Christian Fox and the four Nantuck brothers imprisoned at the Tagish police post in the summer of 1898.

his grandfather. They've got flour and, well, they ask for baking powder. "This looks like the one that cooks bread." Well, nobody can read you know.

They cooked the bread. It raised the bread, too! Then they gave it to the dog, first time. But the dog died too slow; that was the trouble. Then the boy died, and then his grandpa died.

Used to be they didn't kill people for nothing, long ago time. When they get over it, then they're friends together. This way, however many people died, they're going to·pay them. Then they're good friends again, see? Sometimes two chiefs, three chiefs—they kill them to make it even. Then they make a big party. They make a big song....

The two dead were from the Crow clan. In May, 1898, four young Crow men sought a blood price for the death of their relatives from two members of the "white" clan. However, the language and cultural barriers left the two white men, "Billy" Meehan and Christian Fox, unaware of their intentions. Fox described their meeting at the later trial:

We were building our boat and Frank and Jim [Nantuck] came.... They said they were hungry...we gave them their supper, and they camped with us that night.... They stopped around outside the camp until about noon and shot a duck...presently they left camp. The following day...they both came back and Dawson Nantuck with them. We had broken through the ice and our stuff was all wet and we had it spread out on the beach all around and if they ever took anything I don't know it. They seemed to be perfectly honest. The boys were in camp, they came there every day and were very friendly.[38]

On the morning of May 10, Fox and Meehan packed up their camp and pushed off down the river. Sam Steele, now NWMP Superintendent of the Upper Yukon District, reported the crime:

On their way [down the river] they were shot at by several Indians, the first volley killing Meehan and wounding Fox, one bullet passing through him. He managed however to paddle the boat to the other side of the river and arriving at Mr. MacIntosh's camp gave the alarm.

William MacIntosh, a trader operating at Lake Laberge during the rush, later recalled the events of that day:

[Upon learning of the shooting] I called a miners' meeting.... Gathered all the Indians who were camped near the Post...and put guards over them. [He also seized their weapons and ammunition.] I chose 16 men, all fully armed. These men proceeded up the river and the first day found the boat but no trace of Meehan's body.... The 3rd day we captured Jim Nantuck, the leader of the Indian gang...and ascertained that the other 3 Indians had gone into the hills. My desire was to capture them without bloodshed, so...I saw the 2 Chiefs of the Lake Laberge Indians, and by negotiations with them I induced them to secure the 3 Indians...and deliver them to my foreman at Marsh Lake.[39]

It appears two First Nations men were instrumental in having the affair end peaceably. Jim Boss, one of the chiefs of the Lake Laberge people, helped persuade the boys to give themselves up when they came and saw him in the evening. Sam Faller, an Indian scout employed by the Mounties, accepted a reward for bringing in the three boys.

After their surrender, the four brothers were brought to the Tagish Post of the NWMP to await trial. In late July, the boys were then sent downriver to the court at Dawson City. Their trials were brisk, each one lasting only a part of a day. Only Frank Nantuck offered any reason in defence:

White-men had killed two of their friends; that they found one of the bodies and the other they never did find. [This happened] about a year and the other was about 2 years.[40]

Rev. R.M. Dickey of the Presbyterian Church visited the Nantuck brothers at Tagish and wrote on June 10, 1898:[41]

For the four poor boys held as prisoners on a charge of murder my heart is sad. The youngest is 14 and the eldest 18 or 20. They have never been taught either by Church or by Government, and have no conception whatever of the gravity of the crime they have committed.... Poor lads.... They have committed a terrible crime and do not deny it. But surely the nation and the Church, who failed to teach these poor children of nature, share with them the guilt of the crime, which, in their dense ignorance, they have committed.

The evidence seemed clear and the separate juries took only a few minutes to find all the boys guilty of murder. Bishop William Bompas, the Anglican prelate for the Yukon, immediately appealed for leniency and some respect for, or at least acknowledgement of, the aboriginal judicial system:

> *I have been considering that the Indian laws of retaliation are very strict, and though they would doubtless expect that the life of one Indian be exacted for that of a white man, yet I fear that if four Indians are killed, their tribe may think that the lives of 3 more white men must be sacrificed to balance the account.*

This appeal was rejected. The three older boys were sentenced to hang. Frank, the youngest, had his sentence commuted to life imprisonment. Frank and Joe Nantuck died in the Dawson jail of scurvy and consumption in February, 1899. Jim and Dawson Nantuck were hanged in the yard of the jail on August 3 the same year. Kitty Smith concludes the story:

> *When her son was hanged, my grandma said: "I don't know if I can forget it, that Whitehorse River way. I wish they'd throw me in the water when I die so I could follow down. My son got lost that way."…Four people died for that man. Well, they don't know, that time…. They don't know policeman business.*

Clapped in chains and tied to an anvil the four Nantuck boys were displayed to the hordes of travellers on their way to Dawson while imprisoned at the Tagish police post during June and July of 1898.

The 20th Century:

Tourists & First Nations

An effusive 1913 White Pass and Yukon brochure intoned:

To go to Skagway and not see the interior is like going to the threshold of a fairyland and foregoing all the interest and enchantment to be enjoyed within the magic region.[1]

(preceding page) The tourist train arrives back in Skagway, about 1910.

White Pass and Yukon Railway used exquisite artistry and romantic imagery to promote its train and boat excursions. Brochures such as these were distributed as early as 1907 and continued until the late 1930s.

Skagway underwent a radical change during its first three years of life. In August, 1897, the site was transformed from a one-family homestead to an important transportation and commercial centre. Tens of thousands of people streamed through the town on their way to the Klondike goldfields. In the spring of 1898, Skagway's population was estimated at 8,000, with 1,000 more stampeders arriving each week.[2] The construction of the WP&YR —the Yukon's primary connection to "Outside"—guaranteed the town's commercial importance. From 1898 to 1900, railroad construction and the discovery of new goldfields in the Canadian interior continued to give Skagway a boom town atmosphere.

After 1900, Skagway's frontier character began to change. Clubs, churches and schools reflected the arrival of a stable, newcomers' society. The operation of the railway encouraged the development of a relatively steady work force. With the passing of the gold rush, a large number of the local supply stores, saloons, hotels and restaurants closed down. The remaining businesses depended, directly or indirectly, on railway revenues.[3]

Skagway's appearance also changed. The cheap and rough frontier architecture of the gold rush was slowly replaced with more substantial buildings, larger and more elegant than their predecessors. Businesses made a concerted effort to be respectable; false fronts, double recessed doors and elaborate woodwork became commonplace on commercial buildings. The town's residences improved as well, and intermittent civic campaigns encouraged people to tear down the many shacks left by the stampeders.[4]

With its combination of history and natural beauty and a wealth of frontier architecture, Skagway quickly became an important stopping point for tourists. The southeastern Alaska Inside Passage route had been popular with excursion ships since the mid-1880s. When the gold rush exploded, these vessels merely added an extra day to their itinerary to visit the new town.[5] Skagway's first tourist steamer arrived in July, 1898. Visitors joined local residents to celebrate the inaugural train on a newly-completed section of the railway. The following year, the chamber of commerce was urging local residents to prepare for the upcoming tourist season, and the first Skagway Clean-up Day was scheduled to beautify the streets and yards. (Clean-up Day has been held each spring ever since.)[6]

THE SAGA OF MA PULLEN

ALMOST EVERY SKAGWAY tourist for half a century knew about Harriet "Ma" Pullen. She was the proprietor of the Pullen House, the best-known hotel in Alaska. The drama of her life, presented in a stirring, theatrical fashion either in the hotel parlour or across the garden pond, was known around the world.

Pullen, a mother of four, arrived in Skagway in September, 1897. She worked in a tent restaurant where, on her first day on the job, she hammered tin cans into pie plates and baked dried-apple pies. Before long, she was able to bring her children north to be with her. With their help, she went into the horse-packing business and prospered. She purchased Captain William Moore's large home, converting it into the Pullen House, a hotel she ran for almost 50 years.

Pullen claimed she knew Soapy Smith—she said he gave candy to her children—and she witnessed the epic Reid-Smith gun battle. (One wag noted that if all those who claimed to have seen the shooting were laid end to end "the line would extend to the Equator and back again.") She described herself as a widow. However, those who knew her private side were aware she was no widow. Pullen had separated from her husband in early 1897. He later moved to Skagway, and it was not until he left town again, in 1906, that Pullen proclaimed her "widowhood" to the summertime tourists. Nevertheless, her life—stripped of its embroidery—was still dramatic and notable. Through courage and sheer hard work, Pullen was able to ascend, quickly and honestly, from poverty to a position of security, fame, and community respect. She died in Skagway in August, 1947.

Pullen played a major role in post-gold rush Dyea as well. In 1915, she homesteaded most of the historic townsite. She planted a market garden and kept a small herd of dairy cows so that her guests could enjoy fresh milk and cream. She vowed never to tear down any gold rush structure, and often took guests on tours. The family retained control of the area until the late 1970s when the land was sold to the National Park Service.[7]

Ma Pullen with her horse-drawn carriage in front of the Pullen House.

The *Princess Alice*, a regular visitor to the Skagway harbour.

Until about 1910, Skagway tourism remained at a low level. Just before World War I, however, the number of tourists and ships steadily increased, and Skagway developed a number of attractions to lure the summer trade. The WP&YR began producing elaborate brochures inviting tourists to visit the Canadian interior. Special half-day tourist trains ran to the summit of the White Pass; soon afterward, the line instituted day-long trips to Bennett.[8] Over the next several years, the WP&YR added excursions to romantic Ben-My-Chree on Tagish Lake and longer trips on lake steamers to Atlin. Truly adventurous travellers took trips on Yukon River sternwheelers like the *S.S. Klondike* (now preserved in Whitehorse as a National Historic Site), all the way to Dawson City.

Tourism and the railway were Skagway's most important industries. Local tour guide Martin Itjen told visitors at the railyards: "All the people in this town who don't work the tourists, work here."[9]

The Great Depression of the early 1930s proved difficult for everyone. Both railroad freight volume and tourism dropped off, and the railway reduced its Skagway-Whitehorse service to two trains per week. Later that decade, tourism to Skagway rebounded. Canadian Pacific and Canadian National ships made additional sailings. Although this meant more passenger traffic, freight tonnage remained low.[10]

The U.S. government's decision to build the Alaska Highway from Dawson Creek, British Columbia to Fairbanks, Alaska during World War II brought new life to Skagway. The construction of the highway turned the town into a major supply point, as the railway was the main access route for the mid-section of the road. About 5,000 troops were sent to Skagway, remaining there until early 1946.[11]

CHAPLIN'S CHILKOOT—HOLLYWOOD NORTH?

CHARLIE CHAPLIN'S *THE Gold Rush* is one of the most famous movies of all time, loved by audiences and praised by critics. Released in 1925, the film is endearing largely because of a catchy plot line and excellent character development. The scenery is secondary, and most of it is an obvious Hollywood creation. But the opening scene shows a long line of hikers surmounting a steep mountain summit, and the scene is strongly reminiscent of the world-famous photographs of the Scales and the Chilkoot Pass taken during the spring of 1898.

At one time, Hollywood considered shooting this scene on the Chilkoot. Skagway resident George Rapuzzi, in his mid-20s at the time, had already climbed the trail several times when, in the summer of 1924, he was approached by a Metro-Goldwyn-Mayer film crew scouting locations. (At the time, the idea of shooting a movie in Alaska was remarkable. Almost all U.S. films were shot in southern California, and most Alaskan feature films up to that time had been travelogues and documentaries.) Rapuzzi led the Hollywood scouts to Sheep Camp and beyond. They were amazed to find many buildings in Sheep Camp still standing, and they considered refurbishing several of them to recreate a gold rush camp scene. In the end, however, the isolation of Alaska and the relatively inaccessible shooting locale demanded an alternative site. Chaplin's opening scene was shot instead in the Sierra Nevada between Donner Pass and Truckee, California.[12]

The prosperity following World War II assured years of profitability for the WP&YR. By the late 1940s, more tourists than ever were travelling to Alaska and the Yukon. Skagway continued to be served by ships from both the Canadian National and Canadian Pacific companies, and two Alaska Cruise Lines ships which started service in 1957.[13]

Early hiking on the Chilkoot

The WP&YR was completed to Bennett in July, 1899. By the time it reached Whitehorse a year later, it carried nearly all the traffic headed for the Canadian interior. For the first time in hundreds of years, the Taiya River valley was no longer a commercial transport corridor. For the next 60 years, the Chilkoot Trail existed in name only, unused and unmaintained. Access to the Dyea trailhead remained difficult. No road connected Skagway with Dyea until 1948, and small boats found it treacherous to navigate between the two places.

Even as the last stragglers of the stampede moved on and the brush grew back over the ragged ruins of the trail communities, a few tourists and hikers began to explore the trail, reliving the excitement of the rush.[14] Harriet Pullen would entertain visitors by taking them for strolls through the ruins of Dyea, and many locals visited the Taiya valley for picnics, berry picking and hunting.

In 1906, International Boundary Commission surveyors retraced the Chilkoot Trail as they laid out the boundary and set up monuments. O.M. Leland, chief of the American party, reported that:

> ...the trail is overgrown and rough, and the old bridges of 1898 were dilapidated so...many traces of the Klondike "rush" of 1898 remain in the Taiya valley and near the Chilkoot Pass.... Most of the buildings at Sheep Camp are still standing and two at the Scales.... These buildings might be very useful to a party...as they were to us, and many of the old implements are useful when the difficulty of packing things up from Dyea is considered.[15]

Recreational hiking of the trail was sporadic. This was due not only to the condition of the trail but also the hazards of simply reaching the trailhead. In late July, 1928, Florence

BILL MATTHEWS, "MAYOR OF DYEA"

DYEA BECAME A lonely, empty ghost town after the gold rush. One of those who knew Dyea best was William C. Matthews, a Tlingit fondly remembered as the "mayor of Dyea." He arrived in the gold rush port while still a boy; his family may have been in the packing business. His father, William E. Matthews, filed on a 160-acre homestead at Dyea. He cultivated 15 acres of cabbage and other vegetables and grazed some stock.

The elder Matthews died in the mid-1920s; a few years later his wife, Floris, and their son, Bill, moved to Skagway. Bill carved out a successful career as a member of the White Pass longshore crew. But when he could, he returned to Dyea. His many years of residence there gave him an intimate familiarity with the old townsite. A more compelling reason for his repeated visits was the family members interred in the Dyea cemetery. Matthews became the self-appointed cemetery caretaker, maintaining the markers and keeping cattle out. His residence in Skagway, and his visits to Dyea, continued until the mid-1970s. Advanced age and ill health, however, forced a move to the Sitka Pioneers' Home, where he died on March 2, 1977.[16]

Clothier and her brother Lou went to Dyea to hike the trail. Unable to find the homesteader who would ferry them across the Taiya River, they borrowed his boat and almost drowned crossing the swirling waters. Soaking wet, their first night on the trail was uncomfortable. However, they made use of one of the cabins still standing:

> It's an old shack left over from '97 and '98 but it has a roof and glassed or canvassed windows. Also best of all it has the remains of a stove, cut wood, and a filthy looking bed.... We got a fire going and a candle lighted. Lou chopped more wood and I got supper—beans, franks, bouillon, oranges and hard-tack. I slept on the bed and Lou on the floor in front of the stove. It was good.

After three full days of struggling through the bush, the pair made their way up the rocks of Long Hill and climbed the Golden Stairs wrapped in thick fog:

> A high cairn—the summit—we'd triumphed over Chilcoot and reached the summit.... [I felt] a surge of exultation. Tiredness seemed somehow to drop off. We could not look back and see what we had conquered, angry nature had drawn over it her grey impenetrable curtain but ahead the way beckoned and the world looked brighter.... In a few minutes we saw Crater Lake dipped into by the fingers of many glaciers. All around lay relics—cans, old sledges, pick and shovel handles and ancient wheels.... Chilcoot remained shrouded in mist.[17]

By the 1930s, increasing numbers of people were using the trail and the first organized trips took place. Beginning in 1933, Father G. Edgar Gallant, superintendent of Skagway's St. Pius X Mission, took small groups of students over the Chilcoot.[18] Also starting annual tours in 1933 was Bayne Beauchamp, a schoolteacher from Honolulu, Hawaii. "Beauchamp's Boys," as they were labelled by the northern press, usually hiked the trail and then built boats to float down the Yukon River as far as Circle City, Alaska. In 1936, Robert Storm, a 20-year-old college student from Omaha, Nebraska, joined Beauchamp's group.[19]

Storm's experiences on the trail have many similarities with today's hikers. The group had a late start from Skagway:

> The heavy pack and the fact that I didn't get to bed until 3:00 the night before—we met a couple of swell little girls on the boat—worked together to make me a wee bit tired.

In 1936, Robert Storm joined Bayne Beauchamp's tour and helped build this scow at Bennett for a float down the Yukon River to Dawson and beyond.

Not only was Storm's pack heavy—35 kg (77 lbs.)—it was primitive compared to today's sophisticated equipment:

> We used a Civil War pack which is made in the following manner. You lay out your pair of Hudson's Bay blankets flat on the ground. Then you pack your coat and all personal effects in one end and your share of the food in the other. Then you turn back the ends a little and roll the pack up. Then you tie the ends up with rope. When you have finished, you have a nice, heavy, clumsy pack to throw over your shoulder or around your neck.

The group also chanced to meet Father Gallant on the boat to Alaska. He provided them with information on the harsh condition of the trail. Their hike was plagued with rain and clouds, and they were often almost overwhelmed by the challenges of bushwhacking through the rainforest.

Once over the pass, the group missed the historic ford crossing at Deep Lake leading to Lindeman. On the wrong side of the canyon, they struggled through bogs and mosquitoes until they hit the railway tracks. Finally, at lunchtime on the fourth day, they made it to the Bennett railway station:

> ...with a big dining room. We ate dinner first thing. And we had our dollar's worth! "Roast Beef" never tasted quite so good. We finished off with a third of a pie apiece and a big dish of cherries and plate after plate of cookies! On the hike we had nothing but cornmeal—no sugar— a little bacon—an apple a day and a few hard tack. Oh yes, we had 3 cans of corned beef and a can of peaches.

By the 1940s, interest in the Dyea area increased. From 1940 to 1948, the Alaska Road Commission carved out a 13 km (8 mi.) road to Dyea.[20] Several homesteads were claimed north of Dyea. This improved access and the growth in northern literature, especially the publication in 1958 of Pierre Berton's *Klondike*, fuelled a growing interest in hiking the trail.

There was one plant that caused us untold misery. It was a tall plant that had huge leaves in a cluster at the top giving it a parasol effect. The long stalk was bristling with sharp stickers. Breaking a trail through a big patch of these was like tunnelling through a pile of needles. And to top it off, every little barb was poisonous. We were soon covered with a mass of little red spots that burned and itched for days. Our clothing was no protection from these "stinging devils."

• Robert Storm describing devil's club in the rainforest, July 5, 1936

Ed Kalen, long-time Skagway resident, setting up camp at Stone Crib near the Chilkoot summit, 1957.

AN ALUMINUM PLANT IN DYEA?

IN 1952, THE Aluminum Company of America (ALCOA) announced a plan to build a huge aluminum smelter at Dyea. Company officials predicted a city of 20,000. A wave of euphoria swept over Skagway. A large-scale industrial development seemed to be on its way to the area.

Planning for the project began in 1946. The Bureau of Reclamation concluded the Taiya River valley had an enormous water development potential—if (and only if) Canada would agree to provide water from Lindeman Lake and Bennett Lake. The bureau proposed a dam near Whitehorse to raise the lakes some 12 to 15 m (40 to 50 ft.) and a 12 m (40 ft.) wide, 20 km (12 mi.) long tunnel under the Chilkoot Pass to feed hydro-electric generators.

In early 1948, the U.S. Bureau of Land Management withdrew more than 50,000 acres around Dyea from settlement. ALCOA became interested in the project at this time. Access to the cheap electricity of the project prompted the company to propose an aluminum reduction plant for Dyea. Canadian officials, generally supportive of the project, set aside thousands of acres surrounding Marsh, Tagish, Bennett, and Atlin lakes for flooding. British Columbia lands officials made a similar withdrawal on Bennett and Lindeman lakes.

In May, 1949, an ALCOA competitor, the Aluminum Company of Canada (ALCAN), made a preliminary decision to build its own aluminium smelter at Kitimat, British Columbia, 740 km (460 mi.) south of Dyea. Consequently, the British Columbia government took a closer look at the ALCOA scheme and concluded their province would "not benefit economically in any way from the contemplated development."

Despite these setbacks, ALCOA officials forged ahead with their plans. In August, 1952, ALCOA official Leon E. Hickman told the All-Alaska Chamber of Commerce that the company was "ready, without reservation, to proceed with the construction of a large aluminum-smelting project in Alaska, just as soon as the necessary land can be purchased and the required governmental approvals can be obtained."

Unbridled optimism followed Hickman's announcement. Alaska newspapers, and even the *New York Times*, ran lengthy articles on the project. In Skagway, property prices rose sharply, and "mysterious buyers appeared and were interested in purchasing or optioning almost everything in town," according to an *Anchorage Daily Times* report.

Skagway's enthusiasm, however, was not reflected in Canada. No progress was made in convincing either the British Columbia or Canadian governments to back the project. In November, 1952, more bad news followed. A Canadian company submitted plans for a hydro-electric project on the nearby Alsek River. A Dominion official informed ALCOA they would actively fight the Taiya project. The maximum benefit from any power development, he maintained, must go to Canada.

By January, 1953, the *Engineering News-Record* reported: "Canada has slammed the door conclusively in the face of the Aluminum Company of America's plans for development of hydro power in Alaska." ALCOA continued to press its case, although with less and less success, and on March 1, 1957, the company abandoned all plans for the Taiya project.[21]

Proposed tunnel construction under the Chilkoot Pass. Adapted from a sketch published by the *New York Times*, August 24, 1952.

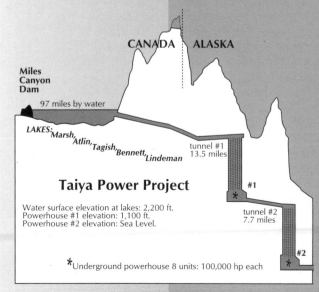

CANADA   ALASKA

Miles
Canyon
Dam

97 miles by water

LAKES: Marsh, Atlin, Tagish, Bennett, Lindeman

tunnel #1
13.5 miles

Taiya Power Project

Water surface elevation at lakes: 2,200 ft.
Powerhouse #1 elevation: 1,100 ft.
Powerhouse #2 elevation: Sea Level.

#1
*

tunnel #2
7.7 miles

*Underground powerhouse 8 units: 100,000 hp each

* #2

First Nations on the land

Elders tell stories of their long and continuous use of the Chilkoot area. Stone flakes from tool making, hunting blinds on the hillsides, meat-drying camps, and old fire rings are witness to the life of the Tagish and Tlingit peoples who have travelled and hunted here. The memories of the elders bring these places back to life for us today.

Artifacts found in the coastal areas of Alaska show that aboriginal people have inhabited the region for at least 9,000 years.[22] Flaked stone tools, approximately 4,500 years old, have been found near Carcross. Copper tools appear to have been first used about 1,200 years ago. Scattered finds of stone tools have also been recorded at the northern end of the Chilkoot Trail. While it is difficult to determine the dates of these sites, they likely were temporary camping places for people travelling between the coast and the interior.

The stone and copper tools indicate hunting and the processing of food and clothing. The source of the tool-making material can provide valuable information about trade and travel networks. The way artifacts are grouped at old camps may give insight into social organization and the division of labour. Further research is required on the Chilkoot sites to learn more.

Three pre-19th century sites have been recorded on the sand hills between the foot of Lindeman Lake and the head of Bennett Lake. One site is south of Bennett in a sand dune area. Its elevated location provides a view of both Lindeman and Bennett lakes and the immediate vicinity. Hundreds of rock flakes, as well as scraping tools, are present. Scraping tools were generally used for hide or fish processing. More modern artifacts found include a tinkler cone—decorative dress accessories made from the lids of baking powder tins—and various brass cartridges.

Native Americans from the Skagway and Haines region returned to the area south of the White Pass and Chilkoot summits shortly after the gold rush. The Tlingit used the area for several decades after the rush, and eulachon fishing around Dyea continues to the present day.

The Tlingit remain an identifiable group, and their regional corporation, the Sealaska Corporation, is one of the most profitable Native American groups in Alaska. They continue to live in towns and villages throughout southeastern Alaska.

Carcross-Tagish children at Carcross, September, 1950.

James "Skookum Jim" Mason (KESH) (ca.1860-1916)

Skookum (strong) Jim, of the Dakhl'wedi clan of the Wolf moiety found a nugget on Rabbit (Bonanza) Creek in August, 1896. This gold strike was the spark for the Klondike Gold Rush. He made the discovery while on a journey down the Yukon River to find his sister Kate and her husband George Carmack.

Well-known as a packer on the Chilkoot Trail, Skookum Jim was renowned for his legendary exploits and physical abilities. He always believed his Frog Spirit had guided him to the gold strike. Jim became very rich but remained a generous man who never forgot his obligations to his community at Carcross. The Skookum Jim Friendship Centre in Whitehorse is a part of his legacy.

North of the summits, First Nations people continued to live and work at Lindeman, Bennett, and elsewhere in the area. The region has long provided opportunities for hunting, fishing, trapping, and berry picking.

The way local people make use of the land often tells something of the way they feel about it as well as their ability to survive in it.[23] The Johnson family of the Ishkìtàn (Frog) clan have lived and worked in the Bennett area since the 1920s. This family, and others from Haines, Klukwan, Skagway and Carcross, have long hunted game and picked berries around Log Cabin. In the old days, the nearest other camps were at Bennett, on the shores of Tutshi Lake, and possibly at Teepee, southeast of Log Cabin.[24] Log Cabin was not always a comfortable camp, though, because of the notoriously poor weather.

This area was part of Skookum Jim's land. Carcross-Tagish people talk about Skookum Jim's deal with the WP&YR—the first land claims deal in the Yukon. Jim, famous for his role in the discovery of gold in the Klondike, gave permission for the railway to travel across his land in the White Pass in return for jobs for the people of his community. Older community members remember this commitment being kept until well into the 1950s.[25]

Berry picking

Berry picking has remained important over the years. In the past, large groups of First Nations women and children camped in the Log Cabin area for several days or a week in late summer to harvest blueberries, mossberries, low-bush cranberries and others. This was usually a happy time in the last of the fine summer weather, leaving women and children free of the routine demands of day-to-day life.[26]

Edna Helm remembers the berry picking seasons when she was young: "Berry picking! In late summer we went berry picking. The family, Grandma, Grandpa, Mom and Dad, and us two girls, took the train from Bennett to Fraser where we set up our berry picking camp. Everyone went out to pick berries. Grandpa, who had polio in his 20s and couldn't get

around much, stayed in camp and did all the cooking. The railway delivered our groceries to the berry camp. We really had something going with the railway.

"Kids galore, all over the place. There were always lots of kids out at the camp. We played lots of games there—Fall in the Creek, where we jumped back and forth over a creek until someone fell in, and Play Monkey, with the kids climbing in the trees.

"We used to sell berries in Carcross. We used five-gallon square tins from Blazo (kerosene) for picking. We kids used to fill the buckets with leaves and then cover the top with berries. When Grandma found out she made us fill the pails and then checked to make sure we only had berries in the pail."

The berries were put into large wooden boxes (Blazo shipping crates) and melted moose grease was poured in to preserve the berries. "In winter, whenever you wanted a treat, you went out to the cache and broke off a piece to eat." However, Helm's sister, Jean Desmarais, recalled: "We used to pick a lot of blueberries, but I don't remember ever eating them. Mom must have taken them to the store to pay for groceries."

Good berry patches had camp sites situated close by and were used every year. Tin pails were often hung upside down on tree branches to mark these places. Before the railway shut down in 1982, berry pickers used the train to travel to Log Cabin. Now they can drive there by the highway.[27]

The First Nations way of life sees connections between all things. In berry picking, the Carcross-Tagish remain sensitive to the many different aspects of life that might affect the harvest. A mid-summer inspection of the berry crop is always discreet. One older woman noted: "Just look at them—don't mention their names."

The great respect of the aboriginal peoples for all parts of the environment illustrates their view that they are participants in, rather than merely observers or harvesters of, the world around them.[28]

Hunting

Animals were the chief source of food and clothing for First Nations, and hunting was an ongoing activity. The importance of the hunting lifestyle and its connections to the traditional ways ensure it remains an important part of the lives of many members of the Carcross-Tagish First Nation.

The Johnson and Atlin families' relationship with the land and its resources reflects their deep and special knowledge and their abiding respect for the animals they hunted.

By early spring, it was necessary to go hunting. It was almost impossible to store enough food for the winter; by late winter, dried meat and fish would be in short supply. But once the snow hardened and the weather moderated, usually by late February, small animals and birds began to reappear. Animals such as rabbits, groundhogs, and ptarmigan were an important part of the diet.[29] Meat from these animals often carried families through lean times.

Rabbits were snared or hunted with a .22 rifle.[30] Another favourite was groundhogs. "We seen a groundhog, we get a groundhog! We get them up the hill back of the White Pass Station," recalled Desmarais. Winnie Atlin

Edna Helm remembers how her Grampa Johnson often collected old horseshoe nails and spikes at Lindeman and Bennett. He handed them out freely to the enthralled railway travellers until "one day, they were all gone."

(preceding page) **Berry picking near Carcross. An important part of the winter diet, berries also supplemented a family's cash flow.**

Jimmy James with a squirrel he shot, December, 1950.

After picking berries in late summer the Johnson family travelled to Lindeman to fish and hunt moose: "We stayed until we got a moose. We always got a moose at Lindeman." One good hunting spot overlooked the marshes and thickets of the old White Pass Trail. Edna Helm remembered camping up there in the years that her father worked on the railway section crew out of Log Cabin: "Every day after work, he used to hike an hour up to the camp. Even when the family was back in Bennett there was always a watch kept for moose. From the front door of Gramma's house, the old government telegraph office, there was a great view over the beach and flats."

Louise James scraping a moose hide at Carcross in August, 1949.

remembered her mom "used to skin them, fix the hides [for]...trimming, moccasins, for parkies, for everything."

Ptarmigan moved down from higher elevations in the late winter and were hunted, sometimes with nets.[31] Jean Desmarais remembered: "Never used to get much around here [Bennett] except in springtime when ptarmigan start mating. Used to be flocks of them here. Eat lots of ptarmigan then. Get them up behind the depot, that's where most of them were."

As the days lengthened, hunters looked forward to the spring beaver hunt. Beavers have rich meat and thick pelts after a winter of leisure, eating their stored food.[32] The pleasures of warmer weather and the attraction of fresh beaver meat made these hunts enjoyable despite the softening trails and the dangers of rotting ice and open water.

For the families living around Bennett, goat meat and fish were the main foods. Winnie Atlin remembered: "All we used to eat around Bennett is goat.... I would rather eat goat meat than moose. Now...I am used to goat meat, that's all." Summer hunting trips were long. She took care of her sick father alone when her brothers went off hunting goats. "You had to go far away for goat...they're not that big. Well one goat was good enough for our family then; there wasn't a big family, and...there's nobody to share with." Goats were hunted around Lindeman Lake; there was a good place near the south end of the lake. Goat skin would be tanned and used for mitts and moccasins and kid fur was kept for trimming slippers and mitts. Speaking about Fraser, just south of Log Cabin, Winnie Atlin said: "Yeah, there was goats there too. Goats up that Fraser Mountain, but since all that Customs, all those houses, everything there now, I think the only thing there now is just beaver. It is bad...to go through Fraser to see all our camp grounds torn apart...that place there is all just gravel now and just nothing there.... It really hurts when you see that all torn apart."

Change had been part of Tagish life in earlier times as well. In the early 1800s, caribou were herded into brush corrals by well-organized groups of hunters. They could then be speared or snared. Through the mid to late 1800s, caribou became less plentiful, while moose extended their range north into the area. At about the same time, guns became available and individual stalking of larger solitary moose became common. Today, the annual fall moose hunt remains a central point in people's traditional ways.

Moose were hunted throughout the area. Helm's grandfather used to hunt in the fall with Marvin Taylor, a manager of the WP&YR. They took the casey car to Mile 34 and hiked up the ridge south of the tracks: "Grampa, he comes early in the morning and sits up on the hill here. He never missed his moose.... Grampa used to just sit, call moose and wait for them. Once he called a moose across Lindeman [Lake]. He called and the moose swam across the lake."

A bull moose can weigh over 700 kg (1,500 lbs.) and a cow almost as much. Moving such a weight through the bush was impossible, so meat drying was often done at the kill site. Winnie Atlin recalled a moose kill near Tutshi Lake in the 1940s: "We camped there, that was when it was time for putting meat up, drying meat. My dad got a moose there and we stayed there, oh, about 10 days putting, drying this meat. After you dry your meat it is not so heavy. It is like, when it is really fresh. So we stayed there about 10 days drying that meat and we packed all our [five] dogs, packed them all in our dog packs" for the trip back to Bennett. Hunting along the tracks or at Lindeman, however, allowed the family to haul the butchered meat back to Bennett by casey car or boat.

William Atlin at the family's storage shed, Bennett, 1992.

PATSY HENDERSON

PATSY HENDERSON or Kulsin, his Tagish name, was Skookum Jim's nephew and the youngest person present at the discovery of gold in 1896. In his later years, Henderson became well known for his presentations to the WP&YR tourist trains at the Carcross railway station. While the best known story was his account of the discovery of gold, he also described the traditional ways of the Carcross-Tagish. Using models he built, he told stories about how First Nations used fish traps, deadfall traps and beaver nets in their daily lives. He also demonstrated game calling, the use of bow and arrows, and how to light a fire without matches. Henderson provided community leadership for many years as chief of the Carcross-Tagish Indian Band.

Patsy Henderson was remembered by the *Whitehorse Star* on his death in February, 1966:

Dressed in beautifully beaded caribou-skin clothing made by Edith [his wife, fondly remembered as "Mrs. Patsy"] they were a colourful sight as they met thousands of tourists, visiting politicians, dignitaries such as Governor-General [Vincent] Massey in 1956, and even royalty.

At Bennett, the family had a meat-drying rack just behind their cabins. Helm described drying the meat: "The moose was cut up into strips, like rope, and then we hang it up to dry. Some short pieces and longer pieces, depends on the part of the moose.... We'd cover the moose and light a fire under it. We used rotten stumps...the worst part was looking for stumps. We used them all the time and had to go further and further for them. We looked for them in the summer, usually out in the dunes.... The smoke wasn't supposed to cook it or dry it, just keep the flies off. Didn't want the heat. It usually takes two to three weeks in good weather to dry it out. While the meat dried we'd roast the bones for the marrow, on a grate over the fire. We'd roast it and roast it and then eat it with bread. What we couldn't dry we'd eat right away. We'd roast the head. We'd eat the guts, we'd eat the nose, and what we didn't eat we'd sew up for clothes."

Once the meat was dried and the fat was rendered, the moosehide was carefully scraped clean and washed, and repeatedly soaked and frozen to soften and prepare it for tanning in the spring.[33] Life relaxed briefly before the winter snows signalled the start of trapping: "[Dried moose meat] was all we had in winter. Wasn't easy to get fresh meat. Mostly it was the younger boys who went out with their snowshoes to hunt moose. They were out hauling wood, setting traps, and if they saw moose tracks they go out and follow it."

Through the winter, the women sewed moosehide into clothing for the family and made souvenirs to sell to the summer train visitors.

Dora Austin, standing beneath an open cache at Patsy Henderson's winter cabin, January, 1951.

While no longer as dependent on the annual round of hunting for food and clothing, or trapping for furs, Edna Helm continues to work hard to keep as close to the old ways as she can: "It's not a living but I love the life."

Trapping and fishing

Trapping season started in the fall with the cleaning and preparing of traps. Trap setting began when snow had fallen in the bush, usually in November. Winnie and William Atlin recalled trapping out of Bennett: "They done a lot of trapping...[the men] stay out three or four days [up the King River (Homan River)], and then come back, and then they went Log Cabin way, and Tutshi Lake way [via Partridge Pass]; they stay out two or three, five or six days sometimes, run all their traps.... [Mom] was out everyday, out running our traps, setting them up, we used to get a lot of snow there, and every time it snowed they have to go back out and get the traps. That had to be done just about every other day; it was snowing, we used to get lots of snow there."

Animals trapped or snared for furs included beaver, fox, coyote, wolverine and occasionally mink. Rabbits were snared for eating and the hide was used as bait for lynx, though lynx were uncommon in the Bennett area. And while trapping, people were always aware of other opportunities. "If you see a moose, see moose tracks, well, you go hunting.

"I remember me and Dick, we set up a camp [in King River valley], in a tent. We decided to come home, boy, it snowed so much that night, the snow was up...to the top of the handle bar [on the dog sled]. All day, about seven miles, it took us to get back [to Bennett]."

Edna Helm's trapping cabin at Bennett *(left)* and Helm *(below)* with fox and marten she trapped in December, 1993. The cabin burnt down in December, 1995.

GROWING UP AT BENNETT

THROUGH THE 20TH century, the Carcross-Tagish people gradually changed their land-use patterns and moved into permanent settlements like Carcross and Tagish. Schooling was one of the reasons for this change. After day schools and the Chooutla Residential School opened in Carcross, families began putting their children in classes through the winter. In the 1940s, one of the few families who still lived out on the land was the Johnsons at Bennett.

In winter, Edna, her sister Jean, and cousins Jerry and Kenneth played in the old church, dug tunnels in the huge snowdrifts and went sliding. Winnie Atlin, their aunt, remembered the toboggan her mom had made: "They shot a bunch of caribou, and the shanks off the caribou, my Mom skin them and sew them together and she freeze it outside, we use that for our sleigh for tobogganing. That was something." Even though not in school, the children still learned a great deal. Jean recalls setting snares for rabbits on the hill and around the church at Bennett: "I was too small to shoot the gun I guess so I got to set snares. It was more fun to set snares. I did the night check after supper."

At the end of the school term many Carcross-Tagish families sent their kids off to Bennett. Then there were lots of kids at Bennett. They lived in tents on the beach for most of the summer; picnics and swimming were popular.

White Pass also contributed to the summer's fun for Helm: "White Pass was good to us at Bennett. They sent over the leftover pie for all the kids staying at Bennett. I used to love pumpkin pie but the big kids always started pie fights and my pumpkin pie used to end up flying around.... Their parents would come down after about a month. Then we'd hunt a moose and have a big celebration. At the end of the summer, everybody headed back north to their homes and we had the place to ourselves again."

Edna, Jerry and Kenneth posing with their dog and sled, Bennett, 1948.

Travel in early winter was usually difficult. Frequent and heavy snowfalls not only covered trails but made lake and river ice treacherous. An early layer of snow insulated thin fall ice, keeping it from getting thicker as the weather turned colder. King River had lots of places where it stayed open all winter, and both Lindeman and Bennett lakes often had extensive areas of overflow or soft ice. By spring, the hard-packed snow made travel much easier.

Suckers, whitefish, and trout were an important part of the Johnson family's diet. After the spring melt raised water levels, a long net was run out into the deep water from the White Pass dock at Bennett. In the fall, the net was moved to the old One Mile River wharf; during the moose hunt it was taken up to Lindeman.

Helm recalled that fishing was a lot of work; cotton nets required plenty of attention: "Gramma used to have a hard time with those things. They used to bust easy. Lots of sewing to repair them." Once in the water, the net had to be checked every day: "We would get

about half a tub sometime, and if we get half a tub, then we'd pull the net out and then we'd clean all the fish, and smoke it. And then we'd have fish enough to last us awhile. All summer we kept the net there, but for our winter food, Mom used to go back to Carcross and put all the fish there and then come back here, sometime, about [mid-October] she'd be back here, with dried fish, and salt fish." Fall fishing was especially trying: "Bloody cold cleaning fish down by the lake, you know, on your hands. We didn't know about rubber gloves in them days."

By early spring, the winter supply of dried fish would be gone. Jean Desmarais remembered going ice fishing: "I went up [Lindeman Lake] about halfway with Grampa with the dog team to set a fish net. It was after Christmas, way after. We used a jig to set the net. Left early morning, had three dogs, and set the net. Went back the next day and we had fresh fish. Our lunch was dry meat, maybe dried fish, grease and berries and a sandwich made of good old SPORK or KLIK [laughter] or something like that. We had fish head soup after we came home. We had lots of fun that day, Grampa and I."

Dora Austin and another woman reset the net after pulling it for fish and thawing it with warm water.

Fishing on Little Atlin Lake, January, 1951. Dora Austin and Patsy Henderson arriving to chop a hole in the ice. On the far right is the second hole to which the net will be set.

Winnie Atlin recalls her mother's tourist tent at Bennett:

She used to have a table. At one time she had a tent frame, way down there [by the railway station]. She had a tent frame there, to keep the stuff out of the rain. She used to be real busy person, she used to get lots of orders, all the time. When the tourist is all finished we used to go to Skagway for a nice big treat. It used to cost us only three dollars to go to Skagway [by train] in them days, and that's return.

"Winter—with all the fur in winter." Kenneth, Edna and Jerry are shown on the postcard designed by their grandmother, Martha Johnson and produced for sale at the Bennett railway station.

Getting ready for tourists

A long and close relationship with the WP&YR also shaped the First Nations way of life around Bennett in the 20th century. The railway provided jobs, easy transportation and personal connections.

Bennett's role as a stop on the WP&YR also meant business opportunities based on tourism. The Johnson family were well aware of the attraction the gold rush held for the tourists travelling through every summer. The women at Bennett took the opportunity seriously and organized the children. Edna Helm recalled: "[in winter] we got busy then sewing things to sell to the tourists—purses, glasses cases, dolls, oh, lots of things.... Grandma kept us pretty busy with the sewing." Some of it was fun though, and posing for tourists proved worthwhile. Winnie Atlin remembered: "I just happened to have my own team of huskies.... We used to let the [tourists] take our pictures for money."

Winnie's mom, Martha Johnson, sold crafts to tourists by the railway station in 1938, working there for years. "She had all kinds of postcards; she had a postcard, that one was the biggest seller for her, it was of all the furs they caught in winter, it was all put together in the springtime, just before she took it into Whitehorse, and she had Edna and others, they were all dressed in fur, they had it wrapped around them, and they were holding them, and all you could see was their faces, there was so much furs around them. That was her biggest seller."

The relationship with the railway was not just a commercial one. The family's dogs got scraps from the station restaurant and were among the best fed in the north. Locomotive engineers regularly brought candy for the kids and the company gave Martha and Billy Johnson a free pass for the train between Bennett and Carcross. Winnie Atlin recalled the

Bennett cook who made her wedding cake: "When my Mom ordered a wedding cake he said, 'I never thought I was gonna make Winnie's wedding cake.' I was just a little girl when I first moved there." A powerful sense of belonging developed over the years. Edna Helm described her map of the area by cupping her hands. "I'd put Bennett here in the centre and mark it HOME. God, I love that place. It's our history. It's still in the family."

Commemorating the gold rush trails

Skagway civic and business leaders began to show an interest in preserving and interpreting gold rush resources as early as the 1930s. The idea of a "Chilcoot National Park"—to include the region around Skagway, Dyea, and the old Chilkoot Trail—was forwarded to U.S. National Park Service (NPS) officials in Washington. The idea was dropped after a few years, but interest began to grow again in the 1950s.[34]

An NPS archaeologist, Paul Schumacher, spent time investigating some of Skagway's old buildings in June, 1959. Two years later, in July, 1961, historian Charles Snell evaluated the Skagway and Taiya river valleys for the National Survey of Historic Sites and Buildings. He felt both Skagway and the Chilkoot Trail were "sites of exceptional value" and thus worthy to be nominated as historic sites.[35]

By the 1960s, the Chilkoot Trail had been abandoned for more than 60 years and the route had become almost entirely obscured. But a meeting of state corrections and lands-division personnel revived interest in the trail, and reconstruction began shortly afterward.

In May, 1961, the state of Alaska organized a party to survey the trail. It was brushed out as far as Sheep Camp and a cable for hauling supplies was installed across the Taiya River. Later, the government committed to a long-term program. In 1962 and 1963, a crew built cabins near Canyon City and Sheep Camp, and by the close of the 1963 season, the trail was open all the way to the summit.[37]

Jean Desmarais continues beading and sewing, skills she learned from her grandmother, Martha Johnson.

ARCHITECTURAL PRESERVATION IN SKAGWAY

SKAGWAY STILL RESEMBLES the gold rush town it was more than 90 years ago. Between 1908 and the outbreak of World War II, only two buildings were erected: the National Bank of Alaska (1916)

and the Presbyterian manse (1941). Several major gold rush-era buildings, both residences and commercial structures, were lost during this period, but enough of them remained that tourists began to appreciate the town's historical architecture.

National Park Service officials recognized the value of the town's gold rush buildings as early as the mid-1950s; these resources played a major role in the Interior Department's 1962 designation of Skagway and the White Pass as a National Historic Landmark. Because state and local interests were in no position to undertake a massive restoration effort, it fell upon the federal government to provide the necessary support. The Congressional bill authorizing Klondike Gold Rush National Historical Park provided a partial solution to this problem when it authorized the NPS to purchase selected, privately-owned properties in the Skagway business district.

There were scores of other historical properties that private interests had no desire to sell. In order to ensure the preservation of these properties, the NPS successfully urged the Skagway City Council to adopt a historic preservation ordinance and appoint a Historic Preservation Commission. Since then, the NPS has provided technical assistance to local businesses, information on rehabilitation grants, local workshops and preservation symposia, and other actions designed to preserve and restore the area's privately-owned historical resources. Partly as a result of these efforts, few historical business or residential buildings have been lost since the early 1970s.[36]

(top) **The Arctic Brotherhood Hall in Skagway, 1905.**

(bottom) **The WP&YR depot and administration building at Skagway in 1901. Sold in 1972, they have housed the NPS park headquarters and visitor centre since 1984.**

In 1967, both the National Park Service and Parks Canada began to study various gold rush sites between Skagway and Dawson City. The NPS developed a plan that gave the agency management control over the Chilkoot Trail, a portion of the White Pass Trail and 2.4 acres in Skagway. A bill establishing Klondike Gold Rush National Historical Park passed the U.S. Congress and was signed into law on June 30, 1976.[38]

The Canadian study group reviewing sites produced a series of plans which eventually resulted in the acquisition of the Chilkoot Trail area, the *S.S. Klondike* sternwheeler and a host of buildings and sites in Dawson City and the Klondike goldfields. Parks Canada began a site presence in 1972, but Chilkoot Trail National Historic Site was only established on April 7, 1993.

The Alaskan initiatives of the early 1960s and the interest of the park services in the trail had sparked a response by the Yukon government in Whitehorse. The territorial Department of Justice organized a work camp for jail inmates at Lindeman in 1968. For the next two years, inmates came out to Lindeman to locate and clear a trail from Bennett to the end of the bush at Deep Lake. By 1969, a cleared trail once again ran to the summit on the Canadian side.

In response to these trail projects, recreational use grew to levels not witnessed since the gold rush. A mere smattering of hikers had crossed the trail during the early and mid-

The lunch room at the Bennett railway station, 1950s.

*My deceased husband's
grandfather, Charles E.
Packard, arrived in Dyea in
Aug. [1897], with a group
from Los Angeles. They
began to relay their goods
up the Trail but didn't make
it over the Pass that winter.
Charles brought his 16-yr old
son, Wilbert, who
contracted meningitis and
died in Dyea, Easter Sun.
April, 1898. His grave and
dear marker are in the Slide
Cemetery. I came over the
Chilkoot in memory of all of
them.*

• Lindeman Lake log book,
Kathleen Packard,
Bow, Washington,
September 2, 1985

**Yukon Correctional Institute
inmates at Lindeman
building a bridge.**

1960s. In 1968, fewer than 100 people signed the log book left in the newly-constructed cabin at Lindeman Lake. But in 1970, close to 500 hikers traversed the trail and by 1973, when both the National Park Service and Parks Canada began to place staff along the trail, the number had risen to almost 1,100.[39] By 1978, the annual total had doubled. Since then, trail use has steadied, and some 3,000 hikers now traverse the trail each summer. During the last 30 years, more than 50,000 people have hiked the length of the trail; that total surpasses the number of stampeders that used the trail between 1897 and 1900.[40]

One inevitable outcome of the boom in recreational use has been the loss of trailside artifacts and the deterioration of both the trail and camping areas. During the 1960s and 1970s, hikers frequently encountered horseshoes, clothing, appliances, and other gold rush remnants, and the trail became known as the "world's longest museum." Many of those items, sad to say, have disappeared over the years. Portions of the historical trail distant from today's route still retain most of their relics, and park staff on both sides of the border have attempted, with some success, to inventory the remaining objects and develop alternative forms of informing the public of the trail's history.

The continuing wear and tear on the trail has been as serious as the loss of historic artifacts. Over the last decade, both park services have hardened campsites, rerouted the trail from

especially fragile areas and encouraged trail users to "travel lightly." The sensitivity of visitors today will ensure the Chilkoot experience remains unimpaired for future hikers.

Land ownership in the trail corridor has also emerged as a lively issue. When the trail was opened for recreational use, governments on both sides of the border—the State of Alaska and the province of British Columbia—were confident that there were no outstanding conflicts over land ownership. But Native Americans and Canadian First Nations have a long-standing and important role in the area, and ownership patterns have altered as a result.

On the U.S. side of the trail, three Aleut brothers named Mahle, all from Skagway, claimed a total of 320 acres between Dyea and Canyon City. In 1991, the brothers gained title to their claims, except for a narrow trail easement.[41]

Across the border, in Canada, the Taku River Tlingit filed their land claim over the trail area in the late 1980s. Several years later the Carcross-Tagish First Nation also claimed the Chilkoot Trail area. The British Columbia aboriginal land claims process just got underway in the mid-1990s and negotiations for land claims are well advanced in the Yukon Territory. The Canadian government acknowledges the validity of these claims, and when negotiations are completed the First Nations rights will be recognized.

Archaeological surveys have recovered elements of the cultural heritage on the Chilkoot. This team is working at Lindeman.

The Historic Sites and Monument Board of Canada plaque on the old train station in Whitehorse reads:

White Pass and Yukon Route

Built at the time of the Klondike Gold Rush, the 177 km narrow gauge railway was the heart of the Yukon transportation system for over 80 years. Completed in 1900, it linked the tidewater port of Skagway in Alaska with Whitehorse, head of navigation on the Yukon River. As a result, Whitehorse became the transportation and later, the administrative, commercial and population centre of the Yukon. The scenic line stopped operating in 1982 but was subsequently revived as a tourist excursion train from Skagway during the summer months.

Transportation in the mountain corridors

On July 29, 1900, the last spike of the WP&YR was hammered in at Carcross, linking Skagway with Whitehorse. Though the gold rush was over by then, the railroad prospered for more than a decade. Hauling in heavy dredge equipment to support the mechanization of Klondike placer gold mining, and hauling out copper ore from the mines near Whitehorse, the WP&YR—with its Yukon River shipping subsidiary, the British Yukon Navigation Company—consistently earned a healthy profit.

Lean years in the 1920s and 1930s were followed by slowly increasing tourism and the initiation of silver-lead ore exports from the Stewart River mines near Mayo. The construction of the Alaska Highway during World War II relied largely on the railway for supplies and services. However, heavy wartime usage by the U.S. Army left the railway in poor physical condition with limited prospects for profitable operation in the immediate post-war years.

In 1951, a new Canadian company, the White Pass & Yukon Corporation, took over the obsolete railway and steamboat equipment. A program of modernization produced a highly efficient transportation system that helped introduce "containerization" to the transport world. However, the company's continued reliance upon ore exports led to financial problems in the late 1970s when low world prices for base metals closed most Yukon mines. Without freight, the company shut down rail operations in 1982.

In 1988, White Pass announced it would reinstate summer tourist trains. That same year, the Historic Sites and Monuments Board of Canada announced the railway was of national

historic significance. Since then, thousands of visitors have ridden the rails to the White Pass summit, and on to Bennett, reliving the dramatic days of the gold rush.[42]

During the 1970s, access to both ends of the trail corridor was eased by the completion of the Klondike Highway between Skagway and Whitehorse. Skagway residents had made repeated lobbying efforts, and in one symbolic demonstration, had lengthened the road by using locally-available hand tools. But cost, and the need for international cooperation, prevented the project from getting off the drawing boards. By the end of World War II, the construction of local roads had narrowed the gap somewhat, but more than 80 km (50 mi.) of mountain wilderness remained. Numerous surveys, conferences, and continuing lobbying took place during the 1950s and 1960s. Finally, in 1973, an agreement was reached to fund the road. Construction began in 1974, and the first vehicles drove over the newly-completed road in August, 1978.[43]

The most commonly seen vehicle on the highway today is the large ore truck, each with four muffin-like containers of galena ore. These giant trucks, weighing in at 77 tonnes (85 tons), are the heaviest vehicles in North America licensed for public roads. Travelling 24 hours a day, 365 days a year, they haul ore from the mine at Faro, Yukon to Skagway harbour for shipment to markets throughout the world.

(preceding page) **WP&YR train heading up White Pass from Skagway.**

View from the Klondike Highway.

End of the trail

From the damp lushness of tidewater rainforest, through the harsh bareness of the montaine rock and ice, to the sunny shelter of the dry boreal forests, the Chilkoot Trail is a place of note. The dramatic changes in climate, ecology and geography along its length are striking. Traders, travellers, stampeders, hunters, and hikers have all fallen under the spell of the Chilkoot. Every passage over the trail provides new experiences and a deeper understanding of the relationship between place and people.

The Chilkoot experience is demanding; it is also rewarding. The primary element defining this experience is geography. The linearity of the route, the visual sense of its containment in its own valley, and the obvious relationship between the local topography, the siting of the trail, and the dynamic natural environment are the basis for understanding the importance of the Chilkoot. The views of verdant forest, the rocky skyline that surrounds the summit of the pass, and the sparkling lakes and rivers that lead off to the north, build upon the magical tinkle of running water, the bitter bite of cold, wind-driven rain, and the smell of the ocean chasing travellers up the trail.

People have left an imprint of their presence on the land. Whether a stone fragment from tool making, a carefully

Alaskan Natives drying salmon at their fish camp.

Stampeders and their dog climb the Chilkoot Pass.

Mrs. Patsy Henderson and her grandchildren, Carcross, about 1950.

prepared platform for a tent, or the discarded remains of a winter's menu of tinned food, these tangible reminders speak of the life and experience of those travelling through the pass before us. In addition to these physical reminders, people have told stories and given names to lakes, mountains and bays to remind others of their experience. In this book we have tried to re-tell some of the stories that reflect the many different perspectives and people who have become part of the history of the Chilkoot.

The Chilkoot Trail is known around the world. The challenge we face, as with all the special places which make up this planet, is to keep the legacy of the past, and its lessons for the future, alive and healthy in the Chilkoot. It is only through understanding and care by present users, a continuing respect of all for the different values resting in this special place, and an ongoing concern for the future, that the Chilkoot will remain a healthy and valued region.

Parks Canada wardens at the Chilkoot summit. Each spring Parks staff mark a trail through the snow fields.

References

Endnotes

The Land

1. This chapter is based upon Sharon Thomson and Debbie Verhalle, "'The Meanest 32 Miles in History': Nature and Geology on the Chilkoot Trail," unpublished report, Parks Canada; Scott Home, "Wildlife in Dyea," unpub. mss, KGRNHP Coll.; and NPS, *Final Environmental Statement (FES), Proposed Klondike Gold Rush National Historical Park, Alaska and Washington* (Washington, c. 1974), pp. 29-30, 34-38.

2. David Neufeld observations, October 1995.

3. Karl Baedeker, *The Dominion of Canada with Newfoundland and an Excursion to Alaska* (Leipsic, 1900), 247.

4. Steacy D. Hicks and William Shofnos, "The Determination of Land Emergence from Sea Level Observations in Southeast Alaska," *Journal of Geophysical Research* 70 (July 15, 1965), pp. 3315-3320; Travis Hudson, Kirk Dixon, and George Plafker, "Regional Uplift in Southeastern Alaska," *USGS Circular C-0844* (1981), pp. 132-135.

5. Lt. Frederick Schwatka, "Military Reconnoissance [sic] in Alaska," in *Explorations in Alaska*, in 48th Cong., 2nd Sess., Senate Document 23, p. 294.

6. E. Tappan Adney, *The Klondike Stampede* (New York, 1900), pp. 91-92, 99.

7. Julius M. Price, *From Euston to Klondike: The Narrative of a Journey Through British Columbia and the North-West Territory in the Summer of 1898* (London, 1898), p. 79; Martha Louise Black, *My Ninety Years*, (Anchorage, 1976), p. 24.

8. Thomas S. Scott, "Some Experiences on the Chilkoot Pass," *The Canadian Magazine*, Feb. 1898, p. 333; Sgt. William Yunera to Major L.H. Rucker, Mar. 21, 1898, in Letters Received, Dept. of the Columbia, RG 393, NA; Inge Sjolseth Kolloen, "Crossing the Chilcoot Pass," mss 923.9 K83c v.f., Mar. 29, 1898, AHL.

9. E. Hazard Wells, *Magnificence and Misery* (Garden City, 1984), 60.

10. Robert Oglesby, "Account of a Six Months' Trip Through the Yukon Gold Fields," *Cosmopolitan Magazine*, Sept. 1897, p. 524; *Seattle Post-Intelligencer*, Oct. 13, 1897.

11. William Zimmer to W.P. McBride, Collector of Customs, August 4, 1898, in Letters Received, Sitka, Vol. 13; Records of Alaska Customshouses, 1867-1939, NA Anchorage.

12. *Seattle Post-Intelligencer*, Oct. 13, 1897; Yunera to Rucker, Mar. 21, 1898; Georgia White, "Diary," June 15, 1898, AHL.

13. Adney, *Klondike Stampede*, pp. 110, 113.

14. *Dyea Trail*, Apr. 9, 1898.

15. Adney, *Klondike Stampede*, pp. 113, 114.

16. J.W. (Will) Patterson diary, Apr. 22, 1898, in KGRNHP Collection.

17. Price, *From Euston to Klondike*, p. 86.

18. Robert B. Medill, *Klondike Diary: True Diary Kept by Robert B. Medill on his Trip to the Klondike 1897-1898* (Portland, 1949), pp. 40-42; Black, *My Ninety Years*, p. 22.

19. *Seattle Post-Intelligencer*, Oct. 13, 1897; Adney, *Klondike Stampede*, p. 116.

20. Ella Lung Martinsen, *Black Sand and Gold* (Portland, 1967), 22.

21. David Neufeld observations, March, 1991.

22. Adney, *Klondike Stampede*, 126.

23. Adney, *Klondike Stampede*, p. 116.

24. Adney, *Klondike Stampede*, p. 119.

25. Schwatka, "Military Reconnoissance in Alaska," p. 296.

26. Martinsen, *Black Sand and Gold*, p. 36.

27. Black, *My Ninety Years*, pp. 29-30.

28. Schwatka, "Military Reconnoissance in Alaska," p. 299.

The Coastal Tlingit: Trading Trails to the Interior

1. Aurel Krause, *The Tlingit Indians* (Seattle, 1956), pp. 66, 68. Aurel Krause and his brother, Arthur, were ethnographers from Germany.

2. Krause, *Tlingit Indians*, pp. 120-122. Beth Laura O'Leary, *Salmon and Storage: Southern Tutchone Use of an Abundant Resource, Occasional Papers in Archaeology No. 3* (Whitehorse, 1992) provides a comprehensive view of the use of salmon by an interior First Nation, highlighting the social and economic variables affected by the use of this resource and their inter-related dependence on other sources of food. A description of the 1880s eulachon fishery is in *The Alaskan* (Sitka), June 5, 1886.

3. Krause, *Tlingit Indians*, p. 85 describes villages from his trip in 1881-82.

4. Peter Nabokov and Robert Easton, *Native American Architecture* (New York, 1989), p. 263.

5. Wallace Olson, *The Tlingit; An Introduction to their Culture and History* (Auke Bay, 1991), pp. 60-61, and George Thornton Emmons, *The Tlingit Indians* (Vancouver, 1991), pp. 22-24.

6. The Tlingit clan system has received a great deal of attention. A basic primer is Olson, *The Tlingit*, pp. 24, 32-35 while a more detailed work is Sergei Kan, *Symbolic Immortality; The Tlingit Potlatch of the Nineteenth Century* (Washington, 1989). Emmons, *Tlingit Indians*, Chapter 2 provides 19th century observations.

ABBREVIATIONS

AHL: *Alaska Historical Library, Juneau*

AMHA: *Anchorage Museum of History and Art*

AMNH: *American Museum of Natural History*

ASA: *Alaska State Archives*

CMC: *Canadian Museum of Civilization*

CT: *Chilkoot Trail*

DCH: *Department of Canadian Heritage*

FN: *First Nations*

HSR: *Historic Structure Report*

KGRNHP: *Klondike Gold Rush National Historical Park*

NA: *U.S. National Archives*

NAC: *National Archives of Canada*

NWMP: *North-West Mounted Police*

PABC: *Provincial Archives of British Columbia*

RCMP: *Royal Canadian Mounted Police*

RG: *Record Group*

UAF: *University of Alaska, Fairbanks*

USGS: *U.S. Geological Survey*

UWL: *University of Washington Libraries*

VPL: *Vancouver Public Library*

YA: *Yukon Archives*

7. Krause, *Tlingit Indians*, p. 127.

8. Olson, *The Tlingit*, pp. 34-36, 41.

9. Elizabeth Nyman and Jeff Leer, *The Legacy of a Taku River Tlingit Clan* (Whitehorse/Fairbanks, 1993) is a powerful personal memoir of a Tlingit woman's life and cultural heritage in this area.

10. A detailed description and maps of this route are part of Yukon Historical & Museums Association, *The Kohklux Map* (Whitehorse, 1995). A variety of different routes were once taken over the coastal mountains. These are described in Catharine McClellan, *My Old People Say; An Ethnographic Survey of Southern Yukon Territory* (Ottawa, 1975), pp. 505-507 and Emmons, *Tlingit Indians*, p. 55.

11. McClellan, *My Old People Say*, p. 505.

12. Emmons, *Tlingit Indians*, p. 55.

13. Krause, *Tlingit Indians*, pp. 134-135. McClellan, *Old People*, p. 504 suggests the ritual prohibition against washing was a magical preventative against melting snow and avalanches.

14. Emmons, *Tlingit Indians*, p. 55 and Krause, *Tlingit Indians*, p. 136 note the trail and camp signs while McClellan, *My Old People Say*, pp. 505, 508, 512 describes the camp sites and trading protocols.

15. McClellan, *My Old People Say*, pp. 506-507.

16. The material on Russian activity is from Lydia Black, "The Story of Russian America," in William W. Fitzhugh and Aron Crowell, ed., *Crossroads of Continents; Cultures of Siberia and Alaska* (Washington, 1988), pp. 70-82, while the Hudson's Bay Company perspective comes from Harold A. Innis, *The Fur Trade in Canada* (Toronto, revised, 1956), chapter 10; and Robert Galois and Arthur J. Ray, "The Fur Trade in the Cordillera, to 1857" (Plate 19) in R. Louis Gentilcore, ed., *Historical Atlas of Canada; Vol. II, The Land Transformed 1800-1891* (Toronto, 1993). Theodore J. Karamanski, *Fur Trade and Exploration; Opening the Far Northwest 1821-1852* (Norman, Oklahoma, 1983) provides an explorer's and trader's perspectives on this period. Julie Cruikshank's *Dan Dha Ts'edenintth'e / Reading Voices; Oral and Written Interpretations of the Yukon's Past* (Vancouver, 1991), chapter 5 provides an important framework for understanding the character of the fur trade in the Yukon.

17. Karamanski, *Fur Trade* pp. 29-30 notes the decline in the sea otter trade and the rise in demand for mainland furs. James Gibson, "The Russian Fur Trade" in C.M. Judd and Arthur J. Ray, ed., *Old Trails and New Directions* (Toronto, 1980) provides detail on the reduction of the Russian sea otter catch in the early 19th century.

18. W.T. Easterbrook and Hugh G.J. Aitken, *Canadian Economic History* (Toronto, 1956), pp. 324-334 describes these developments along the Pacific coast in more detail. Also see Karamanski, *Fur Trade*, pp. 80-81.

19. *Alaska Times* (Sitka), June 11, 1869; and Krause, *Tlingit Indians*, p. 134.

20. The HBC's experience during the *Dryad* affair of 1833 illustrates how European factions fell back upon the Tlingit to reinforce their own positions. cf. Karamanski, *Fur Trade*, pp. 112-117 for more details.

21. This account is based on Karamanski, *Fur Trade*, pp. 236, 268-269; McClellan, *My Old People Say*, p. 503ff; Emmons, *Tlingit Indians*, 39; and YHMA, *Kohklux Map*, p. 9. Campbell's letter of 18 Oct., 1851 from the HBC Archives is reproduced in Cruikshank, *Reading Voices*, p. 86. Innis, *Fur Trade in Canada*, pp. 323-324.

22. Charlotte Willard, *Life in Alaska: Letters of Mrs. E. Willard* (Philadelphia, 1884), letter of Feb. 17, 1882, p. 168; Krause, *Tlingit Indians*, p. 134.

23. Karamanski, *Fur Trade*, pp. 188-91 reports on Campbell's near-fatal experience with the Pelly Indians during his first travels in their country in 1843.

24. Krause, *Tlingit Indians*, p. 132, and McClellan, *My Old People Say*, p. 505 describe the various goods added to the trade. Campbell's observation is in Karamanski, *Fur Trade*, pp. 268-270.

25. McGill University Archives, MG1022, C.82 #59, George Dawson, "Private Diaries - 1887," Vol. II, Sept. 23, 1887.

26. Morris Zaslow, *The Opening of the Canadian North 1870-1914* (Toronto, 1971), p. 59 notes Fort Reliance; William. A. Redmond, "Down the Yukon," Yukon Archives PAM 1891-7, 617 also notes the still tentative nature of interior fur trade out to the coast in 1887.

27. Samuel Alexander White quoted in Hubbard MA Thesis, "The Klondike in Literature 1898-1930" (selected photocopies in Parks Canada research files).

28. Charles M. Taylor, *Touring Alaska and the Yellowstone* (Philadelphia, 1901), p. 191.

29. Julia McNair Wright, *Among the Alaskans* (Philadelphia, 1883), pp. 21, 77-78.

30. Bishop Bompas, Yukon correspondance, Church Missionary Society files.

31. Wright, *Among the Alaskans*, p. 45 and Eugene McElwaire, *The Truth about Alaska: The Golden Land of the Midnight Sun* (n.p., 1901), p. 150 for another example.

32. Wright, *Among the Alaskans*, pp. 58, 266-277, 279.

33. Ivan Petroff, footnote to William A. Redmond, "Down the Yukon," p. 628.

34. Willard, *Life in Alaska*, letter of Feb. 17, 1882, p. 169.

35. General background on the local salmon canning industry comes from a brief description in Ted C. Hinckley, ed., "The Canoe Rocks; We do not know what will become of us," *Western Historical Quarterly* 1 (July 1970), p. 271ff; *Juneau City Mining Record*, Apr. 18, 1888.

36. This account is based on Hinckley, "The Canoe Rocks."

37. This material comes from David Neufeld, "'An Unregulated Corner of the Country'; Establishing Order in the Upper Yukon Basin, 1873-1896" (Parks Canada/Yukon District research mss, 1990) and William Ogilvie's *Early Days On the Yukon and The Story of its Gold Finds* (Ottawa, 1913), pp. 86-96. Michael Gates, *Gold at Fortymile Creek; Early Days in the Yukon* (Vancouver, 1994) is another good source on mining in the Yukon in this early period.

38. Dawson, "Private Diaries - 1887."

39. Capt. L.A. Beardslee, "Operations of the Jamestown in Connection with the Indian Tribes of Southeast Alaska," in Exec. Doc. 71, 47th Congress, 1st Session, Vol. 4, 1882, pp. 59-74 summarizes these events from the perspective of the U.S. government. Beardslee's personal and highly informal account of the events was published as "Chilcat and Chilcoot," *Forest and Stream*, Nov. 25, 1880, p. 325.

40. Beardslee, "Operations of the Jamestown."

41. *The Alaskan*, June 5, 1886 for breakdown of packers. *Alaska Free Press*, May 14, 1887 notes two white packers being turned away by the Chilkoots.

42. A sample outfit is described in *Alaska Searchlight*, Jan. 21, 1895. Also see *The Alaskan*, June 5, 1886.

43. *The Alaskan*, June 5 and 12, 1886.

44. 1886 figures from *The Alaskan*, May 29, 1886; 1887 figures from *The Alaska Free Press*, May 14, 1887.

45. Letter of May 7, 1886 in *The Alaskan*, May 29, 1886.

46. Alaska Boundary Tribunal files reproduced in Carcross-Tagish First Nation (Sheila Greer), *Skookum Stories of the Chilkoot/Dyea Trail* (Whitehorse, 1995) p. 55-56.

47. *The Alaskan*, August 21, 1897.

48. Peterson interested several Juneau investors in his project and ran it for several years. Noted in *The Alaska News*, Nov. 2, 1893, *The Alaskan*, Feb. 17, 1894 and *Alaska Searchlight*, Jan. 21 and Feb. 11, 1895.

49. *Alaska Searchlight*, Apr. 22, May 20, 1895 and July 3, 1897.

The Stampede Through the Chilkoot

1. Lyrics from *Canada's Story in Song*, Folkways Album FW3000 (New York, 1960).

2. "Gold," *Encyclopedia Brittanica* (11th edition, 1911).

Relaxing on the trail, Bennett.

3. Roy Minter, *The White Pass, Gateway to the Klondike* (Fairbanks, 1987), p. 55. Additional information available from Gates, *Gold at Fortymile Creek*.

4. Robert Spude, comp., *Chilkoot Trail*, Cooperative Park Studies Unit, Occasional Paper #26, Univ. of Alaska-Fairbanks, 1980, p. 5; Edwin Bearss, *Proposed Klondike Gold Rush National Historic Park, Historic Resource Study* (hereafter *Klondike Park Study*) (Washington, 1970), p. 47.

5. Minter, *White Pass*, pp. 69-70; Pierre Berton, *The Klondike Fever: The Life and Death of the Last Great Gold Rush* (New York, 1958), pp. 104-107.

6. For an extended discussion of this concept see Roderick Nash, *Wilderness and the American Mind* (New Haven, 1967), pp. 145-47.

7. Charles A. Bramble, *A Manual for Gold Seekers* (New York, 1897) p. 76.

8. Berton, *Klondike Fever*, pp. 211-243.

9. Starr's story comes from his autobiographical *My Adventures in the Klondike and Alaska, 1898-1900* (n.p., 1960), pp. iv, v, 1 and 2.

10. NAC, RG 18, Vol. 148 f.145-198, ltr Jan. 21, 1898.

11. *Alaska News*, Feb. 21, 1895, p. 8; May 30, 1895; *Alaska Searchlight*, Apr. 8, 1895; Apr. 15, 1895, p. 9; June 22, 1895, p. 7; J. Bernard Moore, *Skagway in Days Primeval* (New York, 1968), pp. 173-174; Deed Book, Vol. 17, pp. 10-12, Skagway Magistrate's Office.

12. Edward Dean Sullivan, *The Fabulous Wilson Mizner* (New York, 1935), 81-82.

13. Robert C. Kirk, *Twelve Months in the Klondike* (London, 1899), p. 25.

14. Norris, "A Directory of Businesses in Dyea, Alaska," in *Chilkoot Trail Historic Structure Report*, unpub. mss., 1986, in KGRNHP Coll.

15. Addison Mizner, *The Many Mizners* (New York, 1932), 95.

16. Norris, "DKT Co. Wharf Site," p. 1, in *CTHSR*.

17. Fred W. Hart reminiscence, PABC. *Dyea Trail*, January 12, 1898, p. 1 describes his construction activity.

18. Kirk, *Twelve Months in the Klondike*, 43.

19. Norris, "Townsite of Dyea," p. 1, in *CTHSR*.

20. Harry Suydam, "Boom Town," *Alaska Sportsman* 8 (April, 1942), 12.

21. *Dyea Trail*, Jan. 12, 1898, p. 1.

22. *Dyea Trail*, Feb. 11 and May 14, 1898.

23. William Schooley ltr., Dec. 22, 1897, KGRNHP Coll.

24. Berton, *Klondike Fever*, p. 245.

25. Martinsen, *Black Sand and Gold*, 384.

26. Martinsen, *Black Sand and Gold*, 384.

27. "Record of Deeds," Vol. 1, U.S. Commissioner's Office, Dyea," pp. 24-27, 33, 37-38, 42, 50, 182, in Skagway Magistrate's Office.

28. "Record of Deeds," Vol. 1, pp. 89, 124-128, 175, 208, 250-251.

29. *Dyea Trail*, April 16, 1898, pp. 3, 4.

30. "Record of Deeds," Vol. 1, pp. 44, 222, 257-258, 270, 288, 301.

31. *Dyea Trail*, May 7, 1898, p. 1.

32. Arthur C. Spencer, *The Juneau Gold Belt, Alaska*, USGS Bulletin 287 (Washington, 1906), pp. 13-14, 25; Alfred Hulse Brooks, *Preliminary Report on the Ketchikan Mining District, Alaska*, USGS Professional Paper 1 (Washington, 1902), p. 17.

33. Minter, *White Pass*, pp. 74-75; Berton, *Klondike Fever*, pp. 148-149.

34. Berton, *Klondike Fever*, p. 158; NPS, *Final Environmental Statement, KGRNHP*, 1974, p. 26.

35. Minter, pp. 106-09; Berton, pp. 161-65; Bearss, pp. 182-83.

36. Minter, pp. 200-14; Berton, pp. 333-61; Bearss, pp. 185-92.

37. Berton, pp. 162, 229, 257, 262.

38. Berton, pp. 275-76.

39. NAC, RG 18 Vol. 139 f.442-497, letter of Nov. 15, 1897.

40. Louie May diary, in Mss. 13, Box 7, f.1, AHL.

41. Diary entries have been selected and edited from Kolloon, "Crossing the Chilcoot Pass," AHL. The diary was kept in Norwegian and later translated by her daughter.

42. Mrs Lucy Wren, "Chilkoot Trail Oral History Project" from Carcross-Tagish First Nation, *Skookum Stories*, pp. 74-76.

43. *Dyea Trail*, Apr. 9, 1898.

44. *New York Times*, Apr. 10, 1898, June 13, 1898; Martinsen, *Black Sand and Gold*, pp. 376-79. The number of tramway workmen has been estimated as 17, 19 and 23, but published lists of the dead inexplicably indicate that only five were involved. Carl Lokke, *Klondike Saga* (Minneapolis, 1965), pp. 62-63; Robert F. Graham, "Diary," pp. 5-6, KGRNHP Coll.; Samuel B. Steele, *Forty Years in Canada* (London, 1935), p. 307; *Dyea Press*, April 6, 1898.

45. Bearss, *Klondike Park Study*, pp. 116-118.

46. Paul F. Mizony, "Gold Rush; A Boy's Impression of the Stampede into the Klondike During the Days of 1898," p. 7, AHL.

47. *Dyea Press*, Apr. 6, 1898; William R. Hunt, *North of 53* (New York, 1974), p. 49.

48. Bearss, *Klondike Park Study*, pl. 73; *Dyea Trail*, Apr. 9, 1898.

49. Norwegian American Historical Association, *Norwegian-American Studies and Records*, (Northfield, Minn., 1950), p. 136.

50. Harley E. Tuck, *Klondike Diary 1898-1899* (Monroe, Wash., 1974), p. 7; John J. Hjelsing, "My Trip to the Gold Fields of the Klondike," unpub. mss., p. 8, in KGRNHP Coll.

51. Spude, *Chilkoot Trail*, pp. 181-187; Dave Clabaugh, unpub. mss., 1979, in "Tragedies" file, KGRNHP Coll.

52. The following accounts recorded gold rush slide activity: Harvey Condon, [Letters to his wife and family], p. 9, in KGRNHP Coll.; Archie Satterfield, *Chilkoot Pass, the Most Famous Pass in the North* (Anchorage, 1978), p. 136; Esther Lyons, "An American Girl's Trip to the Klondike," *Leslie's Weekly*, January 13, 1898, p. 21; Mizony, "Gold Rush," p. 7; Moore, *Skagway in Days Primeval*, p. 45; Herbert L. Heller, ed., *Sourdough Sagas* (Sausalito, 1967), p. 79; Price, *From Euston to Klondike*, p. 84; White, "Diary," p. 3; Park Beatty, "Alaska Diary, 1898," May 2, 1898, in KGRNHP Coll.; Bearss, *Klondike Park Study*, pp. 114-115; *Victoria Colonist*, Dec. 22, 1898, p. 2.

53. *Dyea Trail*, April 9, 1898; "Snowslide on Chilcoot Pass: On-the-Spot Accounts," *Alaska Sportsman* 28 (Sept., 1962), p. 40.

54. Deed book, Skagway Magistrate's Office, Vol. 5, p. 217; Minter, *White Pass*, p. 93; *Engineering and Mining Journal*, Dec. 11, 1897.

55. *Alaska Mining Record*, Dec. 8, 1897; *New York Times*, Dec. 28, 1897; Spude, *Chilkoot Trail*, p. 198.

56. Deed book, Vol. 5, p. 334, in Skagway Magistrate's Office.

57. William B. Haskell, *Two Years in the Alaskan and Klondike Gold Fields* (Hartford, 1898), pp. 474-475.

58. Adney, *The Klondike Stampede*, pp. 115, 119.

59. Scott, "Some Experiences in the Chilkoot Pass," pp. 329-338.

60. Additional information on Orr & Tukey is available from Margaret Carter, "Orr & Tukey Co. Ltd.," Item #52, *SIA Study Tour of the Yukon and Alaska*, Society for Industrial Archeology, 1990.

61. Many stampeders misspelled the geographic names along the trail corridor. "Chilkoot" and "Lindeman" were two common victims.

62. Scott, "Some Experiences in the Chilkoot Pass," p. 335.

63. NAC, MG30, D46, Florence Hartshorn reminiscences, "Along the Gold Rush Trail."

64. Ward Hall, "My First Trip to Alaska in 1899," KGRNHP Coll.

65. Price, *From Euston to Klondike*, pp. 94-95.

66. Lulu Alice Craig, *Glimpses of Sunshine and Shade in the Far North* (Cincinnati, 1900), 16.

67. Haskell, *Two Years in the Klondike*, pp. 80-82.

68. Price, *From Euston to Klondike*, pp. 101-103.

69. Beak Associates Consulting Ltd., *A Natural Resource Inventory and Analysis of the Proposed Chilkoot Trail National Historic Park*, 1986, pp. 4-10 and ecosite maps.

70. James S. Easby-Smith, "The Real Klondike," *The Cosmopolitan* 24 (Jan., 1898) and Adney, *The Klondike Stampede*, pp. 118-119.

71. More information on miners' meetings is available in Thomas Stone's two articles, "The Mounties as Vigilantes: Perceptions of Community and the Transformation of Law in the Yukon, 1885-1897," *Law & Society Review* 14 (Fall, 1979) and "Flux and Authority in a Subarctic Society: the Yukon Miners in the Nineteenth Century," *Ethnohistory* 30 (1983).

72. Scarth report on trip to Fort Constantine, June 17, 1897 in NAC, RG 18 Vol. 135 f.1897-211.

73. NWMP Report for 1898, p. 35. Flowers, Smith & Co. activities are described in Robert E. King, "Boats on a Mountain," *Alaska Magazine* 48 (Sept. 1982) and Norris, "Knockdown Boats," *CTHSR*.

74. Clarence L. Andrews Coll., at UAF, noted in Spude, *Chilkoot Trail*, p. 194. Smith subsequently went on to run a hotel at Canyon City and may have been involved in a toll bridge nearby. Flowers apparently returned to his native Seattle. Norris, "Knockdown Boats," *CTHSR*.

75. NAC, RG 18, Vol. 161, f.93-99.

76. Edited excerpts from Tuck, *Klondike Diary*, pp. 11, 13-14, 16, 22, 25.

77. Leon Boillot, *Aux Mines d'or du Klondike; du lac Bennett à Dawson City* (Paris, 1899), p. 60.

78. *Dyea Trail*, Aug. 1898, p. 15.

79. William E. Patterson diary, KGRNHP Collection.

80. Norris, "A Directory of Businesses in Dyea, Alaska," in *CTHSR*, KGRNHP Collection; *Douglas Island News*, Apr. 3, 1901, May 15, 1901, June 5, 1901, June 12, 1901; *Skagway Alaskan*, Aug. 29, 1903; Bob DeArmond to Frank Norris, Oct. 30, 1986; Willette P. Janes to Karl Gurcke, Sept. 18, 1992.

81. R.M. Dickey, June 10 letter in *The Westminster*, July 16, 1898, p. 72.

82. Tuck, *Klondike Diary*, pp. 18, 20-23, 25.

83. Aurel and Arthur Krause, *Journey to the Tlingits* (Haines, 1981), p. 63 describes the forest at Lindeman in May, 1882 while Haskell, *Two Years in the Klondike*, p. 93 provides a good description of the forest profile from Deep Lake to Lindeman in the mid-1890s. Esther Lyons, "An American Girl's Trip to the Klondike", p. 23 notes the state of the Lindeman site in 1897. The Kerry Canadian sawmill is noted in Almon Kerry, *Sixty Years of Logging and*

Autobiography of Almon Aaron Kerry (McMinnville, Ore., 1962) p. 21. Other sources on Chilkoot forests include Omar Maris, *Sketches from Alaska* (Chicago, 1897) p. 25; *Alaska Searchlight*, May 15, 1897; Adney, *Klondike Stampede*, pp. 116, 120; and Beak, *Natural Resource Inventory*, pp. 4-28, 4-35, 4-47.

84. Haskell, *Two Years in the Klondike*, p. 93.

85. Tuck, *Klondike Diary*, pp. 69-70. Tuck was mistaken regarding the railroad; the WP&YR did not reach the summit of White Pass until February 1899.

86. NAC, RG 18 Vol. 161, f.93-99; RG 18, Vol. 194 f.609-00; and NWMP Report for 1900, p. 15.

87. Price, *From Euston to Klondike*, pp. 107-111.

88. Adney, *The Klondike Stampede*, p. 110.

89. Adney, *The Klondike Stampede*, pp. 120-121.

90. Starr, *My Adventures*, pp. 10-16.

91. NAC, RG 18 A1 Vol. 154, f.445-98, Periodic Reports-Tagish District for May, 1898 (hereafter Tagish Reports).

92. Arthur T. Walden, *A Dog-Puncher on the Yukon* (Montreal, 1928), p. 196.

93. Wells, *Magnificence and Misery*, pp. 43-47 describes the Rudolph mill at Bennett. Sawmills are visible in photos of both Lindeman and Bennett during this period. Dr. E.O. Crewe, *Gold Fields of the Yukon and How to Get There* (Chicago, 1897), p. 28.

94. Josiah Edward Spurr, *Through the Yukon Gold Diggings; A Narrative of Personal Travel* (Boston, 1900), pp. 69-70.

95. Tagish Report for July, 1898. Price, *From Euston to Klondike* describes the rapids and evidence of scow wrecks on this creek, pp. 116-118.

96. Price, *From Euston to Klondike*, p. 113; Tagish Reports for May and June, 1898; and Canada, Sessional Papers, No. 15, North-West Mounted Police Reports for 1899, pt. II, Yukon Territory, p. 14.

Boom Towns & the Railway

1. Taylor, *Touring Alaska* pp 209-210, 219-220.

2. NAC, RG 18 A1 Vol. 146 f.89-98 and Vol. 154 f.445-98.

3. NAC, Tagish Reports; *Skagway News*, Oct. 15, 1897; and NAC, James A. McRae Diary, Apr. 3, 1898.

4. Hartshorn reminiscences.

5. Boillot, *Aux Mines d'or du Klondike*, pp. 54, 56-57. St. Crepin was a Christian missionary who worked as a shoemaker to meet people and convert them, thus saving their souls. The author's original french "savetier" has a double meaning of either a cobbler who fixes boots too worn to be worth repairing (this is quite appropriate to the White Pass Trail!) or a bungler. Boillot appears to be playing on both senses of the word.

6. Boillot, *Aux Mines d'or du Klondike*, pp. 56-57.

7. James M. Sinclair, *Mission Klondike* (Vancouver, 1978), pp. 92-93.

8. Tagish Report for April, 1898. Noted in Wells, *Magnificence and Misery*, pp. 43-47.

9. Quote from Lyons, "An American Girl's Trip to the Klondike," Jan. 20, 1898. Canada, Houses of Parliament, Sessional Paper #15, NWMP Report for 1898, p. 50.

10. NAC, Sifton Papers MG27 D15 Yukon Correspondence 1897-1900 Vol. 25, Dec. 15, 1897 and Apr. 27, 1898; Tagish Reports for May, 1898.

11. *Skagway Alaskan*, Apr. 15, 1899 and *Bennett Sun*, Jan. 20, 1900. Photo PA16164, at NAC, shows a pack train filling the central square in front of the Klondike Hotel in April or May, 1898.

12. Henry C. Cryder diary, Apr. 10, 1898, at New York Historical Society; Vancouver Public Library #1270; PABC HP-60270.

13. PABC HP-60270; *Bennett Sun*, Dec. 9, 1899. Information on Rice from *Polk's Alaska-Yukon Directory, 1901*; *Bennett Sun*, May 31, 1899; and Robert L.S. Spude, *Skagway, District of Alaska, 1884-1912; Building the Gateway to the Klondike* (Fairbanks, 1983), p. 52.

14. Canada, Houses of Parliament 1898, Sessional Paper #15, Report of the Commissioner of the NWMP for 1897, p. 147. Jan., 1898 description from NAC, RG 18, Series A1, Vol. 154 f.445-98 Periodic Reports-Tagish District, Apr., 1898.

15. W.R. Rant, June 4, 1898, in Records of the Magistrates Court, Bennett and Atlin, B.C., Mar. 14, 1898 to June 2, 1900.

16. NAC, RG 18 Vol. 146 f.78-98 and Series A1, Vol. 154 f.445-98 Periodic Reports Tagish District June 10, 1898. The tramway can be seen in historic photos of Bennett CT 14.1-64 (YA 4450), May, 1898 and tracks noted in David Neufeld's 1991 field survey of Bennett. Louie May diary, Apr. 4, 1898.

17. NAC, RG 18 A1, Vol. 154 f.445-98 Periodic Reports Tagish District May 6, 1898. The spread of the town from the trail to the lake noted in Margaret Carter, "St. Andrew's Presbyterian Church, Bennett, B.C.," *Canadian Parks Service* #26, pp. 168, 171. Population figure from NAC, Sifton Papers, MG 27 D15 Yukon Corres-pondence 1897-1900 Vol. 25 Apr. 27, 1898. Inge Kolloen, "Crossing the Chilcoot Pass," May, 1898. NAC, George Coffey diary, MG29 C46, May 21, 1898.

18. Sinclair, *Mission Klondike*, pp. 51-52; Carter, "St. Andrew's Presbyterian Church," pp. 168, 171.

19. The first meeting was held on either Jan. 9th or 10th, 1898. NAC RG 18 Vol. 146 f.78-98. Other meetings noted in NAC mf 2151, NWMP-Yukon Records, Daily Journal-Lake Bennett, Jan. 23 and Feb. 2 and 3, 1898. Rant's arrival noted Feb. 9 in the same journal. Information on Rant courtesy of Ann ten Cate, Reference Archivist, B.C. Archives from *Seattle Post Intelligencer*, Feb. 6, 1898, and *Victoria Colonist*, Oct. 5, 1898 and Jan. 22, 1930. McLeod and Sullivan are noted in Canada, Sessional Paper #15, NWMP Report for 1898,

Lily Tugwell (left) and a friend enjoy a fine spring day on the boardwalk between Log Cabin Hotel and the train station (visible in background), about 1905.

pp. 35, 41 and PABC, Map CM/C886, "Townsite of Bennett City," June 17, 1898.

20. NAC, RG 18 Vol. 2183 RCMP 1897 Commissioner's Office pt. 3, Dec. 21, 1897. Commissioner of the Yukon James Walsh added his own bitter assessment of the Mounties' early Yukon performance in a letter to Clifford Sifton of Dec. 10, 1897; "[The police] have been educated only in idleness. They are the laughing stock of the people all along the trail even to our dog drivers and Indian boatmen. They are thoroughly incapable of taking care of themselves let alone being of assistance to anybody else..." in NAC, MG27 II D15 Sifton papers, Yukon Correspondence 1897-1900 (Vol. 295). Walsh was later recalled for irregularities in his administration of the territory.

21. Deficiences in clothing are noted in NAC, Tagish Reports for June, July, and Sept., 1898; RG 18 Vol. 2183 RCMP 1897 Commissioner's Office pt. 3, Nov. 20, 1897; RG 18 Vol. 2183 RCMP 1898 Commissioner's Office, Jan. 29, 1898.

22. NAC, RG 18 Vol. 139 f.442-97, Dec. 1, 1897; Tagish Report for Sept., Oct. 31, 1898; and NWMP Report for 1898, Sessional Papers #15, p. 35.

23. NAC, RG 18 Vol. 156 f.552-98, Dec. 17, 1897; RG 18 Vol. 173 f.488-99; RG 18 Vol. 162, f.119-99, May 26, 1899; and Tagish Report for July, 31 July 1898.

24. NWMP Report for 1898, Sessional Paper #15, p. 35; NAC, RG 18 Vol. 152 f.296-98, Oct. 23, 1898; and Tagish Report for Sept., 1898.

25. Upper Yukon vessels noted in NAC MG27 II D15 Sifton Papers-Yukon Correspondence, Mar. 6, 1898 and Tagish Reports for May and June, 1898. BL&KN is noted in Tagish Report for June, 1898 and *Bennett Sun*, Aug. 5, 1899. Additional material on the BL&KN is in *Victoria Colonist*, July 9, 1898 and A.A. Barrett & R.W. Liscombe, *Francis Rattenbury and British Columbia: Architecture and Challenge in the Imperial Age* (Vancouver, 1983), pp. 62-91. Shipping noted in NAC RG 18 Vol. 171, f.391-99.

26. Minter, *White Pass*, pp. 170, 180. Minter's work is the best source for the construction of the WP&YR railway. Sources on Log Cabin include NAC RG 18 A1 Vol. 161 f.93-99, the monthly reports from the Tagish NWMP post; NAC, *Diary of a trip to the Yukon* by John Alexander McDougall.

27. Minter, *White Pass*, pp. 95-101; 150-152.

28. Minter, *White Pass*, pp. 189, 219-221.

29. Minter, *White Pass*, pp. 228-230, 243-245, 256-257.

30. Minter, *White Pass*, pp. 266-269.

31. The railway hospital is well described in Yukon Archives, WP&YR Records, Hospital, while Sinclair's involvement is noted in B.C. Prov. Archives, John Sinclair Papers, A-1205 and A-1206 and *The Westminster*, Jan. 21, 1899, p. 81.

32. David Neufeld, *Chilkoot Trail; Yukon Gateway* (Whitehorse, 1993), p. 56; Bearss, *Klondike Park Study*, pp. 264-266.

33. *Dyea Trail*, July 30, 1898.

34. Bearss, *Klondike Park Study*, pp. 273-274; Spude, *Chilkoot Trail*, p. 136; Minter, *White Pass*, pp. 293-296, 303-304.

35. U.S. Census Bureau, *Twelfth Census of Population, 1900, Alaska* (RG 29, T 623), Vol. 5, Southern District, E.D. #7, pp. 1-11; Spude, *Chilkoot Trail*, p. 53; *Skagway Alaskan*, Aug. 19, 1903; Robert D. Jones, "A Municipal Farmer," *Alaska-Yukon Magazine*, Aug. 1907, p. 488.

36. *Bennett Sun*, May 31 and Aug. 5, 1899.

37. UBC Special Collections v.f. #92, Joseph L. Near papers.

38. Inga Kolloon, "Crossing the Chilcoot Pass," May 27, 1898.

39. NWMP Tagish Report for June 1898; Ltr Jan. 27, 1899 to NWMP Commissioner; Records of the Magistrates Court, Bennett and Atlin, B.C., Mar. 14, 1898 to June 2, 1900. The Mar. 15, 1898 entry in the Louie May diary (Mss. 13, Box 7 f.#1, AHL) describes the commercial packers' concern about the welfare of all animals on the trail. Also see PABC, Sinclair Papers, Feb. 27, 1900.

40. Joseph L. Near papers.

41. Taylor, *Touring Alaska and the Yellowstone*, p. 227.

42. PABC, Sinclair Papers, Feb, 1900. *Bennett Sun*, Aug. 5, Dec. 9, 1899, and Jan. 20, 1900, *Atlin Claim*, Mar. 10, 1900. More information on Sinclair, the Bennett Church, and church activities is available in Carter, "St. Andrew's Presbyterian Church."

43. *Bennett Sun*, May 31 and Dec. 9, 1899. See photos CT 14.1-44, 14.8-10, 14.8-18.

44. The post office appears in YA photo 9422. AHL Photo PCA 232-202 shows the government building under construction in Apr. or May, 1899 and the completed building in CT 14.1-26, June 1, 1899 and YA 2465 June 9, 1899. Tagish Report for Nov., 1898, *Bennett Sun*, Jan. 20, 1899, and Canada, Parliament, Sessional Paper #15, NWMP Report for 1899, pp. 34-35.

45. PABC, Sinclair Papers, undated newspaper clipping and NAC, MG29 C46 George Coffey diary, May, 1898.

46. Scharschmidt later moved to Whitehorse where he started the *Northern Star* and became the general manager of the British Yukon Navigation Co., a White Pass river subsidiary. *Skagway Alaskan*, May 10, 1899; *Bennett Sun*, July 7, 1900; and *Atlin Claim* Nov. 9, 1901.

47. Customs information from Canada, Parliament, Sessional Paper #15, NWMP Report for 1899, p. 28. Orr & Tukey information from *Bennett Sun*,

Aug. 5, 1899; *Skagway Alaskan*, May 25, 1899; and *Dawson Daily News*, Aug. 17, 1906.

48. *Bennett Sun*, Aug. 5, 1899, CT 14.2-22 and *Bennett Sun*, July 7, 1900.

49. *Bennett Sun*, May 31, 1899, Aug. 5, 1899, and *Atlin Claim*, Dec. 9, 1899.

50. *Bennett Sun*, July 7, 1900; *Atlin Claim*, June 23, 1900 and Sept. 22, 1900.

51. The Merchants Bank had not been built by June, 1898 (CT 14.1-28b) but it was in its plank house by Apr. 20, 1899 (CT 14.2-2) and still there into June, 1899 (CT 14.1-26 and CT 14.2-3). By late summer, 1899 (CT 14.1-7, CT 14.2-4, and CT 14.2-23) it was in the new log building across from the Grand Palace Hotel. The bank appears to have remained open in Bennett at least until mid-summer, 1900. *Bennett Sun*, July 7, 1900.

52. Editorial in the *Bennett Sun*, May 31, 1899.

53. PABC, Sinclair Papers, ltrs, Feb. [n.d.] and Apr. 3, 1900.

54. Taylor, *Touring Alaska and the Yellowstone*, p. 227.

55. *Bennett Sun*, May 31, 1899 and G. Blair, Personal Communication.

56. *Yukon Sun*, Apr. 17, 1900.

57. NAC C48211 shows the hotel in its new location. *Bennett Sun*, Feb. 20, 1901 describes the new place in Whitehorse.

58. Sawmill information from NAC RG 18 A1 Vol. 192 f.495-00, ltr Apr. 13, 1900. *Bennett Sun*, July 7, 1900. NAC, RG 18 A1 Vol. 192 f.495-00.

59. Hudson Stuck, *Voyages on the Yukon and its Tributaries* (New York, 1917), p. 15.

60. Winnie Atlin interview with Sheila Greer for Chilkoot Native History Project, July 12, 1991, pp. 13-14; Carcross-Tagish First Nation, *Skookum Stories of the Chilkoot/Dyea Trail*, p. 101.

61. Spude, *Skagway, District of Alaska*, pp. 42-44.

Indian camp at Dyea. Drawing by Madame Paule Crampel.

Politics & Justice

1. Lyons, "An American Girl's Trip to the Klondike," *Leslie's Weekly*, Jan. 13, 1898, pp. 21, 23.

2. Joaquin Miller, "To Chilkoot Pass, 1897;" Hubbard MA Thesis, "The Klondike in Literature 1898-1930" (selected photocopies in Parks Canada research files).

3. NAC, MG29 C46, George Coffey diary, May 20, 1898.

4. Lewis Green, *The Boundary Hunters* (Vancouver, 1982), pp. 181-182.

5. Neufeld, "An Unregulated Corner of the Country."

6. The best account of these early days comes from M.H.E. Hayne and H.W. Taylor, *The Pioneers of the Klondyke* (London, 1897); and Ken S. Coates and William R. Morrison, *Land of the Midnight Sun; A History of the Yukon* (Edmonton, 1988) pp. 72-75.

7. The various interpretations of the boundary are described in Norman Penlington, *The Alaska Boundary Dispute: A Critical Reappraisal* (Toronto, 1972).

8. J.M. Dobson, *America's Ascent: The United States becomes a Great Power, 1880-1914* (De Kalb, Ill., 1978); Penlington, *The Alaska Boundary Dispute*; and E.R. May, *American Imperialism; A Speculative Essay* (New York, 1968).

9. Dianne Newell, "Publicizing the Klondike" (Univ. of Western Ontario. M.A. thesis).

10. NA, M-802, Special Agent's Division of Dept. of Treasury 1867-1903, Alaska file, ltr. Jan. 28, 1896 and ltr. May 18, 1896.

11. NA, M-802, Special Agent's Division of Dept. of Treasury 1867-1903-Alaska file, ltr. Aug. 21, 1897; M-430, Secretary of the Interior, Ltrs Received, Aug. 19, 1897; and NAC, RG 18, Vol. 139, f.442-97, pt.2.

12. Historic Sites and Monuments Board of Canada Board Paper 1977-33, Tagish Post, Yukon.

13. NAC, RG 18, Vol. 156, f.552-98 and Vol. 2183, RCMP 1897 Comm. Office pt. 3.

14. NAC, RG 18, Vol. 139, f.442-97; RG 18, Vol. 146, f.78-98 and *Seattle Post-Intelligencer*, Jan. 25, 1898.

15. NAC, RG 18 Vol. 2183 RCMP Comm. Office pt.3 and Vol. 164 f.176-99 and Minnesota Historical Society, George Brackett Papers, ltr., Dec. 17, 1897. NAC, RG 18 Vol. 146 f.78-98. T.D. Regehr, *The Canadian Northern Railway* (Toronto, 1976) p. 66. NAC, RG 18 Vol. 2183 RCMP Comm. Office pt.3. and Vol. 156, f.552-98.

16. *Seattle Post-Intelligencer*, Jan. 25, 1898 and NAC RG 18 Vol. 164 f.176-99 and RG 18A1 Vol. 145 f.70-98, RG 18 Vol. 146 f.78-98, and map noted in Norris "Knockdown Boats," *CTHSR*; map dated Jan. 10, 1898, filed in Deed Book, Vol. 53, pp. 59, 70, 138, in Skagway Magistrate's Office; T.D. Regehr, *Canadian Northern*, p. 66. Quotation is the handwritten addenda of Clifford Sifton, Canada's Minister of the Interior.

17. NAC, RG 18 (Tagish Report for Apr., 1898), MG27 II D15 Sifton Papers, ltr of Apr. 9, 1892, and *Seattle Post-Intelligencer*, Mar. 6, 1898. NA, M-430, Secretary of the Interior, Ltrs Received Feb. 3, 1898; *Seattle Post-Intelligencer*, Mar. 7, 1898; and Edwin Bearss, *Klondike Park Study*, pp. 156-157.

18. Bearss, *Klondike Park Study*, pp. 160-161. Dept. of State letter reported in *Seattle Post-Intelligencer*, Mar. 10, 1898. Editorial in paper of Mar. 11, 1898. NAC, RG 18 Vol. 168 f.229-99.

19. This material based on John Ellis, *The Social History of the Machine Gun* (New York, 1975) and

20. NWMP Annual Report for 1898.

21. NWMP Annual Report for 1898, p. 113. Evidence of all buildings and even the flag pole is still visible at the site. NAC, RG 18 A1 Vol. 163 f.137-99. Report of Jan., 1899.

22. NAC, RG 18 A1 Vol. 159 f.29-99 and Vol. 161 f.93-99 and NWMP Report for 1898, pp. 113-114.

23. M.H.E. Hayne, *The Pioneers of the Klondike* (London, 1897).

24. Bearss, *Klondike Park Study*, p. 163; Melody Webb, *The Last Frontier; A History of the Yukon Basin of Canada and Alaska* (Albuquerque, 1985) p. 146; T.D. Regehr, *Canadian Northern*, p. 68.

25. J. Thompson, "Drawing the Line," 2386-87.

26. NAC, RG 18 Vol. 154 f.445-98, Tagish Reports for Apr. and May, RG 18 Vol. 164 f.176-99, and MG27 II D15, ltr. Apr. 20, 1898; Bearss, *Klondike Park Study*, pp. 161, 164.

27. Berton, *Klondike Fever*, pp. 26-27, 30; Allen Wright, *Prelude to Bonanza; the Discovery and Exploration of the Yukon* (Whitehorse, 1980) pp. 258-271; Coates and Morrison, *Land of the Midnight Sun*, p. 75; William R. Hunt, *Distant Justice; Policing the Alaska Frontier* (Norman, Okla., 1987), p. 69.

28. Gov. John G. Brady to Secretary of the Interior, Sept. 14, 1900, in Alaska Territorial Papers, NA Anchorage; Norris, "Officials in the Skagway/Dyea Area During the Gold Rush," 1988, KGRNHP Collection.

29. Berton, *Klondike Fever*, pp. 160-161.

30. Berton, *Klondike Fever*, pp. 261-262; Hunt, *Distant Justice*, p. 58; Bearss, *Klondike Park Study*, pp. 113-114.

31. Bearss, *Klondike Park Study*, pp. 158-159, 162.

32. Bearss, *Klondike Park Study*, pp. 164-165, 167-168, 175-76.

33. Bearss, *Klondike Park Study*, pp. 164-165; Norris, "Officials in the Skagway/Dyea Area During the Gold Rush," in KGRNHP Collection; L. J. Campbell, "Skagway, Legacy of Gold," *Alaska Geographic* 19:1 (1992), pp. 58-61.

34. William Zimmer to W.P. McBride, Collector of Customs, August 4, 1898, in Letters Received, Sitka, Vol. 13; Records of Alaska Customshouses, 1867-1939, NA Anchorage.

35. *Alaska Free Press*, Apr. 9, 1887 and Col. J.W. Kelly writing in the *St. Louis Post-Dispatch* reproduced in *Juneau City Mining Record*, Aug. 15, 1889. Emphasis added.

36. The *Alaska Free Press* regularly commented on the complications arising from the dual justice systems operating in the region, cf. Feb. 12, 1887, July 30, 1887.

37. This account is based upon the stories of Kitty Smith in Julie Cruikshank, Angela Sidney, Kitty Smith and Annie Ned, *Life Lived Like a Story* (Lincoln, Nebr., 1990) and developed in her article "Oral Traditions and Written Accounts: An Incident from the Klondike Gold Rush, *Culture* 9 (1989), pp. 25-33. NWMP reports and Justice records come from NAC, RG 18 Vol. 154 f.445-98 and RG 13 C1, Vol. 1434 f.Nantuck Bros. Permission to use Kitty Smith's stories from her granddaughter, Judy Gingell.

38. p. 3 of trial transcript, RG 13 C1, Vol. 1434 f.Nantuck Bros.

39. NAC, RG 18 Vol. 3153 f.596, Letter, Oct. 7, 1920.

40. p. 22 of trial transcript, RG 13 C1, Vol. 1434 f.Nantuck Bros.

41. Dickey, in *The Westminster*, July 16, 1898, p. 72.

The 20th Century: Tourists & First Nations

1. WP&YR, "Travels in Alaska and the Yukon Territory," 1913.

2. Spude, *Skagway, District of Alaska*, p. 41.

3. Berton, *Klondike Fever*, pp. 358-365; Spude, *Skagway, District of Alaska*, pp. 60, 62.

4. Spude, *Skagway, District of Alaska*, 65; Alaska Federation of Women's Clubs, *1936-1937 Year Book*, p. 99.

5. Ted C. Hinckley, "The Inside Passage: A Popular Gilded Age Tour," *Pacific Northwest Quarterly* 56 (Apr. 1965), pp. 69-71.

6. *Skagway Alaskan*, July 25, 1898; May 10, 1899.

7. Berton, *Klondike Fever*, p. 442; Howard Clifford, *The Skagway Story* (Anchorage, 1975), pp. 54-63; *Skaguay Alaskan* 6 (June-July 1983); *Skagway Alaskan*, June 18, 1915.

8. Frank Norris, *Gawking at the Midnight Sun; the Tourist in Early Alaska*, Alaska Historical Commission Studies in History #170 (Anchorage, 1985), p. 33; White Pass and Yukon Route, "A Tour Through the Land of Nightless Days," c. 1906; *Skagway Alaskan*, June 23, 1908; July 20, 1908.

9. WP&YR, "A Handbook of Vacation Trips in Alaska, Atlin and the Yukon on the White Pass and Yukon Route," 1928; Martin Itjen, *The Story of the Tour on the Skagway, Alaska, Street-Car* (Skagway, 1938), p. 73.

10. Cy Martin, *Gold Rush Narrow Gauge* (Corona del Mar, Calif., 1974), p. 53.

11. Martin, *Gold Rush Narrow Gauge*, pp. 54-60; Stan Cohen, *Gold Rush Gateway; Skagway and Dyea* (Missoula, Mont., 1986), pp. 104-113.

12. Susan Hackley Johnson, "When Moviemakers Look North," *Alaska Journal* 9 (Winter, 1979), pp. 13, 18-19; Norris, "Popular Images of the North in Literature and Film," *The Northern Review* 8/9 (Summer 1992), pp. 73-81; George Rapuzzi, interview with Frank Norris, Nov. 21, 1983.

13. Mary J. Barry, "Alaska Steamship Company: A Legacy of Nostalgia," in *Transportation in Alaska's Past*, Office of History and Archeology, Publication No. 30 (Anchorage, 1982), p. 287; E. Theed to WP&YR Employees, Dec. 6, 1955, in Parks Canada Collection, Whitehorse; Barbara Kalen to Frank Norris, Nov. 17, 1994; Carl Mulvihill to Frank Norris, Dec. 5, 1994.

14. Robert Spude, NPS, "Historic Use of the Chilkoot Trail," in BLM Case File AA-37758, 1984 provides an overview of trail use from the gold rush to the early 1980s.

15. O.M. Leland, *Report of Work done in 1906 on the Alaska Boundary Survey*, March 26, 1907, in Energy, Mines, and Resources (Canada), files of International Boundary Commission.

16. Norris, "Matthews Cabin" and "Dyea Cemetery," both in *CTHSR*; *North Wind*, Aug. 14, 1975; Mark Lee, interview with Frank Norris, Nov. 18, 1983.

17. UAF, Florence Clothier Collection.

18. George Rapuzzi, interview with Frank Norris, Feb. 27, 1984; Spude, "Historic Use of the Chilkoot Trail," 6-8.

19. YA, Robert Storm Collection.

20. Alaska Road Commission, *Annual Report*, 1948, p. 8; Chuck and Helen Clark, interview with Frank Norris, Mar. 13, 1985; Ludwig Frolander to Ike Taylor, Sept. 2, 1948; R.J. DeLaHunt to H.B. Schultz, Sept. 29, 1952; both in Dyea Road file, RG 30, NA Anchorage.

21. Claus-M. Naske, "The Taiya Project," *BC Studies* 91-92 (Autumn and Winter 1991-92), 7-52.

22. This section is based upon various internal Parks Canada archaeological survey reports prepared by David Hems, Kevin Lunn, Sheila Greer, Byron Ebel and Peter Nieuhoff.

23. This section is based upon David Neufeld's interviews with Edna Helm, Jean Desmarais, Winnie Atlin and William Atlin. This material is supplemented with information from Catharine McClellan, *My Old People Say*. To acknowledge the elders' role as the co-authors of the narrative, none of the quotations have been indented in the following pages.

24. McClellan, *My Old People Say*, pp. 37-45.

25. Jeff Choy-Hee, Executive Director, Carcross Tagish First Nation, Personal communication, May 21, 1991.

26. McClellan, *My Old People Say*, pp. 199-201 offers another description of these berry-picking expeditions.

27. Doris McLean, personal communication, Jan. 20, 1989.

28. McClellan, *My Old People Say*, pp. 200-201. cf. Hans Peter Duerr, *Dreamtime: Concerning the Boundary between Wilderness and Civilization* (New York, 1985), p. 45.

29. Richard K. Nelson, *Make Prayers to Raven: A Koyukon View of the Northern Forest* (Chicago, 1983), p. 122.

30. McClellan, *My Old People Say*, pp. 154-157.

31. McClellan, *My Old People Say*, p. 168.

32. McClellan, *My Old People Say*, p. 147 and Nelson, *Make Prayers to Raven*, p. 134.

33. McClellan, *My Old People Say*, pp. 260-264.

34. Bearss, *Klondike Park Study*, pp. 281, 283-284.

35. Herbert Maier to Director NPS, Apr. 5, 1960, National Register Files, NPS Anchorage; National Survey of Historic Sites and Buildings, *Alaska History, 1741-1910* (Washington, 1961), a, foreword, pp. 172-178, 220.

36. Skagway City Ordinance No. 72-54; *Southeast Alaska Empire*, Oct. 11, 1972, 3; John McDermott to Rodger Pegues, Oct. 27, 1973; Robert Howe to ARD/PNRO, Feb. 15, 1974; both in Correspondence File, KGRNHP Administrative History Coll., NPS Anchorage.

37. Mike Leach to A. Earl Plourde, May 23, 1961; Leach to Plourde, July 25, 1961, both in "Chilkoot Trail History Construction" folder, KGRNHP Coll.; C.W. Pfeiffer to Dick White, June 7, 1961; Youth & Adult Authority to T.D. Gregg, June 9, 1961, both in "Chilkoot Trail Reading Files" folder, Series 136, RG 06, ASA; James R. Lotz, "The Chilkoot Trail To-Day, Dyea to Bennett" (unpub. mss., DIAND, Oct. 1963), p. 1.

38. NPS, *Skagway; A Study of Alternatives* (San Francisco, Mar. 1969), pp. 4, 33-41; George M. Hartzog to Walter Hickel, Dec. 7, 1967, in File 882, Series 41, RG 01, ASA; Theodor Swem, interview by Frank Norris, Nov. 18, 1994.

39. Lake Lindeman "Visitors Book" for 1968, in Parks Canada files, Whitehorse; Don McCune to John A. Rutter, May 13, 1971, in KGRNHP Administrative History files, NPS Anchorage; "Chilkoot Trail Ranger Report," 1973, in Box 1, RG 70, KGRNHP Archives.

40. NPS, *Statement for Interpretation, KGRNHP*, 1994.

41. Mahle Land Claim Files, Lands Office, NPS Anchorage.

42. D. Neufeld, "White Pass & Yukon is back on the track," *SIA Newsletter* 17 (Winter, 1988), p. 3.

43. *Lynn Canal News*, May 21, 1981, p. 6.

Illustrations

All images have been scanned and enhanced for publication.

Front pages

Cover. Climb to the summit
UWL/Special Coll. Division, Child Coll. #11

Dedication. Mrs. Patsy Henderson and grandchildren
CMC, J851

Copyright. Packing up the Chilkoot Pass
YA/MacBride Museum, 3626

Preface. On summit with paddles
YA/MacBride Museum, 3584

Facing contents. Maps of North America, northwest coast and coastal trails
Lost Moose/Peter Long

Contents. Packing over the rocks
AMHA, B70.22.44

Chilkoot: The Mountain Trail

1. Walking along the ledge
D. Neufeld

2. Panorama at the summit
DCH

4. At the foot of the Golden Stairs
YA/Jacobsen Coll., 85/82 #15

5. Indian Days at Tagish
D. Neufeld

The Land

6. Eagle and gulls
KLGO/Richard Frear, D-1970 DV-2 1873

7. Ecozones
DCH

8. Sketch map, Cassiar District
PABC/Map Coll., Neg. #284254

9. Coming into Skagway
Dedman's Photo Shop, 11B

10. Forty canoes at Dyea
KLGO, DV-23/1435

11. Carcross-Tagish family
AHL/Charles H. Metcalf, PCA 34-33

11. Campsite in the rainforest
Glenbow Archives/B.W. Kilburn, Littleton, H.H., NH-876-2

12. Wagon going up trail
DCH/Sinclair

13. Rainforest hikers
D. Neufeld

A fine day on the Chilkoot, during the Klondike gold rush.

14. High alpine view
DCH

15. Modern-day hiker near summit
D. Neufeld

16. Summit in the winter
UWL/Special Coll. Division, Hegg #222

17. High alpine trees
D. Neufeld

18. View of Lindeman Lake
AMHA/Humble Coll., B72.46.63

19. Sledding across Lindeman Lake
D. Neufeld

20. View to Bennett
D. Neufeld

21. Moose
DCH

21. Wild flowers
Dedman's Photo Shop, 24G

The Coastal Tlingit: Trading Trails to the Interior

22. Chilkat potlatch dancers
AMHA/Minnesota Historical Society Coll., Winter and Pond, B 70.73.18

24. House at Klukwan
AMHA/H.I. Smith, 46163

24. Eulachon harvest
AMNH, 13989

25. Graveyard at Klukwan
AMNH/H.I. Smith, 46168

25. Interior trade routes
Lost Moose/Peter Long

26. Tlingit family, Dyea
AHL/Klondike Gold Rush Coll., PCA 232-80

26. Tlingit children
AHL/Winter and Pond, PCA 87-326

27. Interior of house at Klukwan
AHL/Early Prints of Alaska, H.I. Smith, 01-2293

27. Klukwan houses
YA/MacBride Museum Coll., 3652

28. Winnie Atlin and jacket
D. Neufeld

28. Tagish youth
VPL/Cantwell, 32621

28. Houses at Tagish
AHL/Charles H. Metcalf, PCA 34-68

29. Arrival of potlatch canoes
AHL/H.C. Barley, PCA 126-19

30. Chilkat packer
AMNH, 11216A

30. S.S. Beaver
PABC/Maynard, Vancouver, #115, Neg. A-11

31. Woman and two children
AMHA, B87.7.103

32. Winter camp
AHL/Winter and Pond, PCA 87-143

33. Sketch of Chilkoot Pass
Schwatka, Summer in Alaska

34. Decoration Day, 1899
YA/Vogee Coll., 103

34. Healy and Wilson's Trading Post
AHL/Klondike Gold Rush Coll., PCA 232-77

35. The Alert
AHL/Eric A. Hegg, PCA 124-26

36. Chilkat Mission map
Willard, Letters from Alaska (plus digital changes)

37. Mission at Haines, Alaska
Willard, Letters from Alaska

38. Cleaning fish
YA/MacBride Museum Coll., 3874

38. Loading the barge
YA/MacBride Museum Coll., 3727

38. Salmon cannery, Pyramid Harbor
YA/MacBride Museum Coll., 3722

39. Pulling sleds
AHL/Winter and Pond, PCA 87-651

40. Prospector
Glenbow Archives/NA-2426-10

40. Stick gambling
AHL/Winter and Pond, PCA 87-322

41. Indian "John's" map
Dawson Field Notes/NAC, GSC Field Notebook of George Mercer Dawson, 1887, Notebook 2762, RG45, vol.135 (plus digital changes)

42. Klukwan panorama
YA/H.C. Barley Coll., 4758 and 4759

44. Packers struggling up hillside
AHL/Winter and Pond, PCA 21-22

44. Chiefs Doniwak and Issac
UWL/La Roche, 2006

45. Resting on the trail
UWL/La Roche, 2035

46. Dyea street scene
AMHA, B70.22.14

47. Schwatka, Indian guide
AHL/Case and Draper, PCA 39-210

48. Packers and oxen
PABC, A-7417

The Stampede Through the Chilkoot

49. Excelsior heading north
Library of Congress, 29265 262-19412

50. Cartoon
San Francisco Examiner, July 27, 1897

51. Map of Dyea and Skaguay trails
Seattle Post-Intelligencer, no date

52. Vancouver outfitters
VPL, 9493

53. Robinson HBC invoice
NAC, MG 29 V. C42

54. Confusion on the beach at Dyea
AHL/Winter and Pond, PCA 87-661

55. Wagons unloading lighter
YA/University of Washington Coll., 1327

56. Freight yard and wharf
UWL/Special Coll. Division, Hegg #58

56. Landing among the rocks
AHL/Winter and Pond, PCA 87-658

57. Freight yard
Sheldon Museum and Cultural Center

57. Map of Dyea
National Park Service

58. Dyea panorama
UWL/Special Coll. Division, Hegg #51B

59. Pacific Hotel
YA/Atlin Historical Society Coll., 4564

60. Ross Higgins store
Trail of '98 Museum/KLGO, E.A. Hegg, 4185

60. Wagons in front of warehouse
AMHA, B72.46.131

61. Downtown Dyea
UWL/Special Coll. Division, Hegg #52

62. People in front of store
KLGO, DM 22/657

62. Tlingit canoe at Dyea
YA/Vogee Coll., 85

63. Taiya River valley
Dedman's Photo Shop, 61C

64. Eager new arrivals
DCH/Sinclair

64. Ships in Skagway harbour
DCH/Sinclair

65. Soapy Smith
DCH/Sinclair

65. Skagway City Hall
DCH/Sinclair

66. Three women in camp
Missouri Historical Society, #4598, Neg.#outside MO#89

67. Clearing a blockade
DCH/Sinclair

67. At lunch on the Yukon trail
AHL/Winter and Pond, PCA 21-17

68. Wagons and tents in canyon
AHL/P.E. Larss, 41-182

68. Map of Sheep Camp
Lost Moose/Peter Long

68. Two women hauling a sled
Huntington Library, HP-2

69. Seattle Hotel, Sheep Camp
UAF/Historical Photographs Coll., 75-178-17

69. Camping at the foot of the cliffs
AHL, PCA 21-18

70. Climb to the summit
UWL/Special Coll. Division, Child Coll. #11

71. Climber on Golden Stairs
YA/T.R. Lane Coll.

72. Digging out from avalanche
VPL

73. Removing a body
NAC/National Photography Coll., C28654

74. Tramway sketch
PABC/Cassier's Magazine, NWp/972.18 #611

75. Boats on Crater Lake
UWL/Special Coll. Division, Hegg #464

76. Sleds with sails on Crater Lake
UWL/Special Coll. Division, Hegg #95

76. Crater Lake shoreline
UAF/H. Levy Photograph Coll., 67-17-28M

77. Burro and firewood
DCH/Sinclair

77. Fallen horse on trail
McGill University/Tappan Adney Coll., Neg. #636

78. Transfer camp, Long Lake
YA/Charmin Coll., 89/64 7

78. Horses packing turkeys
YA/Faulkner Coll., 83/50 H-241

79. Cooking in the snow
PABC, 67054

79. Interior of restaurant
UWL/Special Coll. Division, Hegg #3100

80. Two women at Bennett
DCH/Sinclair

81. Panorama of Lindeman
UAF/Falcon Joslin Coll., #79-41-22SN

82. Building a boat
YA/University of Washington Coll., 1185

82. Street scene in Lindeman
YA/Frank Charman Coll., Pho 390, 89/64, #13

83. Sketch of camp site
NAC, C84632

83. Courtney's store, Sheep Camp
UAF, 75-178-16

84. Inside bunkhouse
J. Price, From Euston to Klondike

84. Sketch of hotel interior
Leon Boillot, Aux mines d'or du Klondike

85. Tugwell's British Hostelry
PABC, HP30929

85. Tugwell's ad
Bennett Sun, Dec. 8, 1899

85. Olympic Hotel
PABC, 62480

86. Baking bread
NAC, PA 16/41

87. Tree stump
D. Neufeld

Main Street, Lindeman, summer, 1899.

Index

Catharine McClellan with two friends after cutting a Christmas tree, Carcross, 1950. McClellan has devoted her career to working with the aboriginal people of Alaska and the southern Yukon.

A White Pass train meets a cruise ship docking in Skagway.

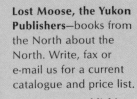

David Neufeld, a Parks Canada historian, has worked on Chilkoot Trail National Historic Site for over ten years. Based in Whitehorse, he does research on the Kluane National Park Reserve, the Yukon River, Dawson City and the Klondike goldfields, and the Yukon north slope. Other work includes *Make It Pay! Gold Dredge #4*, a history of Klondike dredge mining, the history of Canadian air transport, an assessment of the DEW Line and work on several community history projects.

Frank Norris has lived in Alaska since 1983. He spent much of the 1980s in Skagway, where he was a ranger and historian at Klondike Gold Rush National Historical Park. He now works for the National Park Service in Anchorage. The Klondike gold rush remains a favourite research focus. He has also written on topics ranging from homesteading to gardening, tourism, container shipping, and sport fishing, and he's currently writing various histories of Alaska's national park units.

Prospector and two Native American packers in the Dyea River valley, mid-1890s.